WILLIAMS-SONOMA

Savoring

Meat & Poultry

Best Recipes from the Award-Winning International Cookbooks

GENERAL EDITOR

Chuck Williams

AUTHORS

Georgeanne Brennan • Kerri Conan • Lori de Mori • Abigail Johnson Dodge

Janet Fletcher • Joyce Goldstein • Diane Holuigue • Joyce Jue

Michael McLaughlin • Cynthia Nims • Ray Overton • Jacki Passmore

Julie Sahni • Michele Scicolone • Marilyn Tausend

Oxmoor House®

CONTENTS

Top: The milk in Manchego cheese comes from sheep that graze on the high, dry plains of La Mancha, Spain. **Above:** Onions of all colors are mainstays of many Provençale dishes, particularly in rich, slow-simmered stews and daubes. **Opposite:** Saint-Malo was a properous French port in the seventeenth century and local mariners became wealthy through trade and piracy. Its ramparts, once for protection, now offer a view of the sea.

*F**rom the kitchen comes the mouth-watering aroma of roasted meat and the sound of fat sizzling in a roasting pan. The dining-room table wears holiday dress: a formal white linen cloth, the best special-occasion china, decoratively folded napkins, and delicate cut-crystal goblets. When the excited youngsters finally take their seats alongside parents, aunts, uncles, grandparents, and friends, the celebratory roast, an enormous prime rib of beef, is already on the table, its well-browned surface glistening, its rosy juices pooling on the serving platter.*

In Mexico, a similar succulent aroma wafts around a large cluster of family, friends, and neighbors as they crowd around a charcoal grill, waiting to pile platters high with smoky pork ribs that were marinated in orange juice and achiote paste and slathered with roasted-tomato and habanero salsa.

Or imagine an Italian farmhouse trattoria nestled among olive groves and vineyards on a hilltop in Chianti. Inside, a simply laid table stands near a cavernous hearth. Over the embers rests a grill laden with heavy, sizzling *bistecche*, or beefsteaks, alongside half a dozen fresh, sweet sausages dripping their juices onto the coals and releasing their spicy fragrance. And in marketplaces from Portugal to Shanghai, glistening whole roasted suckling pigs are on proud display, waiting to be carved into succulent slices edged with crisp skin.

Whether part of a snack or a haute-cuisine feast, meat and poultry dishes command respect. Around the world, these are the dishes that symbolize abundance and good times, holiday celebrations and family prosperity, whether it's a whole roasted chicken, its skin golden, crispy, and scented with herbs in Provence, or a savory pot of tangy, spicy *birria* (lamb or goat stew) in Jalisco. It is in these dishes, as well, that national and regional pride often resides. An American Southerner may have strong feelings about peach cobbler or sweet tea, but ask about barbecue or fried chicken, and you'll get not just a recipe but an entire history of who makes the best version. And what would Thanksgiving be without a glossy brown turkey on the table, or the Fourth of July (Independence Day) without the neighborhood cookout of burgers and

hotdogs on the grill? From coast to coast, a big night out still usually means a thick steak cooked to order, with the vegetables on the side, the better not to distract from the glory of the meat.

Pork chops and sausages get their due in America, but it is elsewhere in the world that the pig really comes into its own on the table. In Mexico, pork *carnitas* is a favorite filling for everything from a quick tortilla-wrapped snack to a bubbling pan of enchiladas. Roasted with a variety of fresh and cooked salsas, braised in deep, complex mole sauces, or grilled at a roadside stand, pork can be found on every menu from Chihuahua to Oaxaca. The usefulness of the entire pig is part of its worldwide charm. In a French *charcuterie* or an Italian *salumeria,* no part is wasted. The feet, the blood, even the tender cheeks: all become part of a vast array of pâtés, terrines, sausages, and cured meats, from Italy's delicate *prosciutto di Parma,* served in tissue-thin slices wrapped around a wedge of ripe melon or a plump fig, to a chunky wedge of rough-textured French *pâté de campagne,* served with cornichon pickles, grainy mustard, and bread. In Iberia, *jamon* and *presunto* (Portugal's smoky, dark brown cured ham) reign supreme. In Spain, the best is *jamón ibérico,* made from a native black pig raised in forests, where it dines on grasses, acorns, and olives. Around the whitewashed mountain villages, hams hang in drying halls and cellars, filling the mountain air with a rich, nutty fragrance.

In Asia, pork is also held in high regard, used extensively throughout China as a filling for dumplings, a source of stock or broth, and in stir-fries. Chicken, duck, and other fowl are equally popular, in preparations ranging from the famous Peking duck to delicacies like tea-smoked quail, roast duck with hot-and-sour cabbage, and braised spicy ginger chicken. Chicken and pork also dominate the varied cuisines of Southeast Asia, from the curries of Thailand and Malaysia to the tangy pork *adobo* and fried chicken simmered in lime-spiked coconut juice favored in the Philippines.

The extensive use of lamb, poultry, and goat in India's many regional cuisines is due in part from necessity—sheep, chickens, and especially goats can survive in widely varying climates, on much less grazing and foraging space than would be required by cattle—and part from religious restriction. Hindus, Jains, Buddhists, Parsis, and Sikhs do not eat beef; in fact, many Jains, Buddhists, and Hindus are strict vegetarians. Muslims and Jews do not eat pork. Hence, lamb, mutton, goat, and poultry dishes make up the bulk of meat dishes in India's culinary lexicon, in such varied preparations as lamb curry with pumpkin, the much-loved, bright-red tandoori chicken, and Madras-style lamb or goat with coconut.

In the recipes on the following pages, you will find international dishes for every occasion—some familiar, some brand-new, but all delicious and all ready to bring delight to your table every day.

Opposite: A Chinese teahouse is a popular afternoon destination for those with leisure time. **Above, left:** A waiter at Morelia's Villa Montaña Hotel in Mexico prepares the dining room for dinner. **Above, right:** A restaurant in France charmingly advertises its daily menu handwritten on small chalkboards.

NORTH AMERICA

A lthough beef dominates the American table today—in part due to the country's love of the hamburger—its widespread popularity is a modern phenomenon. Early settlers raised primarily pigs and chickens, which were easier to feed and manage. With the country's expansion into the wide-open West—much of it too arid for farming—cattle ranching took off in Texas and Arizona, and beef was brought to Eastern markets on the hoof, via arduous cattle drives. With the advent of the railroad and refrigerated railcars, the stockyards of Chicago and Kansas City became the centers of a giant meatpacking industry that could ship fresh, high-quality Western beef to the East Coast quickly and cheaply. Americans remain enthusiastic beef eaters, but they are choosing poultry and seafood more often, usually with an eye on their health.

A taste for pork persists in New England, a legacy of the self-sufficient farmlands of the region, where the accommodating pig, surviving on scraps from the table or by foraging for roots and acorns in the nearby woods, made the difference between having meat and not. Packed in deep barrels of salt, pork would last through the long winter to flavor innumerable pots of baked beans. Chicken, especially tender young spring chickens, was a company dish, topped with a flaky potpie crust or simmered with plump cornmeal dumplings for Sunday dinner. And it wouldn't be Thanksgiving dinner without a bronze-skinned roast turkey brought proudly to the table.

In the South, tradition reigns, especially when it comes to fried chicken and barbecue, still the benchmarks of the Southern cook. Anyone born south of the Mason-Dixon line will tell you that superlative fried chicken requires a skillful interplay of cook, pan, bird, and batter, and a slow pan sauté will always beat fast-food deep-frying.

From Chicago's steakhouses and Kansas City's rib-and-brisket barbecue joints to Milwaukee's outposts for bratwurst and beer, the Midwest is true meat-and-potatoes country. In the mountain states, including Nevada, Colorado, and Idaho, communities of sheepherders have added rugged, rustic lamb dishes to the table. And while many of

the unique dishes of the Southwest remain strictly regional, many of the area's Mexican-inspired dishes have become part of the nation's culinary repertoire. Americans have embraced tacos, enchiladas, fajitas, and tamales, especially when stuffed with chile-doused chicken, beef, or pork.

Out in the Pacific Northwest, home of a burgeoning wine-making industry, determining what dishes complement a Willamette Valley Pinot Noir or a Columbia Valley Merlot is a pleasurable pastime. Nature in its wisdom has provided for some superb food and wine marriages: flank steak with local Walla Walla sweet onions and fruity Merlot; succulent duck breasts with sweet black cherries and peppery Syrah. In health-conscious California, many markets now offer organic chickens, antibiotic- and hormone-free meats, grass-fed beef, and meat from suppliers dedicated to humane animal husbandry.

Like the United States, Mexico has a long history of cattle ranching and thus has its own indigenous *barbacoa* (barbecue) styles inspired by the open-air techniques of the *vaqueros* (cowboys). At a roadside stand in Tlaxcala or Puebla, the fare is pieces of lamb coated with a chile-rich *adobo,* marinated with *pulque* (a liquor made from agave). In Yucatán, it's pork cooked in garlic, achiote, spices, and the juice of bitter oranges. In Tamaulipas, a main course may be a huge slice of unadorned beef with enchiladas.

But rather than plain grilled or fried meat or poultry, most meaty main courses are served in or with a sauce, and when you order, it is often by the name of the sauce—a *pipián verde* or a *mole negro*. The cooked meat or poultry sometimes seems interchangeable. These dishes are presented alone or, at the most, with a mound of rice, but the vibrant flavors and rustic textures make even the simplest dishes memorable.

Meats (along with beans) are the focus of the country's beloved *antojitos,* little corn *masa* creations that are eaten on the street and in the marketplace throughout Mexico. Stuffed with chicken, rolled, and deep-fried, a tortilla becomes a *flauta;* cupping morsels of fried pork *carnitas* and fresh salsa, it's a taco. Every region has its own variation on these two- or three-bite snacks.

But it is during Mexico's many fiestas that the country's meat and poultry dishes really come into their own. Whether it is a lavish, chocolate-spiked mole rich with turkey served as part of the Christmas feast or an elegant roast chicken stuffed with almonds, onions, apples, and bread crumbs, all perfumed with cumin and cinnamon, these dishes are a delicious opportunity to gather friends and family around the table. There's even a cure for too much revelry: the long-cooked lamb stew known as *birria,* rich with garlic and toasted guajillo chiles, is often claimed as a flavorful and surefire hangover cure throughout the country.

Left: Fresh chiles—*chiles de agua*, jalapeños, serranos, habaneros—impart either a hint of fruity heat or a sizzling shot of fire, depending on which type is used. **Above, left:** So famous that it is known by name throughout America and the world, Chicago-style blues can be heard in clubs and concerts across the city. **Above, right:** Centuries of Spanish Catholicism left an impression upon Mexico's indigenous religions, and today shrines to the dark-skinned Virgin of Guadalupe, who appeared in a trio of visions to a local peasant in 1531, can be found all over the country.

Stuffed Chicken, Zacatecas Style

Gallina Rellena Estilo Zacatecas • Zacatecas • Mexico

With its fragrant, crisp brown skin, succulent meat, and unusual filling, this stuffed chicken is a perfect dish to showcase at a small holiday dinner party. Serve it with baked sweet potatoes and a spinach salad for a family feast.

1 roasting chicken, 5–6 lb (2.5–3 kg)

2 cups (16 fl oz/500 ml) dry sherry

1 cup (8 fl oz/250 ml) white wine vinegar

1 large white onion, sliced into rings

2 bay leaves

1 teaspoon peppercorns

¼ teaspoon ground cumin

STUFFING

2 tablespoons safflower or canola oil

1 lb (500 g) ground (minced) lean pork

1 cup (4 oz/125 g) chopped white onion

2 ripe tomatoes, peeled, seeded, and chopped

1 cup (4 oz/125 g) peeled chopped apple

½ cup (3 oz/90 g) raisins

½ cup (2½ oz/75 g) slivered blanched almonds, toasted

½ cup (2½ oz/75 g) pimiento-stuffed green olives, chopped

2 slices French or Italian bread, lightly toasted and cut into small cubes

1 egg, lightly beaten

1–2 tablespoons chicken stock, if needed

¼ teaspoon ground cumin

¼ teaspoon ground cinnamon

Sea salt and freshly ground pepper to taste

3 tablespoons lard or unsalted butter

6–8 inner romaine (cos) lettuce leaves

8 radishes, sliced

Serves 6–8

1 Rinse the chicken and pat dry. In a bowl, stir together the sherry, vinegar, onion, bay leaves, peppercorns, and cumin to make a marinade. Combine the chicken and marinade in a large bowl, cover, and refrigerate, turning occasionally to marinate the chicken evenly, for 4–6 hours.

2 To make the stuffing, in a frying pan over medium heat, warm the oil. Add the pork and sauté until cooked through, about 5 minutes. Using a slotted spoon, transfer the pork to a plate. Pour off all but 2 tablespoons of the oil and pork fat. Add the onion and sauté until translucent, 3–5 minutes. Stir in the tomatoes, apple, raisins, almonds, and olives and sauté until the tomatoes and apple soften, about 2 minutes. Transfer to a large bowl. Stir in the cooked pork, bread cubes, and beaten egg. Add the stock if the stuffing is too dry. Sprinkle with the cumin and cinnamon, mix well, and season with salt and pepper.

3 Preheat the oven to 350°F (180°C).

4 Remove the chicken from the marinade and pat dry, reserving the marinade in a small saucepan. Bring the marinade to a boil, then set aside. Rub the bird with the lard or butter; sprinkle inside and out with salt and pepper. Loosely fill the body and neck cavities with the warm stuffing. Lap the skin over the openings and secure by sewing with a trussing needle and kitchen string or with skewers or toothpicks. Fold the wing tips under the bird. If desired, truss the legs together with a piece of string. Spoon any remaining stuffing into a lightly buttered baking dish, cover, and slip it into the oven to heat during the last 10–15 minutes the chicken is cooking.

5 Place the chicken on one side on a rack in a roasting pan and roast for 10 minutes, basting often with the reserved marinade. Turn the chicken on its other side and roast for another 10 minutes. Turn breast side up and continue cooking, basting frequently with the marinade, until the juices run clear when a knife is inserted into the thigh joint. Total cooking time is about 1½ hours. Transfer the chicken to a serving platter and let rest for 5 minutes before carving.

6 Clip the strings or remove the skewers or toothpicks. Spoon the stuffing into a warmed bowl, adding the stuffing that was baked separately. Carve the chicken and arrange on a platter garnished with lettuce leaves and radish slices. Strain the pan juices, skim off the fat from the surface, reheat, and pour into a warmed bowl. Pass the pan juices at the table.

Sesame Seed Pipián with Chicken

Pipián de Ajonjolí • Mexico, D.F. • Mexico

Savory *pipianes* are similar to moles in appearance, and for some types of moles the names are interchangeable. So what, if anything, distinguishes a *pipián* from a mole? Just as the *mole poblano* is quite different from a *mole amarillo, verde,* or *manchamanteles,* it helps to think of a *pipián* as just another type of mole. Fewer spices are typically used in a *pipián,* and although it still includes chiles and tomatoes or tomatillos in the sauce, it is more apt to be thickened just with seeds, providing a seductive, creamy texture.

1 To prepare the chicken, in a large pot, bring the water to a boil. Add the chicken thighs, onion, garlic, and salt, skimming off any foam from the surface. Reduce the heat to medium, cover partially, and simmer for 10 minutes. Add the chicken breasts, return the water to a simmer, and cook for 15 minutes. Let the chicken cool in the broth. Lift out the chicken, reserving the broth. Remove the skin and tear the meat into large pieces, discarding the bones. Strain the broth, then spoon off the fat.

2 To make the *pipián,* line a heavy frying pan with heavy-duty aluminum foil, shiny side up (to prevent sticking), and place over medium heat. Add the tomatoes and onion slices and roast, turning occasionally, until the tomato skin is blistered and begins to blacken and the onions are blackened and softened. Carefully trim off and discard the most blackened parts of the tomato skin. Transfer the tomatoes and onions to a blender or food processor. Roast the garlic cloves, turning them frequently, until they soften and their skins blacken, about 10 minutes, then add to the tomatoes and onions. Add 2 cups (16 fl oz/500 ml) of the broth to the blender or food processor, process briefly, add the chiles, and process until smooth.

3 Remove the foil from the frying pan and warm over medium heat. Add the 1½ cups (4½ oz/140 g) sesame seeds and toast, stirring constantly, until golden brown, about 2 minutes. Spread on a plate to cool completely. Finely grind the seeds in a spice grinder. Pour into a small bowl. Finely grind the cinnamon bark, if using, and add to the seeds.

4 In a large, flameproof earthenware casserole or a dutch oven over medium-high heat, warm the oil. When just starting to smoke, pour in the tomato mixture, reduce the heat to medium-low, and simmer, stirring occasionally, until the mixture thickens and changes color, about 10 minutes. Add the ground sesame seeds and cinnamon, salt, and 2 cups (16 fl oz/500 ml) of the broth, whisking until smooth. Add the chicken and simmer over low heat, stirring to prevent the sauce from sticking, until the oil rises to the surface, 10–15 minutes. Add up to ¾ cup (6 fl oz/180 ml) more broth if needed to thin the sauce.

5 Place the chicken on a warmed platter or on individual plates, spoon on the sauce, and garnish with the 2 tablespoons sesame seeds. Serve immediately.

CHICKEN

8 cups (64 fl oz/2 l) water

4 chicken thighs

¼ white onion

2 cloves garlic

1 teaspoon sea salt

4 chicken breast halves

PIPIÁN

4 small ripe tomatoes, about 1 lb (500 g)

2 thick slices white onion

4 cloves garlic, unpeeled

2 dried chipotle chiles, toasted (page 224) or canned *chiles chipotles en adobo*

1½ cups (4½ oz/140 g) plus 2 tablespoons sesame seeds

2-inch (5-cm) piece true cinnamon bark or 1 teaspoon ground cinnamon

6 tablespoons (3 fl oz/90 ml) safflower or canola oil

½ teaspoon sea salt

Serves 8

Duck Breasts with Cherry-Syrah Sauce

The Pacific Northwest · America

The Northwest's sweet cherries peak in late June to mid-July. During the off-season, you can substitute jarred cherries, frozen dark sweet cherries, or ¼ cup (1 oz/30 g) dried cherries that have been plumped in hot water and well drained.

2 duck half breasts, ½–¾ lb (250–375 g) each

Salt and freshly ground pepper to taste

1 cup (8 fl oz/250 ml) Syrah or other medium-bodied red wine

⅓ cup (2 oz/60 g) pitted and halved Bing cherries

2 tablespoons red currant jelly

2 teaspoons minced fresh chervil or flat-leaf (Italian) parsley

Serves 2–4

1 With the tip of a sharp knife, score the duck skin in a diamond pattern, slashing not quite to the flesh. Season the breasts with salt and pepper. Place a heavy frying pan over medium-high heat. When it is well heated, add the duck breasts, skin side down, and cook until the skin is well browned and much of the fatty layer has been rendered, about 5 minutes. Turn the breasts over, partially cover the pan, reduce the heat to medium, and continue cooking until the duck is just pink when cut into at the center, 4–5 minutes longer. Transfer the duck breasts to a cutting board and tent loosely with aluminum foil.

2 Pour out and discard the duck fat from the frying pan. Add the wine to the pan, place over high heat, bring to a boil, and deglaze the pan, stirring to scrape up any browned bits on the pan bottom. Boil the wine until reduced by about three-fourths and slightly thickened, 3–4 minutes.

3 Add the cherries and jelly to the pan and stir to blend evenly, about 1 minute. Taste and adjust the seasoning with salt and pepper.

4 Carve each of the duck breasts on the diagonal into slices about ½ inch (12 mm) thick. Arrange the slices in a slightly fanned pattern on individual plates. Spoon the pan sauce over the duck, sprinkle with the chervil or parsley, and serve immediately.

Chicken Potpie

New England • America

Creamed chicken, carrots, onions, peas, and mushrooms are the staples in this favorite homey dish, but the choice of topping varies widely, from pie pastry to mashed potatoes. This rustic potpie with a biscuit topping is served straight from the frying pan.

FILLING

8 tablespoons (4 oz/125 g) unsalted butter

½ lb (250 g) fresh button mushrooms, brushed clean and thinly sliced

2 carrots, peeled and diced

1 yellow onion, chopped

1 small red bell pepper (capsicum), seeded and diced

Salt and freshly ground black pepper to taste

1 clove garlic, minced

1 teaspoon chopped fresh thyme

1¼ lb (625 g) boneless, skinless chicken breasts or thighs, trimmed of fat and cut into bite-sized pieces

¼ cup (1½ oz/45 g) all-purpose (plain) flour

2 cups (16 fl oz/500 ml) chicken stock

1 cup (8 fl oz/250 ml) heavy (double) cream or half-and-half (half cream)

1 cup (5 oz/155 g) fresh or frozen peas

2 tablespoons dry sherry

2 tablespoons chopped fresh chives

2 tablespoons chopped fresh flat-leaf (Italian) parsley

BISCUIT TOPPING

1 cup (5 oz/155 g) all-purpose (plain) flour

1 tablespoon sugar

2 teaspoons baking powder

½ teaspoon salt

Pinch of ground cayenne pepper

5 tablespoons (2½ oz/75 g) unsalted butter, chilled, cut into pieces

½ cup (4 fl oz/125 ml) buttermilk

Serves 6

1 To make the filling, in an ovenproof frying pan 11 inches (28 cm) in diameter and 2½ inches (6 cm) deep, melt 2 tablespoons of the butter over medium heat. Add the mushrooms, carrots, onion, and bell pepper and season with salt and black pepper. Cook, stirring occasionally, until lightly browned and just barely tender, about 10 minutes. Add the garlic and thyme and cook, stirring occasionally, until fragrant, about 1 minute. Transfer to a large plate.

2 Raise the heat to medium-high and add another 2 tablespoons butter to the frying pan. When the butter is melted, add the chicken and season with salt and black pepper. Cook, stirring often, until the chicken is lightly browned and barely cooked through, about 4 minutes. Scoop out the chicken and pile onto the plate with the vegetables.

3 Reduce the heat to medium-low and melt the remaining 4 tablespoons (2 oz/60 g) butter in the pan. Add the flour and whisk constantly until bubbling but not browned, about 1 minute, scraping up any browned bits on the pan bottom. Pour in the stock and the cream, raise the heat to medium-high, and bring to a boil. Reduce the heat to low and simmer, stirring occasionally, until thickened, about 3 minutes. Add the reserved vegetables and chicken and the peas, sherry, chives, and parsley. Season with salt and black pepper. Remove from the heat and leave the filling in the pan. Cover with aluminum foil and set aside while you make the topping. (You may make the recipe up to this point and refrigerate the filling for up to 6 hours. Uncover and reheat gently, stirring frequently, while making the biscuit dough.)

4 Preheat the oven to 400°F (200°C).

5 To make the biscuit topping, in a bowl, whisk together the flour, sugar, baking powder, salt, and cayenne pepper until well blended. Add the butter and, using a pastry blender, cut in the butter until the pieces are no larger than peas. Add the buttermilk and stir gently with a rubber spatula until a soft dough forms.

6 Uncover the filling. Bring to a boil over medium-high heat, stirring occasionally, about 3 minutes. Reduce the heat to medium-low. Using 2 tablespoons, scoop up small amounts of the biscuit dough and drop onto the hot filling. The topping will almost completely cover the filling.

7 Bake the potpie until the biscuits are lightly browned and a toothpick inserted into the center of one comes out clean, about 25 minutes. Spoon immediately onto warmed individual plates and serve.

Chicken Enchiladas with Tomatillo Sauce

Enchiladas Verdes • Mexico, D.F. • Mexico

These traditional green-sauced enchiladas from Mexico City are a favorite of chef Ricardo Muñoz Zurita. The recipe comes from nearby Xochimilco, where, long before the Spanish conquest, the Aztecs were raising vegetables, chiles, and herbs on floating gardens encircling Tenochtitlán, their island capital.

CHICKEN

2 lb (1 kg) chicken breasts

¼ white onion

1 head garlic, halved crosswise

1 tablespoon sea salt

SAUCE

3 lb (1.5 kg) tomatillos, husked and rinsed

9 serrano chiles

3 cloves garlic, chopped

¼ cup (2 fl oz/60 ml) safflower or canola oil

1 tablespoon sea salt, or to taste

ENCHILADAS

⅓ cup (3 fl oz/80 ml) safflower or canola oil

18 purchased thin corn tortillas

1 cup (8 fl oz/250 ml) *crema* (page 224)

1 white onion, thinly sliced

1 cup (5 oz/155 g) crumbled *queso fresco*

Serves 6

1 To prepare the chicken, place in a saucepan with the onion, garlic, and salt and add water to cover. Bring to a boil over high heat, reduce the heat to medium, cover, and simmer until the chicken is cooked through, 20–25 minutes. Let cool and lift out the chicken, saving the broth for another use. (The chicken can be wrapped and refrigerated for up to 1 day before continuing.) Discard the skin and bones and shred the meat with your fingers. There should be 4 cups (1½ lb/750 g) chicken.

2 To make the sauce, in a saucepan, combine the tomatillos and chiles with water to cover. Bring to a boil over medium-high heat and cook until tender, 10–15 minutes. If some of the tomatillos remain firm, the pan should still be removed from the heat. Drain and, working in batches, place the tomatillos and chiles in a blender along with the garlic. Process until a smooth sauce forms.

3 In a frying pan over medium-high heat, warm the oil until it is smoking. Quickly add the tomatillo sauce and fry, stirring constantly, until the sauce begins to bubble. Reduce the heat to low and cook until the sauce thickens, 5 minutes longer. Add the 1 tablespoon salt; taste and add more salt if needed. Keep warm. When the sauce is combined with the tortillas and chicken, the taste of salt will be quite diminished; it should be highly seasoned at this point. You should have about 3 cups (24 fl oz/750 ml) of sauce. If needed, add some of the chicken broth.

4 Preheat the oven to 350°F (180°C).

5 To make the enchiladas, in a frying pan, heat the oil over medium-high heat until sizzling hot. Using tongs, quickly pass each tortilla through the oil to soften and drain on absorbent paper.

6 Using your fingers, dip each tortilla briefly in the warm sauce, place on a plate, put a large spoonful of shredded chicken near one edge, roll up the tortilla, and place, seam side down, in a baking dish. Cover with the remaining sauce. Place in the oven and bake until thoroughly heated, about 10 minutes.

7 Remove the enchiladas from the oven and top with the *crema*, onion slices, and crumbled cheese. Alternatively, arrange the enchiladas on individual warmed plates and garnish before serving. Serve immediately—enchiladas become soggy quickly.

CINCO DE MAYO

It's 7:00 AM on a spring day so clear that the gently steaming volcano, Popocatépetl, slowly being topped with a crown of white-fringed, purple-bellied plumes, seems framed against the blue of the sky. As she has every morning for a dozen years, Emelia López, joined by her young daughter, has created an instant kitchen on the street outside Puebla's busiest market.

As the first customer appears, the daughter scoops out blue corn *masa* with two small cupped hands, forms it into a ball, and gives it to her mother. Emelia pats the *masa* into a large, thick oval tortilla and deftly slips it into hot melted lard, where it is instantly surrounded by soft popping bubbles. She flips the tortilla, frying the other side, takes it out, spreads on black beans, adds pungent epazote and other toppings, and presents the finished *memela* to the waiting man.

This is not just any day. It is Cinco de Mayo, a day of special significance in Puebla. For here, over three hundred years ago, on the fifth of May, a ragtag group of Mexican ex-guerrillas drove off a powerful army of six thousand French invaders. Nevermind that the city was eventually conquered, resulting in the Viennese prince, Maximilian, being installed by Napoleon as emperor of Mexico. This holiday represents the Mexican spirit to survive.

By midday the downtown streets will be filled with marching bands from local schools and legions of exuberant workers. The central plaza, transformed into an outdoor eatery, will draw Emelia and her mobile kitchen to sell her special regional *masa* snacks to the festive throngs. On a nearby hilltop, at the site of the Fort of Loreto, one of the main defense points during the victorious battle, a mammoth fair draws its share of excitement seekers. High-spirited families and friends gather to celebrate with games, cockfights, and, of course, food.

In other parts of Mexico, Cinco de Mayo is a legal holiday, though the festivities are rather muted. But here in Puebla, where the struggle took place, it is a full-blown celebration.

Chicken and Cornmeal-Cheddar Dumplings

The Midwest • America

This version of chicken and dumplings adds a little texture to the dumplings with cornmeal and enriches them with cheddar cheese. As a first choice, use a stewing hen or roasting chicken, both of which are larger and more flavorful than young fryers.

CHICKEN

1 chicken (see note), 6–7 lb (3–3.5 kg)

3 carrots, peeled and cut into chunks

3 celery stalks, cut into chunks

2 yellow onions, quartered

1 head garlic, unpeeled, with top sliced off to reveal cloves

4 bay leaves

1 small bunch fresh flat-leaf (Italian) parsley

2 teaspoons black peppercorns

2 teaspoons kosher salt or coarse sea salt

1 teaspoon coriander seed

1 bunch fresh chives

DUMPLINGS

1¼ cups (6½ oz/200 g) stone-ground yellow cornmeal

1¼ cups (6½ oz/200 g) all-purpose (plain) flour

1½ teaspoons baking powder

¼ teaspoon baking soda (bicarbonate of soda)

½ teaspoon kosher salt or coarse sea salt

¼ teaspoon freshly ground white pepper

¼ cup (2 oz/60 g) chilled unsalted butter

¼ lb (125 g) sharp cheddar cheese, shredded

½ cup (4 fl oz/125 ml) buttermilk

2 eggs

Serves 6

1 Several hours before serving, rinse the chicken and place in a large stockpot. Add the carrots, celery, onions, garlic, bay leaves, parsley, peppercorns, salt, and coriander seed. Add water to cover the chicken. Cover with a lid and bring to a boil. Pick out several chives and add to the pot. Reserve the remainder for the dumplings. When the chicken reaches a boil, reduce the heat to medium-low, cover partially, and cook until the meat starts to fall off the bone, about 2 hours. Remove from the heat, uncover, and let the chicken rest in the liquid for 30–60 minutes.

2 Lift the bird from the pot, leaving all the seasonings and vegetables behind, and set aside to cool. Strain the broth through a fine-mesh sieve into a saucepan and skim off the fat. Place the pan over low heat and bring the broth to a simmer. Cook, uncovered, to reduce a little and concentrate the flavor. Remove the meat from the chicken carcass in large pieces. Set aside in a bowl, or refrigerate if dinner is more than a couple hours away.

3 About 30 minutes before serving, start the dumplings: Chop the reserved chives. You should have about ½ cup (⅔ oz/20 g). Pour 1 cup (8 fl oz/250 ml) of the broth into a large, deep frying pan with a tight-fitting lid. Add water to bring the depth to 2 inches (5 cm). Add the chicken meat to the remaining broth and heat through. Taste and adjust the seasoning. Keep warm.

4 In a large bowl, combine the cornmeal, flour, baking powder, baking soda, salt, white pepper, butter, and all but ¼ cup (1 oz/30 g) of the cheese. Using a pastry blender, cut the butter and the cheese into the dry ingredients until the mixture resembles coarse meal. In a bowl, beat the buttermilk and the eggs until well blended. Stir in ¼ cup (⅓ oz/10 g) of the chives. Fold the buttermilk mixture into the dry ingredients and stir just until moistened. The dough will be firm but not dry. Adjust the flour and the buttermilk as needed.

5 Gently press the dough into a large disk about 1 inch (2.5 cm) thick. Using a 2-inch (5-cm) biscuit cutter or drinking glass, cut out the dumplings. Gather the scraps and cut out more dumplings. You should have 12–14. Bring the liquid in the frying pan to a slow boil over medium heat. Carefully slip in the dumplings in a single layer. They can get a little crowded, as they will remain separate. Set any extra dumplings aside for a second batch, which can be cooked after the first batch is served.

6 Reduce the heat to a steady gentle boil, cover, and cook until the dumplings puff up and are light and a toothpick inserted into the center comes out clean, 10–15 minutes. Sprinkle with the remaining cheese and chives and cover while you serve the chicken. In each bowl, put a little broth and some chicken pieces. Top with 1 or 2 dumplings and serve.

Roast Chicken with Acorn Squash

The Great Plains • America

Hearty vegetables played a crucial role in the early Great Plains farm diet. This cold-weather classic can move easily into more temperate-weather months. Simply substitute summer squashes, asparagus, or stuffed tomatoes for the acorn squash and adjust the cooking times accordingly.

1 chicken, 3–4 lb (1.5–2 kg)

1 tablespoon *each* olive oil and melted unsalted butter

1 tablespoon kosher salt

Several fresh thyme sprigs

2 shallots, peeled but left whole

2 acorn squashes

1½ cups (12 fl oz/375 ml) fresh orange juice

Serves 4

1 Rinse the chicken and pat dry. Set in a large roasting pan. In a bowl, combine the olive oil, butter, and salt. Coat the chicken, inside and outside, with the mixture. Stuff the thyme sprigs and shallots into the cavity. Remove the wing tips and truss or tie the legs together. Position the bird, breast side down, in the pan and let come to room temperature. Preheat the oven to 425°F (220°C). Cut the squashes lengthwise into quarters or eighths and remove the seeds.

2 Place the pan in the oven and roast the chicken until lightly browned, 15–20 minutes. Turn the bird and pour ½ cup (4 fl oz/125 ml) of the orange juice into the pan. Add the squashes, skin side down, and brush with the pan juices. Reduce the oven temperature to 400°F (200°C). Continue to roast, brushing the chicken and the squashes with the pan juices every 15 minutes and adding more orange juice if the pan is dry, until an instant-read thermometer inserted into the thickest part of the thigh away from the bone registers 165°F (74°C), 50–60 minutes. Transfer the chicken and squashes to a warmed platter. Place the roasting pan over medium-high heat, pour in the remaining orange juice, and stir to scrape up any browned bits on the pan bottom. Pour the pan juices through a fine-mesh sieve placed over a serving bowl, and skim off any fat from the surface.

3 Carve the chicken and serve with the squashes. Pass the pan juices at the table.

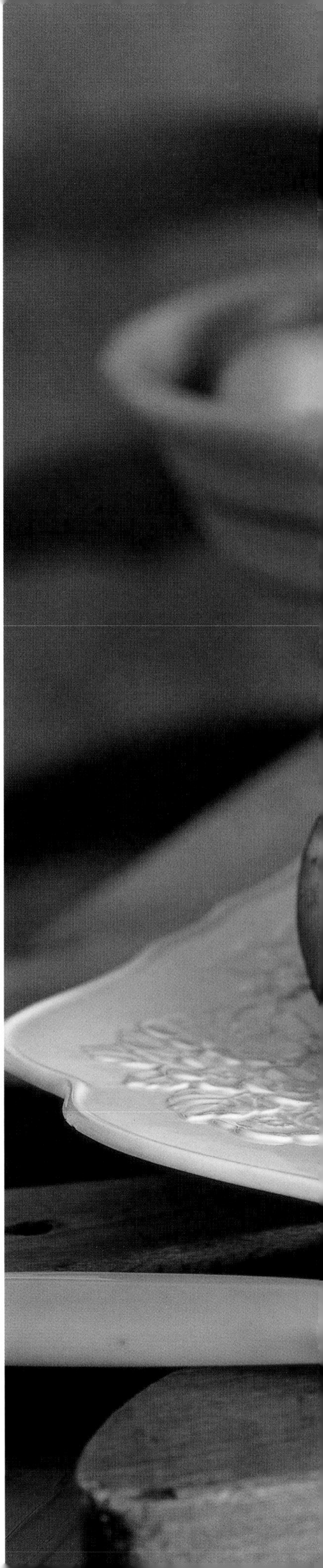

Cornmeal-Crusted Fried Chicken

The South • America

Ask nearly anyone to name the quintessential dish of the South and "fried chicken" will invariably be the answer. Every cook in the region claims to have the ultimate recipe for this centerpiece of the southern Sunday dinner, which usually involves little more than dredging the pieces in flour, dipping them in egg, rolling them in cornmeal, and then frying them, sometimes covered, sometimes not. The two most important qualities of the best fried chicken? A crisp crust and a moist interior are vital.

1 chicken, 4 lb (2 kg), cut into 8 serving pieces

8 cups (64 fl oz/2 l) water

½ cup (4 oz/125 g) kosher salt

¼ cup (2 oz/60 g) sugar

2 cups (16 fl oz/500 ml) buttermilk

1 egg, beaten

1 teaspoon Tabasco sauce or other hot-pepper sauce

1 cup (5 oz/155 g) yellow cornmeal

2 cups (10 oz/315 g) all-purpose (plain) flour

1 teaspoon salt

1 teaspoon freshly ground pepper

1 teaspoon paprika

1 teaspoon celery seed

1 teaspoon garlic powder

1 teaspoon onion powder

2½ cups (1¼ lb/625 g) solid vegetable shortening

Serves 4

1 Rinse the chicken pieces and pat dry with paper towels. In a large bowl, combine the water, kosher salt, and sugar and stir to dissolve. Place the chicken pieces in the water, and weight down with a small plate to immerse totally. Cover and refrigerate for at least 12 hours or for up to 24 hours.

2 In a bowl, mix together the buttermilk, egg, and Tabasco. Remove the chicken from the brine and place in the buttermilk mixture, turning to coat evenly. Let stand for 15 minutes.

3 In a shallow baking dish, stir together the cornmeal, flour, salt, pepper, paprika, celery seed, garlic powder, and onion powder.

4 Remove each piece of chicken from the buttermilk, allowing the excess to drip away. Dredge the chicken pieces in the seasoned flour and place on a large baking sheet. After 10 minutes, dip each piece into the buttermilk a second time and then dredge in the seasoned flour again. Return to the baking sheet.

5 In a large, deep frying pan over medium-high heat, melt the shortening and heat to 365°F (185°C). Place the chicken, skin side down, in the hot shortening, putting the pieces of dark meat in the center and the pieces of white along the sides. Allow the pieces to touch slightly, but do not crowd the pan. Reduce the heat to medium and cook the chicken until golden brown on the first side, about 12 minutes. Using tongs, turn over the chicken pieces, cover, and continue to cook for 10 minutes. Uncover, turn the chicken once more, and cook until the chicken skin is crisp and the meat is cooked through, 8–10 minutes longer. Using tongs, transfer the pieces to paper towels to drain.

6 Serve the chicken at once, allow to cool and serve at room temperature, or chill and enjoy cold, straight from the refrigerator.

Chicken in a Clay Pot

Pollo a la Cazuela • Oaxaca • Mexico

This recipe comes from Socorrito Zorrilla and is her version of the traditional Mexican chicken in a clay pot: here, pieces of chicken are flavored with toasted chiles, garlic, and avocado leaves, then wrapped in banana leaves before being baked.

4 guajillo chiles, seeded and toasted (page 224)

1 can (14½ oz/455 g) diced tomatoes, drained

1 tablespoon finely chopped white onion

4 cloves garlic, coarsely chopped

1 tablespoon fresh oregano leaves or 1 teaspoon dried, preferably Mexican

Sea salt to taste, plus 1 teaspoon

Freshly ground pepper to taste, plus ½ teaspoon

3–4 lb (1.5–2 kg) chicken pieces (12–16 pieces)

4 fresh or thawed frozen banana leaves

16 avocado leaves (optional) (page 223)

Serves 4–6

1 In a small bowl, soak the chiles in boiling water to cover until soft, 10–20 minutes. Drain and tear them into pieces. In a blender, combine the chiles, tomatoes, onion, garlic, and oregano. Blend until very smooth. Strain through a medium-mesh sieve. Season with salt and pepper.

2 Preheat the oven to 350°F (180°C). Rinse the chicken, pat dry, and season with the 1 teaspoon salt and ½ teaspoon pepper.

3 Cut the banana leaves into 8-inch (20-cm) squares and soften them by passing over a burner. Set each leaf on a 10-inch (25-cm) square of aluminum foil. Center 2 avocado leaves (if using) on each banana leaf. Douse the chicken with the chile sauce. Place 3 or 4 chicken pieces on the leaves. Cover with 2 more avocado leaves (if using). Fold the foil tightly around the chicken. Place the packets on a baking sheet. Bake until the chicken is cooked throughout, about 30 minutes.

4 Remove the foil and the top avocado leaves. Slide the chicken and bottom leaves onto individual plates or combine in a shallow clay pot. Serve at once.

Fiesta Black Turkey Mole

Mole Fandango de Guajolote • Querétaro • Mexico

Both the turkey and the mole can be cooked in advance and combined right before serving. In fact, the flavors will mellow if the mole is allowed to rest at least overnight.

1 whole turkey breast, 6–8 lb (3–4 kg), halved

6 cloves garlic

1 white onion, thickly sliced

Sea salt to taste

MOLE

12 ancho chiles

15 dried pasilla chiles

15 cascabel chiles

7 tablespoons (1½ oz/45 g) sesame seeds

8 tablespoons (4 oz/125 g) lard (page 226) or (4 fl oz/125 ml) safflower oil

6 tomatillos, husked, rinsed, and quartered

1 white onion, finely chopped

2 cloves garlic, minced

¼ teaspoon aniseeds

¼ teaspoon ground cumin

1 bay leaf

1 day-old corn tortilla

1 slice day-old French bread or French roll

25 almonds

30 peanuts

2 tablespoons raisins

About ½-inch (12-mm) piece true cinnamon bark or 1 teaspoon ground cinnamon

3 whole cloves

1 disk Mexican chocolate, about 1½ oz (45 g)

1 teaspoon sugar

1 teaspoon sea salt, or to taste, if needed

Serves 10–12, with extra for enchiladas or tamales

1 In a large pot, combine the turkey, garlic, onion, salt, and water to cover. Bring to a slow boil over medium-high heat, skimming off any foam from the surface. Reduce the heat and simmer until the turkey is partially cooked, about 30 minutes. Remove from the broth. Strain the broth. Cover the turkey and broth and refrigerate until needed. Before using the broth, spoon off the congealed fat from the surface.

2 To make the mole, seed the chiles, reserving the seeds, then devein. Put 1½ tablespoons of the seeds of each chile type in a heavy frying pan over medium heat. Toast until golden, then pour into a dish. Toast the sesame seeds lightly. Set 2 tablespoons of the sesame seeds aside. Add the rest to the chile seeds.

3 In a large frying pan, warm 2 tablespoons of the lard or oil over medium heat. Add the tomatillos and onion and cook until deeply browned, 10–15 minutes. Stir in the garlic and fry until soft, 3–4 minutes. Stir in the aniseeds, cumin, and bay leaf. Transfer to a blender. Process until a smooth paste forms.

4 Wipe out the pan and add another 2 tablespoons of the lard or oil. Place over medium-high heat and heat until shimmering. Line a baking pan with absorbent paper. Quickly fry the tortilla, turning once, and drain on the paper. Fry the bread, turning once, until golden, just a few minutes; drain on the paper. In the following order, one at a time, fry the almonds, peanuts, raisins, cinnamon, and cloves for just a few seconds, immediately draining on the paper. Add along with about 1 cup (8 fl oz/250 ml) of the broth to the blender holding the tomatillo paste. Process to form a thick paste.

5 Add the remaining lard or oil to the same pan and place over medium heat. Fry the chiles, a few at a time and tossing constantly, until blistered, just a few seconds. Discard any burned chiles. Place the chiles in a bowl, add hot water to cover, and soak for about 30 minutes. Drain and tear into small pieces. Add with ½–1 cup (4–8 fl oz/125–250 ml) of the broth to the blender. Process until a smooth purée forms.

6 Pour off most of the fat from the pan, leaving about 1 tablespoon. Place over medium-high heat, add the seed, tomatillo, and tortilla mixture, reduce the heat, and simmer, stirring often, about 3 minutes. Add the puréed chiles and stir well for several minutes. Break the chocolate into chunks and add it with the sugar, stirring until it melts. Slowly stir in 4 cups (32 fl oz/1 l) of the broth and simmer for about 2 minutes. Season with salt.

7 Place the turkey in the mole. Simmer, turning occasionally and basting often, for about 45 minutes. An instant-read thermometer inserted into the thickest part should register 150–155°F (66–68°C). Remove from the heat and let stand in the mole for 10–15 minutes. Lift out the turkey, scraping off the sauce, and cut into thick slices. Arrange on a serving platter or individual plates and spoon the mole over the top. Sprinkle with the 2 tablespoons sesame seeds and serve immediately.

Roast Turkey

New England · America

The stuffing for this Thanksgiving bird calls for apples and apple cider, two pantry items stocked in nearly every New England kitchen come fall.

APPLE STUFFING

½ cup (4 oz/125 g) unsalted butter, plus extra for dotting top

2 yellow onions, chopped

4 large celery stalks, chopped

2 large red apples, cored and chopped

2 cloves garlic, minced

½ cup (¾ oz/20 g) chopped fresh flat-leaf (Italian) parsley

3 tablespoons chopped fresh sage

2 tablespoons chopped fresh thyme

1½ cups (12 fl oz/375 ml) apple cider

1 loaf coarse country bread, about ¾ lb (375 g), cubed and lightly toasted

2½ teaspoons kosher salt, or to taste

1 teaspoon freshly ground pepper, or to taste

1 turkey, 13–14 lb (6.5–7 kg)

10–12 fresh sage leaves

1 navel orange, thinly sliced crosswise

Kosher salt and freshly ground pepper to taste

½ cup (4 oz/125 g) unsalted butter

2 large carrots, peeled and quartered crosswise

2 yellow onions, each quartered lengthwise

1½ cups (12 fl oz/375 ml) apple cider, plus extra for drizzling

GRAVY

2–3 cups (16–24 fl oz/500–750 ml) chicken stock

½ cup (2½ oz/75 g) all-purpose (plain) flour

Serves 10–12

1 To make the stuffing, in a large, heavy frying pan over medium heat, melt the ½ cup butter. Add the onions, celery, and apples and cook, stirring frequently, for 10–12 minutes. Stir in the garlic, parsley, sage, and thyme and sauté for about 3 minutes. Transfer to a bowl. Pour the apple cider into the pan, raise the heat to high, and bring to a boil, stirring to loosen any brown bits on the pan bottom. Boil until reduced to 1 cup (8 fl oz/250 ml), about 2 minutes. Add the reduced cider to the vegetables along with the bread cubes, 2½ teaspoons salt, and 1 teaspoon pepper. Toss to coat. The stuffing should just hold together when mounded on a spoon. Adjust the seasoning. Cover with plastic wrap and refrigerate until cold.

2 Position the oven rack in the lower third of the oven and preheat to 325°F (165°C). Remove the neck, giblets, and liver from the turkey and reserve for stock or gravy, if desired. Rinse the turkey inside and out and pat dry. Beginning at the tail cavity, gently slide your fingers under the skin to loosen it. Place a sage leaf on each orange slice and slide each slice and leaf under the skin, sage leaf up, spacing them evenly to cover the entire breast. Season both cavities with salt and pepper, then loosely stuff with the stuffing. Return any leftover stuffing to the refrigerator. Fold the wings back to secure the neck skin and loosely tie the legs together with kitchen string.

3 Place the stuffed bird in a large, heavy roasting pan with sides no higher than 2 inches (5 cm). Sprinkle with salt and pepper and smear with the butter. Scatter the carrots and onions around the bird. Pour in the 1½ cups (12 fl oz/375 ml) apple cider. Bake, basting every 30 minutes, until the thigh juices run clear when pierced and an instant-read thermometer inserted into the thickest part of the thigh away from the bone registers 175°F (80°C), 4–4½ hours.

4 Spoon the reserved stuffing into a buttered baking dish, drizzle with apple cider, and dot with butter. Cover and bake alongside the turkey during the last hour of roasting. For a crispy topping, uncover during the last 30 minutes.

5 When the turkey is done, transfer it to a platter. Spoon the stuffing from the cavities into a serving dish and keep warm. If the separately cooked stuffing is ready, remove from the oven and keep warm. Tent the bird loosely with aluminum foil and let rest for 15 minutes before carving.

6 To make the gravy, pour the juices from the roasting pan through a large sieve set over a 2-qt (2-l) glass measuring pitcher. Allow the fat to rise to the top. Spoon off ½ cup (4 fl oz/125 ml) of the fat into the roasting pan, then spoon off and discard the remaining fat. Add enough chicken stock to the reserved juices to total 6 cups (48 fl oz/1.5 l). Set the roasting pan over medium heat, whisk in the flour, and whisk constantly for about 3 minutes. Pour in the juices-stock mixture and whisk until blended. Cook, whisking frequently, until the gravy boils and thickens, about 5 minutes. Adjust the seasoning.

7 Carve the turkey. Pour the gravy into a bowl and serve alongside with the stuffing.

Crispy Chicken Tortilla Flutes

Flautas de Pollo Deshebrado • Jalisco • Mexico

The secret to making these long rolled tacos is the *raspadas,* tortillas that have had the top layer literally rasped off and discarded before they are wrapped around a tasty filling and fried until crisp. If you do not want to spend the effort to make them extra thin, you can still prepare delicious *flautas* using whole tortillas.

1 To make the filling, place the chicken in a large saucepan and add the water and onion piece. Bring to a boil, reduce the heat to medium, cover, and simmer until the chicken is cooked through, 15–20 minutes. Remove the chicken and set aside to cool, reserving the broth for another use. Remove the skin from the chicken and discard. Shred the meat, discarding the bones.

2 In a frying pan over medium heat, warm the oil. Add the chopped onion, chiles, and garlic and sauté just until softened, about 3 minutes. Raise the heat to medium-high, add the tomato, and cook, stirring occasionally, until the color of the tomato deepens and the excess moisture is absorbed, several minutes longer. Remove from the heat and stir in the shredded chicken and salt. Set aside to cool.

3 If making the *raspadas* (see note), heat a hot, dry *comal,* griddle, or large, heavy frying pan over low heat. Place a tortilla on it and allow it to just dry out. It should take only 3–5 minutes; do not allow it to brown. Remove from the pan and immediately use a table knife to scrape and then pull off the top layer of the tortilla, which, with luck, will have puffed up to make it easier. Repeat with the remaining tortillas.

4 Just before filling the tortillas, pour about 3 tablespoons oil into a deep, heavy frying pan over medium-high heat. When the oil is hot but not smoking, pass each tortilla briefly through it, turning once. Transfer to paper towels to drain.

5 To form each *flauta,* put a spoonful of the shredded chicken mixture along the center of a tortilla, roll it up tightly, and secure with a toothpick placed almost horizontally.

6 Add oil to a depth of ¾ inch (2 cm) into the same frying pan and place over medium-high heat until hot. Working in batches, add the *flautas* to the oil and fry, turning several times to cook evenly, until lightly browned and crisp, about 2 minutes. Using tongs, lift the *flautas* out of the oil, allowing any excess oil to run off, and lean them against a pan on absorbent paper so they can completely drain. Keep warm in a low oven while frying the rest of the *flautas.*

7 The *flautas* should be served immediately. Place on individual plates atop some shredded cabbage and drizzle with the *crema.* If using, garnish with the radishes and serve the salsa and guacamole on the side.

FILLING

2 chicken breast halves

4 cups (32 fl oz/1 l) water

¼ white onion

1 tablespoon safflower or canola oil

½ cup (2 oz/60 g) chopped white onion

3 serrano chiles, chopped

1 clove garlic, minced

1 large ripe tomato, finely chopped

Sea salt to taste

TORTILLAS

12 purchased thin corn tortillas, 6–7 inches (15–18 cm) in diameter

Peanut or safflower oil for frying

ACCOMPANIMENTS

2 cups (6 oz/185 g) thinly shredded cabbage seasoned, if desired, with juice of 1 lime (optional)

1 cup (8 fl oz/250 ml) *crema* (page 224)

12 radishes, sliced or cut into flowers (optional)

Pico de gallo (page 49) or good-quality purchased salsa

Guacamole, homemade or purchased (optional)

Serves 6

Grilled Duck with Tamarind

Pato con Tamarindo • Guerrero • Mexico

Using tamarind with Muscovy duck is a contemporary idea, but one that seems a natural. Tamarind pods can be found in some Asian or Indian grocery stores, as well as many Latin American markets. It is necessary to start this dish a day in advance.

1 lb (500 g) tamarind pods

2 tablespoons unsalted butter

8 cloves garlic, mashed

1 cup (8 fl oz/250 ml) chicken stock

2 tablespoons honey

1 tablespoon Worcestershire sauce

1½ teaspoons ground cayenne pepper, or more to taste

Sea salt to taste

4 boneless Muscovy duck breasts with skin intact, 12–14 oz (375–440 g) each

Serves 6–8

1 Place the tamarind pods in a bowl, add boiling water to cover, and let soften for 1 hour. Drain, squeeze out the seeds, mash the pulp, and pass through a sieve. In a frying pan over medium heat, melt the butter. Add the garlic and sauté for 3 minutes. Stir in the tamarind and stock and simmer for 5 minutes. Add the honey, Worcestershire sauce, cayenne, and salt and simmer several more minutes, stirring often. Let cool. Set aside half for serving, cover, and refrigerate. Score the skin sides of the breasts down to the meat in a diamond pattern. Roll in the marinade, seal in a covered container, and refrigerate at least 8 hours.

2 Prepare a medium-low fire in a charcoal grill. Lift the duck from the marinade. Pour the marinade into a small saucepan and bring to a boil, adding water if needed to thin it slightly. Place the breasts, skin side down, on the grill rack and grill, basting with the heated marinade, until brown and crisp on the first side, 10–12 minutes. Turn and cook on the second side for about 3 minutes for medium-rare. Transfer to a cutting board, cover loosely with aluminum foil, and let rest.

3 Reheat the reserved tamarind mixture. Slice each breast on the diagonal. Fan the slices out on individual plates, top with the warm sauce, and serve.

Red Mole with Chicken, Pork, and Fruit

Manchamanteles · Mexico, D.F. · Mexico

This light red mole with the delightfuly descriptive name of *manchamanteles,* or "tablecloth stainer," is a stewlike dish found throughout central Mexico. Combining fruit and meat is a common practice in Mexico, with the fruit adding a slightly sweet and welcome tart flavor. Serve with fresh corn tortillas and steamed white rice.

¼ cup (2 fl oz/60 ml) safflower or peanut oil, or as needed, plus 1 tablespoon

1 white onion, coarsely chopped

6 cloves garlic, coarsely chopped

6 ancho chiles, seeded, deveined, and torn into large pieces

4–4½ cups (32–36 fl oz/1–1.1 l) chicken stock

½ cup (4 fl oz/125 ml) water, or as needed

20 almonds

¼ cup (1 oz/30 g) pecans

1 lb (500 g) boneless pork shoulder, cut into 1½-inch (4-cm) pieces, trimmed of excess fat

Sea salt to taste

1 lb (500 g) chicken thighs, halved

½ lb (250 g) good-quality chorizo, crumbled (optional)

½-inch (12-mm) piece true cinnamon bark or ½ teaspoon ground cinnamon

6 peppercorns or 2 large pinches of freshly ground pepper

4 whole cloves or 2 pinches of ground cloves

½ teaspoon dried oregano, preferably Mexican

1 tablespoon unsalted butter

2 slices pineapple, cored and cut into large cubes

1 small ripe plantain or green banana, about ¼ lb (125 g), peeled, quartered lengthwise, and cut into large cubes

1 small jicama, about ½ lb (250 g), peeled and cut into large cubes

Serves 8

1 In a large frying pan or *cazuela* over medium heat, warm the ¼ cup (2 fl oz/60 ml) oil. Add the onion and fry until lightly browned and soft, about 5 minutes. Add the garlic and cook until softened, a few more minutes. Using a slotted spoon, transfer the onion and garlic to a blender. In the same pan, quickly fry the chiles, flattening them with a spatula until they just start to blister and change color, only a few seconds. Using the slotted spoon, transfer to a work surface and let cool, then tear into small pieces and add to the blender. Add 1 cup (8 fl oz/250 ml) of the chicken stock and process until smooth, adding an additional ½ cup (4 fl oz/125 ml) stock or the water only if necessary to create a good consistency. In the oil remaining in the pan, quickly sauté the nuts until fragrant, and transfer to the blender.

2 Raise the heat to medium-high and add more oil if necessary. Working in batches, add the pork in a single layer, salt lightly, and brown well on all sides, turning as needed. Using the slotted spoon, transfer to absorbent paper to drain. Add more oil to the pan if it is dry and heat over medium-high heat. Fry the chicken in the same manner, until lightly browned on all sides. Drain on absorbent paper. Add the chorizo (if using), brown it, and drain on the paper.

3 Grind the cinnamon bark, peppercorns, and cloves in a spice grinder and add to the blender holding the nuts, or add the preground spices. Process thoroughly, adding more water if needed to create a very smooth sauce. If it is too granular, strain through a medium-mesh sieve.

4 Reheat the oil remaining in the frying pan over medium-high heat until it starts to smoke, scraping up any meat particles from the pan bottom. Pour in the chile sauce, stirring constantly, being careful that it doesn't splatter. Add the oregano, then stir in the remaining 3–3½ cups (24–28 fl oz/750–875 ml) stock and bring to a simmer. Reduce the heat to low, add the pork, season with salt, cover, and cook until tender, about 45 minutes.

5 Meanwhile, melt the butter with the 1 tablespoon oil in a separate frying pan over medium heat. Add the pineapple and fry, turning as needed, until browned on all sides, about 5 minutes. Using a slotted spoon, transfer to a plate. Repeat with the plantain or banana and jicama in separate batches.

6 When the pork is tender, add the chicken, chorizo, pineapple, and plantain or banana, cover, and simmer over low heat, stirring occasionally, until the chicken is cooked throughout, about 10 minutes longer. Add the jicama, taste for salt, and add a bit of water if the sauce is too thick.

7 Transfer the chicken and chunks of meat and fruit to a warmed serving bowl. Spoon the sauce on top and around them. Serve immediately.

Grilled Pork Ribs

Costillas al Carbón • Yucatán • Mexico

Silvio and Angelica Campos serve these ribs at their home in the village of Tixkokob. You can substitute a mixture of orange, lime, and grapefruit juices for the bitter orange juice.

4 lb (2 kg) meaty pork back ribs, cut into sections of 4 or 5 ribs each

Sea salt to taste

2 tablespoons achiote paste (page 223)

½ cup (4 fl oz/125 ml) fresh bitter orange juice or Seville orange juice

4 cloves garlic, minced

2 large ripe tomatoes

¼ white onion

1 habanero chile, roasted (page 224)

¼ cup (⅓ oz/10 g) coarsely chopped fresh cilantro (fresh coriander)

Serves 4–6

1 Place the ribs in a large pot. Add water to cover and the salt. Bring to a boil, skimming off any foam on the surface. Reduce the heat to low, cover, and simmer until nearly cooked, about 35 minutes. Transfer the ribs to a glass bowl. In another bowl, dissolve the achiote paste in the orange juice. Stir in the garlic and salt. Pour over the ribs, mix well, cover, and refrigerate for at least 6 hours or up to 24 hours.

2 Prepare an indirect-heat fire in a charcoal grill. Meanwhile, line a heavy frying pan with aluminum foil and place over medium heat. Add the tomatoes and onion and roast, turning occasionally, until their skin is blistered and begins to blacken and the interior of the tomatoes softens. Carefully trim off the most blackened parts of the tomato skin. Remove the ribs from the marinade, place on the grill rack, and grill, turning often, until brown, about 15 minutes.

3 Combine the tomatoes, onion, and chile in a blender or food processor and blend until smooth. Pour the purée into a saucepan and heat to serving temperature.

4 Remove the ribs from the grill and cut into 1-rib portions. Add the ribs to the sauce and simmer, uncovered, over low heat, for 10 minutes. Arrange the ribs on a platter, spoon the sauce over them, and sprinkle with the cilantro. Serve at once.

Pulled Pork Sandwiches

The South · America

South of the Mason-Dixon line, every state and county seems to boast the best barbecue. In this version, the pulled (shredded) pork is doused in a not-too-sweet, not-too-sour sauce.

1 bone-in pork shoulder, about 6 lb (3 kg)

2 teaspoons red pepper flakes

1 tablespoon salt

1 tablespoon freshly ground black pepper

1 tablespoon mustard seed

1 cup (8 fl oz/250 ml) water

1 cup (8 fl oz/250 ml) cider vinegar

4 yellow onions, thinly sliced

1 green bell pepper (capsicum), seeded and finely chopped

SAUCE

½ cup (4 oz/125 g) unsalted butter

3 yellow onions, chopped

3 cloves garlic, chopped

2 cups (16 fl oz/500 ml) canned whole tomatoes, puréed

2 tablespoons tomato paste

1 cup (10 oz/315 g) peach preserves

½ cup (4 oz/125 g) coarse-grain Dijon mustard

½ cup (4 fl oz/125 ml) aged Kentucky bourbon

½ cup (6 oz/185 g) honey

⅓ cup (2½ oz/75 g) firmly packed dark brown sugar

1 cup (8 fl oz/250 ml) cider vinegar

2 tablespoons Worcestershire sauce

1 tablespoon Tabasco sauce or other hot-pepper sauce

Salt and freshly ground black pepper to taste

1 tablespoon chopped fresh rosemary

12 sesame seed–topped sandwich buns, warmed

Bread-and-butter pickle slices

Serves 12

1 Preheat the oven to 300°F (150°C). Lightly oil a large baking pan.

2 Place the pork shoulder in the prepared pan and rub with the red pepper flakes, salt, black pepper, and mustard seed. Pour the water and the vinegar over and around the pork. Scatter the onions and the bell pepper over and around the meat. Cover with aluminum foil and roast in the oven for 4 hours. Remove the foil and continue to roast until an instant-read meat thermometer inserted into the thickest part of the pork away from the bone registers 180°F (82°C) and the juices run clear, about 1 hour longer. Remove the pork from the pan and let stand for 1 hour. Using 2 forks, shred the pork by steadying the pork shoulder with 1 fork and pulling the meat away with the other, discarding any fat as you shred. Place the pork in a bowl. Using a slotted spoon, lift the roasted vegetables from the baking pan and ladle over the pork, then mix well.

3 Meanwhile, in a saucepan over medium heat, melt the butter. Stir in the onions and the garlic and cook, stirring occasionally, until the onions are soft and beginning to brown, about 10 minutes. Add the puréed tomatoes, tomato paste, peach preserves, mustard, bourbon, honey, brown sugar, vinegar, Worcestershire sauce, Tabasco sauce, salt, and black pepper. Bring to a boil, then reduce the heat to very low and simmer gently, uncovered, stirring occasionally, until the sauce is very dark and thick, about 2 hours. Stir in the rosemary and cook for 10 minutes. Remove from the heat and let cool for 15 minutes.

4 Mix half of the sauce with the shredded pork. Mound on a large serving platter with the sandwich buns and the pickle slices on the side. Pass the remaining sauce at the table. Diners make their own sandwiches, topping them with pickle slices.

TACOS IN OAXACA

Just across the street from Oaxaca's busy Mercado Benito Juárez, smoke drifts through the narrow corridor of the large brick building that houses many *fondas*. Packed with hungry snackers at all hours of the day, it attracts locals who come for their favorite tacos of grilled meats.

As you enter the long hall, you see long, flat market tables crammed with various salsas, avocados, radishes, green onions, and the feisty regional *chiles de agua*. One of the women at these tables hands you a large, flat wicker basket, into which you are to place the chiles and onions that you will want to have grilled for your taco.

To continue your taco making, you must then choose from a variety of hanging meats: links of chorizo, fresh *tasajo* (thinly sliced beef), salted and aged *tasajo,* wide ribbons of intestines, and spicy *cecina* (air-dried strips of pork). The vendor puts your selection on the grill along with the chiles and onions from your basket. Now you pay, but just for the meat, and you wait for the grilled food to be returned to your basket. Then you make your way back through the crowds to the first woman, who offers salsas and other condiments. A third woman appears with a basket of tortillas to wrap the meat and accompaniments.

Your taco is complete, so you look for a seat, joining your fellow diners on an upside-down Pepsi crate in front of a nearby low concrete slab. Order a can of soda and you are ready to enjoy the taco. Sometimes, a blind violinist led by his small grandson will be there to play a cheerful melody to eat by. Eventually, just as you start to leave, someone—usually a young boy—will stick a piece of paper in your hand stating the amount of pesos needed to finish paying for the meal.

Grilled Chile-Coated Pork Tacos

Tacos con Cecina a la Parrilla • Oaxaca • Mexico

If you were to order *cecina* in most other parts of Mexico, it would be thinly sliced beef, but in Oaxaca it consists of long, thin strips of chile-marinated pork.

PORK

6 cloves garlic, unpeeled

5 guajillo chiles, seeded and toasted (page 224)

4 ancho chiles, seeded and toasted (page 224)

Boiling water to cover

¼ cup (2 fl oz/60 ml) mild white vinegar

½ teaspoon dried oregano, preferably Mexican

10 peppercorns or ¼ teaspoon freshly ground pepper

½-inch (12-mm) piece true cinnamon bark or ½ teaspoon ground cinnamon

1 whole clove or pinch of ground cloves

1 generous teaspoon sea salt, or to taste

1 pork tenderloin, about 1 lb (500 g), trimmed of excess fat

ACCOMPANIMENTS

12 large green (spring) onions, root ends trimmed

12 small Anaheim chiles

2–3 tablespoons safflower or canola oil

4 limes, halved

2 avocados, pitted, peeled, and sliced

Pico de gallo (page 49)

12 small radishes with leaves attached

12 corn tortillas, warmed

Serves 4–6

1 Line a heavy frying pan with aluminum foil, add the garlic cloves, and roast, turning them frequently, until they soften and their skins blacken, about 10 minutes, then set aside. Place the chiles in a bowl, add boiling water to cover, and let stand until soft, about 20 minutes. Drain, reserving the soaking water, tear into small pieces, and place in a blender. Peel the garlic and add with the vinegar and oregano. If using whole spices, put in a spice grinder and pulverize. Add the spices and the salt to the blender and pulse to form a thick *adobo,* or sauce. If necessary, add a few drops or so of the chile soaking water.

2 Using a very sharp knife, accordion-cut the meat: Lay the pork horizontally in front of you. Pushing down firmly with one hand, begin making a slice ⅛ inch (3 mm) thick along the surface, from one end to about ½ inch (3 mm) from the opposite end. Do not cut through. Turn the meat 180 degrees. Still pushing down with one hand, slice back to the other side. Unfold the wide ribbon of meat as you complete a slice, and continue slicing back and forth until the entire piece is stretched out. Rub the *adobo* on both sides, fold the meat back into the original shape, and spread the outside with any remaining *adobo.* Seal in plastic wrap and refrigerate for at least 2 hours or as long as 12 hours.

3 Prepare a fire in a charcoal grill. When the coals are hot, lay 2 sheets of heavy foil on the coals. Rub the green onions and chiles with oil and place on the foil, with the white part of the onions over the coals. Grill, turning frequently, until browned, about 10 minutes. Place in a bowl and toss with some lime juice. Cut the meat into long slices and lay on the grill rack. Brush with oil and grill, turning once, until browned, 2–3 minutes on each side.

4 Place the green onions, chiles, limes, avocados, *pico de gallo,* and radishes in separate bowls. Serve each guest a portion of meat and 2 or 3 tortillas. Pass the fixings at the table.

Beer-Braised Bratwursts

The Midwest • America

Beginning in the mid-1800s, German immigrants settled throughout the Midwest, where pockets of their culinary influence still thrive, as in this signature dish of plump bratwursts and tangy sauerkraut that is still a staple dish in Milwaukee.

6 cups (3 lb/1.5 kg) sauerkraut

2 tablespoons safflower oil

3 yellow onions, chopped

3 cloves garlic, crushed (optional)

1 teaspoon paprika

½ teaspoon caraway seed

1 tablespoon light brown sugar

Pinch of cayenne pepper (optional)

1 bottle (12 fl oz/375 ml) beer, preferably ale

8 bratwursts, 1½–2 lb (750 g–1 kg) total weight

Kosher salt or coarse sea salt and freshly ground white pepper to taste

Spicy brown mustard for serving

Serves 6–8

1 Preheat the oven to 375°F (190°C). Place the sauerkraut in a colander, rinse briefly, and drain. Rinse again if you prefer a milder taste. In a large, deep ovenproof frying pan over medium-high heat, warm the safflower oil. Add the onions and fry, stirring often, for 3–4 minutes. Stir in the garlic (if using), reduce the heat to medium-low, and cook, stirring occasionally, for 10 minutes. Sprinkle with the paprika, caraway seed, brown sugar, and cayenne (if using). Toss to coat and heat until fragrant. Stir in the sauerkraut and beer, raise the heat to medium-high, bring to a boil, and remove from the heat.

2 Using a fork, prick each bratwurst in a couple of places. Arrange on top of the sauerkraut, pushing them into the mixture a bit. Cover tightly, place in the oven, and braise until most of the liquid is absorbed and the sausages are plump, 40–45 minutes. Taste and adjust the seasoning with salt and white pepper.

3 To reduce the juices further, remove the sausages and keep warm. Place the frying pan over medium-high heat and cook the sauerkraut, stirring often, until the juices have thickened. Divide the sausages and sauerkraut among individual plates and serve with spicy brown mustard on the side.

Pork Chops with Vidalia Onion Gravy

The South • America

The Southern fondness for gravy shows up in many dishes, such as this pairing of juicy pork chops and sweet onions. Dishes sauced with gravy are often referred to as "smothered."

2 cups (10 oz/315 g) all-purpose (plain) flour

3 tablespoons cornstarch (cornflour)

1 teaspoon each onion powder and garlic powder

Salt and freshly ground black pepper

¼ teaspoon ground cayenne pepper

6 bone-in loin pork chops, about ½ lb (250 g) each

⅓ cup (3 oz/90 g) unsalted butter

⅓ cup (3 fl oz/80 ml) olive oil

3 Vidalia onions, chopped

2 celery stalks, chopped

1 large carrot, peeled and chopped

3 cups (24 fl oz/750 ml) chicken stock

Serves 6

1 In a large, lock-top plastic bag, combine the flour, cornstarch, onion powder, garlic powder, 1 teaspoon each salt and black pepper, and cayenne. Seal and shake the bag to mix. Add the pork chops, then seal and shake the bag to coat the chops. In a large frying pan over medium-high heat, melt the butter with the olive oil. Reduce the heat to medium, add the chops (reserving the seasoned flour), and cook, turning once, until browned, about 5 minutes on each side. Transfer to a plate and keep warm.

2 Add the onions, celery, and carrot to the frying pan over medium heat and cook for 5–7 minutes. Add ½ cup (2½ oz/75 g) of the reserved seasoned flour and cook, stirring occasionally, for 3 minutes. Raise the heat to medium-high and add the stock. Bring to a boil, stirring constantly and scraping up any browned bits on the pan bottom. Reduce the heat to low, stir in any accumulated juices from the chops, and nestle the meat in the gravy. Cover and simmer over very low heat until the gravy is very thick and the meat is fork-tender, about 1 hour.

3 Transfer the chops to a warmed platter. Season the gravy with salt and black pepper. Spoon the gravy over the chops and serve.

Tiny Rustic Tamales

Tamalitos Rancheros • Mexico, D.F. • Mexico

Noted Mexican cook Margarita Carrillo de Salinas prepares the *masa* and filling in advance and then gets friends or family together to assemble these tasty tamales.

MEAT

½ white onion

2 whole cloves

1½ lb (750 g) boneless pork butt or shoulder, cut into large chunks

4 cloves garlic

About 1½ teaspoons sea salt

SAUCE

6 ancho chiles, seeded and deveined

½ lb (250 g) tomatillos, husked and rinsed

1 white onion, coarsely chopped

4 cloves garlic

¾ teaspoon ground cumin

⅛ teaspoon ground allspice

6 tablespoons (3 fl oz/90 ml) safflower or canola oil

2 bay leaves

Sea salt to taste

TAMALES

50 corn husks

⅔ cup (5 oz/155 g) lard or vegetable shortening

4 cups (2½ lb/1.25 kg) *masa harina* (page 226) for tamales

1½ teaspoons baking powder

1½ teaspoons sea salt, or to taste

Makes about 40 tamales; serves 8–10

1 To prepare the meat, stud the onion with the cloves and put it into a large pot. Add the pork, garlic, salt, and water to cover and bring to a boil, skimming off any foam from the surface. Reduce the heat to low, cover, and simmer for 1½–2 hours. Let the meat cool in the broth, then remove, reserving the broth. Shred the meat very finely. Skim off as much of the fat from the broth as possible.

2 To make the sauce, in a bowl, soak the chiles in hot water to cover for 15–20 minutes. Drain, reserving the water. In a saucepan over medium-high heat, combine the tomatillos with water to cover, bring to a boil, and cook until soft, about 8 minutes. Drain well. In a blender, combine the chiles, the tomatillos, half of the chopped onion, the garlic, the cumin, the allspice, and ½ cup (4 fl oz/125 ml) of the chile water. Blend until smooth.

3 In a deep, heavy frying pan over medium-high heat, warm the oil. Add the remaining onion; sauté for about 5 minutes. Add the chile purée and bay leaves and let sizzle for a few seconds. Reduce the heat to low and simmer uncovered, stirring occasionally, until the sauce begins to thicken, about 15 minutes. Stir in the meat, season with salt, and cook until the sauce becomes thick and a little dry, about 20 minutes. If it becomes too dry, add a little broth.

4 To make the tamales, rinse the corn husks and soak in very hot water until pliable, about 15 minutes. In a bowl, using an electric mixer, beat the lard until fluffy, about 5 minutes. Add the *masa harina,* baking powder, and salt and mix well. Reheat the broth and stir 3 cups (24 fl oz/750 ml) into the *masa harina* mixture, 1 cup (8 fl oz/250 ml) at a time, adding more broth if it is too dry. Beat for at least another 10–15 minutes. The dough should be very light. Taste and add more salt if necessary. The *masa* (dough) is ready when a spoonful of it dropped into cold water floats to the surface.

5 Drain the husks and pat dry. Put 4 or 5 of the torn ones in the bottom of a steamer basket. Line up the husks, *masa,* and meat on a work surface. Hold a husk in the palm of your hand, with the pointed end on your wrist. Spread 1 tablespoon of the dough in the center of the upper half, leaving a margin on all sides. Put 1 rounded teaspoon of the meat filling in the center of the dough. Fold the sides of the husk over the filling and bring up the pointed end until even with the cut or cupped end. If desired, tie the open end with narrow strips of soaked husks.

6 Place each tamale vertically in the steamer basket, folded side down. Start in the center, propping the tamales around an inverted small funnel. Fill a large pot with water to a depth of at least 2 inches (5 cm), but not enough to touch the basket once it is in the pot. Bring the water to a low boil. Add the basket, cover the tamales with corn husks and a kitchen towel, then cover the steamer with a tight lid.

7 Steam, without uncovering, for 1 hour. Remove a tamale, unwrap it, let it sit for several minutes, then break into it to see if the dough is firm. Serve the tamales hot, piled on a platter, letting each person unwrap his or her own tamales.

Pot Roast with Winter Vegetables

New England • America

Transforming a tough piece of beef into a hardy, tender stew through slow cooking is one of the great culinary lessons New Englanders learned from their colonial forefathers, who passed on the secret to coaxing flavor and texture from even the most sinewy meat. This pot roast recipe reflects the colonists' reliance on the larder. Roots and tubers like potatoes, parsnips, and carrots, stored for use during winter, were often added to the pot.

1 Preheat the oven to 325°F (165°C).

2 Put the bouquet garni ingredients on a square of cheesecloth (muslin), bring the corners together, and tie with kitchen string; set aside. Starting at the stem end, cut the onion into 6 wedges, stopping just short of the root end. Set aside. Rub the roast with the salt and pepper. Dust the entire surface of the roast with the flour and tap off any excess.

3 In a large Dutch oven or other heavy, lidded, ovenproof pot over medium-high heat, warm the canola oil until hot but not smoking. Add the roast and brown well on all sides, about 15 minutes. Transfer to a plate and set aside. Add the garlic, onion, and bouquet garni and cook, stirring frequently, until fragrant, about 2 minutes. Add the tomatoes, beer, beef stock, and brown sugar. As the foam subsides, scrape up the browned bits on the pot bottom. When the liquid is boiling, return the roast to the pot, cover, and bake for 2 hours, turning the roast every 30 minutes.

4 Remove the pot from the oven and lift off the lid. Scatter the carrots, potatoes, sweet potatoes, and parsnips around the roast and baste with the juices. Cover the pot and return to the oven. Bake, basting the roast and vegetables occasionally, until the vegetables and meat are tender when pierced with a fork, 1–1½ hours longer.

5 Transfer the meat to a large carving board and snip off the strings. Using a slotted spoon, arrange vegetables on one side of the carving board. Tent the meat and vegetables with aluminum foil. Remove and discard the bouquet garni. Spoon off any fat from the pan juices, then taste and adjust the seasoning. Pour into a warmed serving bowl.

6 Slice the meat and serve on warmed individual plates with the vegetables and some of the pan juices. Pass the remaining juices at the table.

Bouquet garni of 3 large fresh flat-leaf (Italian) parsley sprigs, 1 fresh rosemary sprig, 2 fresh thyme sprigs, and 1 small bay leaf

1 large yellow onion

1 boneless beef bottom round or rump roast, 3½ lb (1.75 kg), tied

1½ teaspoons kosher salt

¼ teaspoon freshly ground pepper

2 tablespoons all-purpose (plain) flour

2 tablespoons canola oil

6 cloves garlic, peeled but left whole

1 can (14 oz/440 g) whole tomatoes, drained and diced

1 bottle (12 fl oz/375 ml) beer

1 cup (8 fl oz/250 ml) beef stock

2 tablespoons light brown sugar

3 carrots, peeled and cut into 1½-inch (4-cm) lengths

3 Yukon gold or other boiling potatoes, peeled and halved

2 large sweet potatoes, peeled and cut into 3-inch (7.5-cm) chunks

2 parsnips, peeled and cut into 2-inch (5-cm) lengths

Serves 6

Meatballs in Spicy Tomatillo Sauce

Albóndigas en Salsa Verde • Mexico, D.F. • Mexico

Well-known cook Margarita Carrillo de Salinas prepares these plump balls of ground meat in the classic Mexican fashion, with a hidden surprise of chopped egg.

1 lb (500 g) tomatillos, husked and rinsed

2 small white onions, 1 quartered and 1 finely chopped

2 cloves garlic, unpeeled

2 *chiles chipotles en adobo*

1 cup (8 fl oz/250 ml) beef or chicken stock, plus up to 1 cup (8 fl oz/250 ml), if needed

Sea salt to taste, plus 1 teaspoon

2 lb (1 kg) ground (minced) lean beef

1 cup (4 oz/125 g) fine dried bread crumbs soaked in ¼ cup (2 fl oz/60 ml) milk

2 eggs, lightly beaten

6 tablespoons (½ oz/15 g) finely chopped fresh cilantro (fresh coriander)

½ teaspoon freshly ground pepper

3 eggs, hard-boiled and cut into cubes

Serves 6-8

1 Line a heavy frying pan with heavy-duty aluminum foil, shiny side up (to prevent sticking), and place over medium heat. Add the tomatillos and roast, turning occasionally, until their skin is blistered and begins to blacken and their interior softens and begins to ooze. Carefully trim off only the most blackened parts of the skin. Add the onion quarters and roast, turning occasionally, until blackened in spots and softened. Carefully remove the aluminum foil from the pan. Add the garlic cloves and roast, turning them frequently, until they soften and their skins blacken, about 10 minutes. Peel the garlic and place in a blender with the tomatillos and roasted onion. Add the chiles and the 1 cup (8 fl oz/250 ml) stock and process until smooth. Pour into a saucepan and bring to a boil. Reduce the heat and simmer, uncovered, for 10 minutes. Season with salt.

2 Mix the meat, bread crumbs, beaten eggs, chopped onion, 4 tablespoons (⅓ oz/10 g) of the cilantro, salt to taste, and pepper in a bowl. For each meatball, flatten 1 rounded tablespoon of the mixture. Add several cubes of egg and wrap the meat around them. Shape into a ball. Drop the balls into the simmering sauce, cover, and cook, stirring occasionally, 20–30 minutes. Add more stock as needed.

3 Spoon onto a warmed serving platter, sprinkle with the remaining 2 tablespoons cilantro, and serve.

Fajitas with Pico de Gallo

The Southwest • America

This example of how the Texas attitude transforms Southwestern fare into something larger than life is based on Mexican *arracheras,* beef rubbed with garlic and lime juice and grilled.

FAJITAS

⅓ cup (3 fl oz/80 ml) fresh orange juice

3 tablespoons fresh lime juice

2 tablespoons *each* tequila and olive oil

4 cloves garlic, finely chopped

1 tablespoon *each* honey, soy sauce, and Worcestershire sauce

1 tablespoon minced canned *chiles chipotles en adobo*

2½ lb (1.25 kg) skirt steaks

PICO DE GALLO

5 tomatoes, halved and seeded

⅔ cup (3½ oz/105 g) finely chopped yellow onion

2 jalapeño chiles, coarsely chopped

3 tablespoons fresh orange juice

2 tablespoons fresh lime juice

3 cloves garlic, coarsely chopped

¾ teaspoon salt, plus salt to taste

4 green Anaheim chiles, roasted and peeled (page 224), then chopped

⅓ cup (½ oz/15 g) chopped fresh cilantro (fresh coriander)

5 tablespoons (2½ fl oz/75 ml) olive oil

4 cloves garlic, finely chopped

2 large red bell peppers (capsicums), seeded and julienned

2 large poblano chiles, julienned

2 large yellow onions, thinly sliced

¾ teaspoon salt

½ teaspoon freshly ground pepper

24 flour tortillas, each 6 inches (15 cm) in diameter

16 large green (spring) onions

Guacamole and sour cream for serving

Serves 8

1 To make the fajitas, in a food processor or blender, combine the orange juice, lime juice, tequila, olive oil, garlic, honey, soy sauce, Worcestershire sauce, and chipotles and process until completely smooth.

2 Arrange the steaks in a single layer in a shallow dish and pour the orange juice mixture over them. Cover and marinate, turning occasionally, at room temperature for at least 3 hours, or refrigerate overnight. Bring to room temperature before proceeding.

3 To make the *pico de gallo,* coarsely chop half the tomatoes and place in a food processor. Add half the yellow onion along with the jalapeño chiles, orange juice, lime juice, garlic, and ¾ teaspoon salt. Process, stopping to scrape down the sides of the bowl, until finely and evenly chopped. Transfer to a bowl. Dice the remaining tomatoes and add to the bowl along with the chiles and the cilantro. Let stand at room temperature, stirring once or twice, for no more than 30 minutes. Taste and adjust the seasoning.

4 In a large frying pan over medium heat, warm 3 tablespoons of the olive oil. Add the garlic and cook, stirring once or twice, for about 2 minutes. Add the bell peppers, poblano chiles, yellow onions, salt, and pepper. Raise the heat to high and cook, tossing and stirring the vegetables, until they are lightly browned and becoming tender, 5–7 minutes longer. Remove from the heat and keep warm.

5 Prepare a hot fire in a grill with a cover. Preheat the oven to 400°F (200°C). Divide the tortillas into 4 equal stacks of 6 tortillas each. Wrap each stack tightly in aluminum foil. Set the packets in the oven for 10–15 minutes to warm the tortillas.

6 Lift the steaks from the marinade, reserving the marinade. Lay them on the grill rack 6 inches (15 cm) from the fire. Cover and grill, basting the meat with the marinade and turning occasionally, until the meat is done to your liking, 8–10 minutes for medium-rare. Stop basting at least 5 minutes before the meat is done. Transfer the steaks to a cutting board and tent loosely with aluminum foil. Brush the green onions with the remaining 2 tablespoons oil. Lay them on the grill rack, cover, and cook, turning once, until lightly marked by the grill rack and beginning to soften, about 4 minutes total.

7 Carve the steaks across the grain and on the diagonal into thin strips. Transfer to one end of a large platter. Spoon the reserved bell pepper mixture onto the other end of the platter. Top with the grilled green onions. Serve immediately with the *pico de gallo,* guacamole, sour cream, and tortillas. Diners arrange the steak, bell peppers mixture, *pico de gallo,* guacamole, and sour cream on the tortillas—along with the whole green onions—and fold the tortillas to enclose them.

Yellow Mole of Beef and Vegetables

Mole Amarillo de Res • Oaxaca • Mexico

Abigail Mendoza, who lives in the valley of Oaxaca, serves this hearty yellow mole with hot corn tortillas to scrape up every bit of the smoky, spicy sauce.

2 lb (1 kg) boneless stewing beef

1 beef soup bone

1 tablespoon sea salt, or to taste

4 guajillo chiles, seeded and toasted (page 224)

2 ancho chiles, seeded and toasted (page 224)

4 cloves garlic, coarsely chopped

⅛ teaspoon ground cumin

½ cup (2½ oz/75 g) *masa harina* for tortillas (page 226)

1 lb (500 g) new potatoes

1 chayote, peeled, seeded

1 lb (500 g) green beans

1 teaspoon dried oregano

3 limes, cut into wedges

Serves 6–8

1 Trim the beef and cut into 1-inch (2.5-cm) cubes. Put the beef and bone into a large, heavy pot. Add water to cover and the salt. Bring to a slow boil over medium heat, skimming off any foam from the surface. Cover, reduce the heat to medium-low, and simmer for about 45 minutes. Discard the soup bone.

2 Tear the chiles into large pieces and place in a bowl. Add very hot water to cover and soak for 10–15 minutes. Drain and place in a blender with the garlic and cumin. Add ½ cup (4 fl oz/125 ml) of the broth from the beef. Pulse to form a very smooth purée. Scrape into a bowl. Put 1 cup (8 fl oz/250 ml) broth into the blender, add the *masa harina*, and blend until smooth. Stir into the chile mixture.

3 Cut the potatoes and chayote into chunks, add to the meat, and cook, covered, for 10 minutes. Trim the ends of the green beans and cut into 1½-inch (4-cm) lengths. Add the green beans and cook for about 10 minutes. Stir in the chile-*masa* mixture and then add the oregano. Reduce the heat to low and cook uncovered, stirring occasionally, for about 10 minutes. Taste and adjust the seasoning. Ladle into bowls. Serve with the limes.

MOLES

The most remarkable of Mexico's culinary achievements is the mole—the quintessential fiesta dish since before recorded history. The term may come from *molli*, the Nahuatl word for "sauce" or "mixture." It is a broth that has been thickened with ground toasted nuts, seeds, or even tortillas or bread; flavored by chiles, herbs, and spices; and served with a few pieces of meat or vegetables.

The arrival of the Spanish changed the native mole. Visiting dignitaries were entertained in the convents of seventeeth-century Mexico, and no preparation was as lauded as the silky black mole poblano from the Convent of Santa Rosa in Puebla.

It contained more than a hundred different ingredients from both continents, as well as exotic spices from Asia.

Whenever there is a special event to celebrate, the women of the family will begin the preparation of their treasured version of mole, a dish that spans a full spectrum of colors and flavors. In Oaxaca, it might be *mole amarillo*, its yellow sauce usually surrounding various vegetables and meat, or *mole verde*, with an aromatic fresh herb sauce served with pork and tiny white beans. In Michoacán, a fruity *manchamanteles* with its lighter red sauce is common, while in Guerrero, a brick-red mole rules.

Guadalajara-Style Beef in Broth

Carne en Su Jugo Estilo Tapatío • Jalisco • Mexico

Bold and brash, this simple but unusual beef dish typifies the foods of Tapatíos—a word that identifies a person or thing as being from Guadalajara, the capital of Jalisco.

½ lb (250 g) lean, thin bacon slices, finely chopped

1 lb (500 g) beef sirloin tip or top round, thinly sliced diagonally, then coarsely chopped

4 cups (32 fl oz/1 l) rich beef stock

2 *chiles chipotles en adobo*

2 bay leaves

2 teaspoons sea salt, or to taste

1 teaspoon freshly ground pepper, or to taste

12 large green (spring) onions

2 cups (14 oz/440 g) drained canned pinto beans

½ cup (¾ oz/20 g) chopped fresh cilantro (fresh coriander)

5 serrano chiles, chopped

3 limes, quartered

Serves 4–6

1 In a frying pan over medium-low heat, slowly fry the chopped bacon until crisp. Transfer to absorbent paper to drain. Raise the heat to medium-high, add the beef to the bacon drippings, and fry for about 2 minutes. Transfer the beef to a large, heavy pot.

2 Put about 1 cup (8 fl oz/250 ml) of the beef stock in a blender, add the *chiles chipotles*, and blend until smooth. Add to the pot along with the rest of the stock and the bay leaves, salt, and pepper. Bring to a boil, reduce the heat to low, cover, and simmer until the meat is very tender, about 20 minutes.

3 Meanwhile, roast the green onions: line a heavy frying pan with heavy-duty aluminum foil and place over medium heat. Add the whole green onions and roast, turning occasionally, until blackened in spots and softened. Remove from the heat and set aside. Heat the beans in a saucepan over medium-low heat. Divide among bowls. Ladle the meat with its broth into the bowls and sprinkle with bacon and cilantro. Put 2 or 3 green onions on the side of each bowl. Pass the serrano chiles and limes at the table.

Marinated Steak with Herbs

Carne Asada con Hierbas • Puebla • Mexico

This recipe uses serrano or jalapeño chiles *en escabeche,* pickled peppers that are sold in jars at Latin American markets—juice and all—to create a flavorful marinade.

1 slice of large section beef tenderloin, 2½–3 lb (1.25–1.5 kg) and 2 inches (5 cm) thick

1 can (14 oz/440 g) pickled serrano or jalapeño chiles, with liquid

½ cup (4 fl oz/125 ml) safflower or canola oil

4 cloves garlic

¼ white onion, coarsely chopped

4 large fresh marjoram sprigs or ½ teaspoon dried

4 fresh thyme sprigs or ½ teaspoon dried

2 bay leaves

Sea salt and freshly ground pepper to taste

Serves 4

1 Place the beef in a shallow glass baking dish. In a blender or food processor, combine the chiles, oil, garlic, onion, marjoram, thyme, bay leaves, salt, and pepper. Process to form a purée with some texture. Pour the purée over the steak, cover, and refrigerate for at least 4 hours or as long as 12 hours, turning the steak once or twice.

2 Prepare a hot fire in a charcoal grill with a cover.

3 Lift the meat from the marinade, brushing off any excess. Place on the grill rack and sear for about 10 minutes on the first side. Turn the meat and sear the second side until well browned, about 7 minutes. Push the coals to one side of the grill bed, place the steak on the grill rack not directly over the coals, cover the grill, and grill for about 6 minutes longer for medium-rare. Do not leave the meat too long, as it will continue to cook when it is removed from the grill. Transfer to a cutting board, cover loosely with aluminum foil, and let rest for 5 minutes.

4 Slice the meat diagonally across the grain into strips ½ inch (12 mm) thick. Serve at once on a warmed platter.

Meat Loaf with Ketchup

The Midwest • America

Bread crumbs are often used to bring together ground meat and seasonings into a fine, firm loaf, but many Midwesterners substitute rolled oats soaked in scalded milk. The result is a nutty flavor and creamy texture with no discernible remnants of grain. Homemade chunky ketchup, a piquant sauce passed at the table, pushes this dish toward fancy fare.

KETCHUP

1 tablespoon olive oil

2 cloves garlic, crushed

3 anchovy fillets (optional)

1 teaspoon ground ginger

1 teaspoon dry mustard

1 teaspoon celery seed

2 teaspoons Worcestershire sauce

2 cans (28 oz/875 g each) whole plum (Roma) tomatoes, coarsely chopped, with juice

1 cup (10 oz/315 g) light corn syrup

3 bay leaves

Kosher salt or coarse sea salt to taste

2 tablespoons sugar (optional)

MEAT LOAF

1 tablespoon olive oil

6 green (spring) onions, including tender green tops, minced

2 teaspoons kosher salt or coarse sea salt

1 teaspoon freshly ground pepper

½ cup (4 fl oz/125 ml) milk

1 cup (3 oz/90 g) old-fashioned rolled oats

1 egg, beaten

1½ lb (750 g) ground (minced) pork

1½ lb (750 g) ground (minced) beef round or sirloin

Serves 8–10

1 Several hours or a day before serving the meat loaf, make the ketchup: In a saucepan over medium-low heat, warm the olive oil. Add the garlic and the anchovies, if using, mashing and stirring until soft, about 2 minutes. Add the ginger, mustard, and celery seed and heat until fragrant. Add the Worcestershire sauce and deglaze the pan, stirring to scrape up any browned bits on the pan bottom. Cook until almost fully evaporated.

2 Stir in the tomatoes and their juice, the corn syrup, and the bay leaves. Raise the heat to high and bring to a boil, then reduce the heat to low so the mixture simmers gently. Cook, uncovered, stirring occasionally, until thickened and shiny, about 1 hour. Season with salt, and sweeten with the sugar, if desired. Remove from the heat and let cool.

3 To make the meat loaf, in a small frying pan over medium-high heat, warm the olive oil. Add the green onions and sauté until soft, about 2 minutes. Add 1 teaspoon of the salt and the pepper and stir to distribute evenly. Remove from the heat and let cool.

4 Put the milk in a small saucepan over medium heat and heat until small bubbles appear at the edge of the pan. Pour the hot milk into a large bowl and stir in the rolled oats and the remaining 1 teaspoon salt. Let stand until the liquid is absorbed, about 15 minutes.

5 Preheat the oven to 350°F (180°C).

6 Add the egg, sautéed green onions, and 1 cup (8 fl oz/250 ml) of the ketchup to the rolled oats and stir to incorporate. Fold in the ground meats and mix gently with your hands just until the liquids are evenly distributed. Do not overmix, or the meat loaf will be tough and crumbly. Sear a small patty of the mixture in a hot frying pan until cooked. Taste and adjust the seasoning with salt and pepper.

7 Pack the meat mixture into an 8½-by-4½-inch (21.5-by-11.5-cm) loaf pan, mounding it nicely on top. Place in a baking pan to collect any overflowing juices. Bake the meat loaf for 1 hour. Remove from the oven and pour off the fat. Return to the oven until the juices run clear when the meat loaf is pierced in the center with a sharp knife or an instant-read thermometer inserted into the thickest part registers 165°F (74°C), 30–45 minutes longer. If the top of the loaf is browning too quickly, cover loosely with aluminum foil.

8 Just before the meat loaf is ready, reheat the remaining ketchup. Remove the meat loaf from the oven and let rest for 5 minutes, then cut into slices of desired thickness. Using a flexible metal spatula, carefully remove the slices from the pan and arrange on a warmed platter or individual plates. Pour some of the ketchup around the slices and pass the remaining ketchup at the table.

RANCHING IN THE WEST

Columbus brought the first cattle to the New World in 1494, but it wasn't until the early sixteenth century that the Spanish began ranching in Mexico, later expanding the tradition north of the border into New Mexico, Texas, and Colorado. Spanish cowboys, or *vaqueros,* were responsible for much of the early character of ranching, right down to the origination of the word *rodeo,* which comes from the Spanish for "to go around."

Following the Civil War, Anglo ranchers ran giant herds freely on public land throughout the region. The cattle would graze for months on the virtually untended natural grassland, with a single large house, barn, bunkhouse, and corrals serving as their headquarters. Once they were fattened, the herds were rounded up by cowboys and driven to railheads, then taken by train to Chicago and other Eastern markets.

From this rich mixture of the Spanish *cocina*—rough fare from trail-drive chuck-wagon cooks and home cooking from the ranch-house kitchen—was forged a strong tradition of hearty eating that lives on in the West of today.

Venison with Honey-Glazed Vegetables

The Mountain States • America

The tradition of wild game cooking in the West is very old, and even today the hunting tradition is vital in the region. Nonhunters may consider cooking game a novelty, but local chefs, who are great proponents of venison and other game, ensure a predictable supply of these meats by mail order, which makes turning out spectacular dishes such as this one relatively effortless. Ask your butcher or supplier to french the rib bones, that is, cut away the thin layers of meat from the top 4 inches (10 cm) of each bone.

1½ cups (12 fl oz/375 ml) medium-dry red wine

4 cloves garlic, chopped

5 tablespoons (3 fl oz/80 ml) olive oil

3 tablespoons honey

2 tablespoons red wine vinegar

18 juniper berries, chopped

1 oven-ready 8-chop venison rack, about 2½ lb (1.25 kg), frenched (see note)

2 tablespoons corn oil

12 small, red new potatoes, unpeeled, halved

2½ cups (12 oz/375 g) peeled, cubed butternut squash (½-inch/12-mm cubes)

½ teaspoon freshly ground pepper, plus pepper to taste

¼ teaspoon salt, plus salt to taste

2 Red Delicious apples, peeled, cored, and cut into ½-inch (12-mm) cubes

⅓ cup (½ oz/15 g) finely chopped fresh sage

Serves 4

1 In a food processor, combine the wine, the garlic, 3 tablespoons of the olive oil, the honey, the vinegar, and the juniper berries. Process until as smooth as possible. Place the venison rack in a shallow, nonaluminum pan or dish and pour the wine mixture over the rack. Cover and let stand at room temperature, turning once or twice, for 2 hours.

2 Position a rack in the upper third of the oven and preheat to 400°F (200°C).

3 In a large frying pan over medium-high heat, warm the corn oil. Lift the venison from the marinade, reserving the marinade, and pat the rack dry. Lay in the hot oil and cook until browned on the first side, about 4 minutes. Turn and cook on the other side until browned, 3–4 minutes. Transfer the rack to a shallow roasting pan, positioning it bone side up. Discard the oil from the frying pan but do not clean the pan.

4 Place the frying pan over medium heat and add the remaining 2 tablespoons olive oil. Add the potatoes and cook, stirring once or twice and scraping the browned bits from the pan bottom, until lightly browned, about 7 minutes. Add the squash cubes and cook, stirring once or twice, until they begin to to turn brown, about 7 minutes longer. Stir the ½ teaspoon pepper and the ¼ teaspoon salt into the vegetables and remove from the heat. Stir the apples into the vegetables, then spoon the mixture around the venison.

5 Place the roasting pan in the oven and roast for 8 minutes. Pour the marinade through a fine-mesh sieve and discard the solids. Baste the venison with about one-third of the marinade and stir the vegetable mixture. Return the venison to the oven and roast for another 8 minutes. Then baste the roast with half the remaining marinade and again stir the vegetables. Roast for another 8 minutes, then baste with the remaining marinade and stir the vegetables again. If the vegetables are tender, remove them from the pan and reserve. Continue to roast the venison until an instant-read thermometer inserted into the thickest part of the rack away from the bone registers 120°–125°F (49°–52°C) for rare, about 5 minutes longer, or until done to your liking.

6 Transfer the venison to a platter, tent loosely with aluminum foil, and let rest for about 5 minutes. If the vegetables are not yet tender, continue to roast for a few more minutes, then arrange on the platter.

7 Carve the rack of venison between the bones into chops. Arrange the chops on warmed individual plates, and season lightly with salt and pepper. Stir the sage into the vegetables, then taste and adjust the seasoning. Spoon the vegetables and any pan juices over the venison chops. Serve immediately.

Slow-Smoked Brisket with BBQ Sauce

The Great Plains • America

Texas may stake a claim on BBQ beef, but people in the Great Plains will never cede the right to call pit-cooked smoked brisket their own. The recipe may seem complicated, but the process is rewarding when you build a social gathering around it.

BRINE

1 cup (8 oz/250 g) kosher salt

1 head garlic, unpeeled, with top sliced off to reveal cloves

8 bay leaves

1 whole trimmed beef brisket, 7–9 lb (3.5–4.5 kg)

SAUCE

½ cup (4 fl oz/125 ml) corn oil

2 large white onions, chopped

1 teaspoon kosher salt or coarse sea salt

1 tablespoon New Mexico chile powder

2 teaspoons freshly ground black pepper, plus pepper to taste

½ teaspoon *each* celery seed and ground allspice

¼ teaspoon ground mace

¼ teaspoon ground cayenne pepper, or to taste

¼ cup (2 fl oz/60 ml) *each* distilled white vinegar and Dijon mustard

2 tablespoons light brown sugar

1 tablespoon molasses

2 cans (28 oz/875 g each) whole plum (Roma) tomatoes with juice

Granulated sugar and salt to taste

RUB

1 tablespoon *each* black peppercorns, white peppercorns, celery seed, caraway seed, and mustard seed

1 loaf soft white sandwich bread (optional)

Serves 16

1 Begin brining the brisket 1 or 2 days before smoking. Select a stockpot or other vessel large enough to hold the brisket and about 4 qt (4 l) of water. Pour in 2 qt (2 l) of water. Add the salt, garlic, and bay leaves. Stir to dissolve the salt. Rinse the brisket under running cold water and place in the brine. Add water just to cover. Cover the stockpot and refrigerate for 24–36 hours, turning the meat once or twice.

2 The day before smoking the meat, make the sauce: In a large, heavy nonaluminum pan over medium-high heat, warm the corn oil. Add onions and salt and sauté, stirring often, for 3 minutes. Add the chile powder, 2 teaspoons black pepper, celery seed, allspice, mace, and cayenne and stir and toss to coat the onions. Cook until fragrant, about 1 minute. Pour in the vinegar and stir to scrape up any browned bits on the pan bottom. Stir in the mustard, brown sugar, and molasses. When the mixture comes to a boil, add the tomatoes and return to a boil. Reduce the heat to very low, cover partially, and cook, stirring occasionally and mashing the tomatoes, for 3–3½ hours. Using a blender and working in batches, purée the sauce, adding water as needed to reach the desired consistency. It should be thick but pourable. Adjust the seasoning with granulated sugar, salt, and black pepper. Cover and refrigerate until ready to use.

3 On the morning you will begin smoking the meat, make the rub: In a spice mill or clean coffee grinder, combine the black and white peppercorns, celery seed, caraway seed, and mustard seed and grind finely. Remove the meat from the brine and rinse thoroughly. Pat dry with paper towels and rub with the spice mixture, coating well on all sides. Set aside for 1–2 hours to come to room temperature.

4 Prepare a fire for indirect-heat cooking in a covered grill, building it on one side of the grill bed and starting with about 2 qt (2 l) hardwood charcoal. Light the fire and open the vent beneath it. Place a drip pan on the other side of the grill bed. When the coals are almost all white, spread them a little but keep them to one side. Add a handful of fresh charcoal. Replace the grill rack.

5 Place the brisket, fat side up, on the rack over the drip pan. The fire should not be under the meat. Close the lid and open the vent on the lid so an opening is over the meat. Check the fire every 30 minutes to make sure it is still hot, adding 6 or 7 coals at a time. The goal is to keep the temperature inside the grill around 220°F (105°C). If it is too high, the meat will be dry; if it is too low, microbial growth will occur. Continue smoking the brisket for 8–10 hours. Do not worry if the crust turns very dark. The brisket is ready when it is tender and firm but not dry when cut into at the center and an instant-read thermometer inserted into the thickest part resisters at least 160°F (71°C). Remove from the grill and let rest for 15 minutes.

6 Gently reheat the barbecue sauce. Slice the brisket thinly against the grain and serve with the sauce and with the sandwich bread, if desired.

Slow-Cooked Lamb

Birria • Jalisco • Mexico

Birria, a rustic dish closely identified with Jalisco, is a richly spiced type of the traditional *barbacoa*. No longer steamed in buried underground pots, the chile-marinated meat, usually mutton or kid, is still long-cooked until it turns into a tender stew with plenty of flavorful broth. This sophisticated version contains fresh ginger and sherry.

5 cloves garlic, unpeeled

8 ancho chiles, seeded and toasted (page 224)

6 guajillo chiles, seeded and toasted (page 224)

1 cup (8 fl oz/250 ml) mild white vinegar

2-inch (5-cm) piece true cinnamon bark, ground, or 1 teaspoon ground cinnamon

½-inch (12-mm) piece fresh ginger, peeled and grated

2 teaspoons dried oregano, preferably Mexican

½ teaspoon ground cumin

½ teaspoon freshly ground pepper

1 teaspoon sea salt, or to taste

4–5 lb (2–2.5 kg) bone-in lamb shoulder, trimmed of excess fat

1 lb (500 g) tomatoes, boiled, or 1 can (14½ oz/455 g) chopped tomatoes

½ cup dry sherry (optional)

GARNISH

Shredded cabbage

Finely chopped white onion

Lime wedges

Serves 10

1 Place a heavy frying pan over medium heat. Add the garlic cloves and roast, turning them frequently, until they soften and their skins blacken, about 10 minutes. Remove from the heat and set aside. Put the chiles in a saucepan, add water to cover, and bring to a boil. Remove from the heat, press the chiles down in the water, and let soak until very soft, about 20 minutes. Drain and set aside.

2 Peel the garlic and place in a blender along with the chiles and vinegar. Process until very smooth. Add the cinnamon, the ginger, 1 teaspoon of the oregano, the cumin, the pepper, and the 1 teaspoon salt and blend again. You can add a spoonful of water to be sure the mixture blends smoothly, but this is a paste, so do not add more water than necessary. Taste and add more salt, if needed. If the paste is not perfectly smooth, pass it through a medium-mesh sieve.

3 Place the meat in a bowl and coat evenly with the paste. Cover and refrigerate for at least 5 hours or, preferably, overnight.

4 Preheat the oven to 350°F (180°C).

5 Place a rack in the bottom of a Dutch oven or roasting pan large enough to hold the meat. You may have to devise your own rack. The goal is to allow the steam to rise and the pungent sauce to drip into the water. The pan must have a tight-fitting lid as well. Pour in enough water to reach just to the top of the rack (3–4 cups/24–32 fl oz/750 ml–1 l) and then pile the meat on top of the rack, scraping any chile paste clinging to the bowl over the top. Seal the top of the pan tightly with foil and cover with the lid. Bake for 3 hours.

6 Remove from the oven and raise the oven temperature to 375°F (190°C).

7 Lift the meat from the pan, tear into large pieces, and spread them on a baking sheet, removing any large pieces of fat and gristle and the bones. Reserve the broth in the pan. Brown the meat in the oven for 15 minutes, turning at least once.

8 Pour the broth into a saucepan, skimming off as much fat as possible. In a blender, combine the tomatoes, the remaining 1 teaspoon oregano, and 1 cup (8 fl oz/250 ml) of the broth and purée until smooth. Pour the purée into the saucepan holding the broth. Add the sherry, if using, and bring to a gentle simmer over low heat. Season with salt, if necessary. Simmer gently, uncovered, for 15 minutes to blend the flavors.

9 To serve, spoon the meat into individual bowls and ladle in the broth. Pass the cabbage, onion, and lime wedges in separate small bowls at the table.

ZINFANDEL

California's first Cabernet Sauvignon, Pinot Noir, and Merlot vines came from Europe, but historians puzzled for years over the state's Zinfandel. Where did the original vines come from? Certainly, European vintners grew nothing by that name. Finally, in the late 1990s, with the help of DNA fingerprinting, researchers proved that Zinfandel and southern Italy's Primitivo are the same grape. How its name changed en route to America is still unknown; yet by the 1850s, California nursery owners were selling Zinfandel, and for a while it was the most widely planted wine grape in the state. Most growers today train the vines on trellises, but earlier farmers allowed them to sprawl. Some of the old vines survive, their thick gnarled arms a picturesque sight in winter.

If Cabernet Sauvignon is the serious member of the red wine family, Zinfandel is the fun-loving brother. When made in a light, fruity, zesty style, it complements barbecued ribs, hamburgers, and grilled chicken. Even when made in a weightier, riper style, this California classic seems better suited to informal, straightforward food—a juicy grilled steak, some aged cheese—than it does to a fussy, starched-tablecloth meal.

Braised Lamb Shanks with Zinfandel

California · America

Zinfandel is grown all over California, but regions particularly renowned for it include the Sierra Nevada foothills, Sonoma County, Lodi, and Napa Valley's Howell Mountain. The state's zesty Zinfandels pair beautifully with slow-cooked lamb, both in the sauce and on the table. And because this sauce requires only a small amount of wine, you will have plenty left to pour with the dinner. Serve the lamb with fresh egg noodles or polenta.

4 lamb shanks, 2¾–3 lb (1.4–1.5 kg) total weight

Salt and freshly ground pepper to taste

1 tablespoon extra-virgin olive oil

¾ lb (375 g) plum (Roma) tomatoes

½ yellow onion, finely minced

1 small carrot, peeled and finely chopped

1 celery stalk, finely chopped

2 cloves garlic, finely minced

2 teaspoons minced fresh rosemary

½ cup (4 fl oz/125 ml) Zinfandel

½ cup (4 fl oz/125 ml) water

2 tablespoons chopped fresh flat-leaf (Italian) parsley

Serves 4

1 Season the lamb with salt and pepper. In a high-sided frying pan or Dutch oven over medium-high heat, warm the olive oil. When the oil is hot, add the lamb, reduce the heat to medium-low, and brown on all sides, about 30 minutes. Using tongs, transfer the lamb shanks to a plate.

2 Meanwhile, halve the tomatoes. With your fingers, scoop out and discard the seeds. Grate the tomatoes using the large holes on a box shredder-grater, positioning the cut side of each half against the grater. Discard the tomato skins. You should have about 1 cup (8 fl oz/250 ml) purée.

3 Add the onion, carrot, celery, garlic, and rosemary to the pan. Sauté until soft, about 10 minutes. Add the wine, raise the heat to high, and simmer until the pan is almost dry, about 1 minute. Add the tomato purée and the water and return the lamb shanks to the pan. Bring to a simmer, cover, and adjust the heat to maintain a bare simmer. Cook until the meat is fork-tender and is easy to pull away from the bone, about 2 hours, turning the lamb shanks occasionally in the liquid.

4 Transfer the lamb to a plate. Pour the braising liquid and vegetables into a large measuring cup and refrigerate until most of the fat rises to the top, about 30 minutes. Spoon off the fat and discard, then return the braising liquid and vegetables to the pan. Place over high heat and simmer, uncovered, until thickened to a sauce consistency. Taste and adjust the seasoning.

5 Return the lamb shanks to the sauce and reheat gently until hot throughout. Stir in 1 tablespoon of the parsley.

6 Divide the shanks among warmed individual plates. Spoon the sauce over them. Garnish with the remaining parsley and serve at once.

Basque Leg of Lamb with Peppers

The Mountain States • America

The Basque cuisine of the Mountain States, primarily Nevada, is distinctive but not as well known as other culinary specialties of the West. Basque food is typically bold and rugged, like the Basques themselves. Often featuring mutton or lamb and frequently seasoned with herbs and spices that recall those of Euskadi, the Basque homeland, this is simple, rib-sticking fare that is easy to like.

1 leg of spring lamb, about 5½ lb (2.75 kg)

2 large cloves garlic, each cut into about 12 slivers, plus 18 whole large cloves, unpeeled

About 24 small fresh rosemary sprigs

2 tablespoons sweet Spanish or Hungarian paprika or medium-hot pure chile powder

6 tablespoons (3 fl oz/90 ml) olive oil

8 large red bell peppers (capsicums), seeded and quartered lengthwise

½ teaspoon salt, plus salt to taste

½ teaspoon freshly ground pepper, plus pepper to taste

¾ cup (6 fl oz/180 ml) beef stock or chicken stock

½ cup (4 fl oz/125 ml) medium-dry red wine

Serves 8

1 Ask the butcher to remove the aitchbone, or hipbone, from the lamb leg for easier carving, or do it yourself. Set the lamb, skin side down, on a roasting rack on a work surface. Using a paring knife, make a deep slit in the meaty portion of the upper surface of the lamb. Insert a sliver of garlic and a sprig of rosemary in the slit. Repeat, making 11 more evenly spaced slits and inserting a garlic sliver and a rosemary sprig in each one. Evenly dust the upper surface of the lamb with 1 tablespoon of the paprika, patting it firmly to adhere. Turn the lamb skin side up on the rack and repeat the process of making evenly spaced slits and filling them with the remaining garlic slivers and rosemary sprigs. Dust the upper surface with the remaining 1 tablespoon paprika, and pat it into place. Set the rack in a shallow, flameproof roasting pan large enough also to hold all the bell peppers without excessive crowding. Drizzle the upper surface with 1 tablespoon of the oil. Cover loosely with aluminum foil and let come to room temperature, about 1½ hours.

2 Position a rack in the lower third of the oven and preheat to 450°F (230°C).

3 Uncover the lamb, place in the oven, and roast for 15 minutes. Scatter the bell pepper quarters and garlic cloves in the roasting pan around the rack. Drizzle with the remaining 5 tablespoons (2½ fl oz/75 ml) olive oil and sprinkle with the ½ teaspoon salt and the ½ teaspoon pepper. Stir well to coat evenly with the oil. Return the pan to the oven, reduce the oven temperature to 350°F (180°C), and continue to roast, stirring the bell peppers and garlic every 10–15 minutes to promote even cooking, until an instant-read thermometer inserted into the thickest part of the lamb away from the bone registers 135°–140°F (57°–60°C) for rare to medium-rare, about 1 hour, or until done to your liking. The bell peppers will be tender and lightly browned, and the garlic cloves will be soft inside their peels. Transfer the lamb to a platter, tent with aluminum foil, and let rest for 10 minutes. Using a slotted spoon, transfer the bell peppers and garlic to the platter, arranging them around the lamb.

4 Set the roasting pan over medium-high heat on the stove top and add the stock and the wine. Bring to a brisk simmer and deglaze the pan, stirring to scrape up any browned bits from the pan bottom. Cook until the liquid is reduced by half and is becoming syrupy, about 5 minutes. Taste and adjust the seasoning. Pour through a fine-mesh sieve into a warmed gravy boat.

5 Carve the lamb into thick slices and arrange on individual plates. Mound some of the bell peppers and garlic over the lamb. Drizzle with a bit of the pan sauce and serve immediately, passing the remaining sauce at the table.

ASIA

Preceding pages: A family picnics beside one of the Sasbahu temples, part of the massive fortress of Gwalior, in India. **Top:** Watched over by stone Buddhas, a Burmese monk meditates in the magnificent Shwedagon Pagoda. **Above:** Garlic is hung in rural Indian houses to ward off insects, snakes, and evil. **Right:** Staple crops like rice are traditionally grown near Indian temples, such as this one near the Betwa River, to provide the temple an income.

I*n China, the pig reigns supreme on the nation's tables. An estimated 70 percent of China's meat dishes contain pork. This sometimes mild, sometimes richly flavored meat is particularly revered in the south, where roast suckling pig is essential to any festive occasion. Every day, along China's snaking rail lines, trains speed cargoes of live pigs from vast piggeries to markets in Hong Kong and Guangdong, and to specialty restaurants farther north.*

In northern China, the taste shifts. The Muslim preference for sheep and goat meat is far more evident in restaurants, where menus offer mutton kabobs, tender stir-fried lamb with honey and cilantro, and the famous lamb hotpot. This Chinese-style fondue uses lamb cut so thin that it is said a good chef can produce a hundred slices from a pound (500 g) of meat. When the marauding Mongols were hungry during a campaign, they threw a shield over a fire, slaughtered a sheep, and grilled the meat on the hot metal. During their dominance of the north of China (AD 1215–1368) this tradition was translated to the kitchen and the shield became the ribbed iron grid seen in many Mongolian restaurants.

Chicken and duck are consumed in vast quantities and with equal gusto. Peking duck is possibly one of the best-known dishes in the world and is a treat not to be missed on a visit to Beijing. Fujian, on the east coast, also has a reputation for duck and goose dishes, and part of the secret is the use of local citrus and vinegar in the preparation. Duck, quail, or other poultry smoked over camphor or tea is a favorite in Sichuan. Chicken comes slow-simmered to gelatinous tenderness, is succulent in a stir-fry, is sublimely moist as "white cut" poached chicken, might be baked in a clay shell like Hangzhou beggar's chicken, or is served with rice and a salty shallot and oil sauce on Hainan Island. Nothing is too humble to be a potential star in the Chinese cooking pot. Even peripheral ingredients such as chicken feet, ducks' webs and tongues, pigs' ears and tails, and beef tendons are transformed into desirable dishes in the hands of skillful cooks throughout the country.

With thousands of miles of coastline, it's no surprise that many peninsular and island nations of Southeast Asia depend on fish for protein. However, meat and poultry, although generally not as plentiful and usually more costly, do appear on the region's tables. In Indonesia and Malaysia, where Islam is widespread, lamb and beef are popular, primarily in curries and in the region's popular charcoal-grilled satays, an adaptation of Arab traders' kabobs, given an Asian flavor with a dip of spicy-sweet peanut sauce. Elsewhere pork is added to the list, turned into such dishes as pork stewed in coconut juice in Vietnam and pork *adobo* in the Philippines. In Vietnam, beef appears in the renowned shaking beef (named to evoke the flipping of the beef in a pan of hot oil) and in the cooked-at-the-table dish of beef fondue, in which the beef is simmered briefly in a vinegar-laced broth, then rolled in rice paper with crunchy raw vegetables and dipped in salty *nuoc cham*. Chicken, however, is popular throughout the region, simply grilled in Cambodia and Laos, poached and served with rice in Singapore, crisply fried in Indonesia, simmered in green curry in Thailand, stir-fried in Vietnam, and coated with a lemongrass curry sauce in Malaysia.

In India, lamb and goat are the most commonly consumed red meats, as Hindus, Buddhists, Jains, and Sikhs are forbidden to eat beef, while Muslims and Jews shun pork. Pork and beef dishes like the Portuguese-influenced *sorpotel* (pork in hot and sour sauce) are thus found only in predominantly Christian areas, such as Goa and Kerala on the southwest coast. And while mutton technically refers to the meat of a mature sheep, in India it also denotes lamb and goat. (This confusion dates from the British Raj when the English *memsahibs* called all red meat "mutton.") Goats are adaptable, making them better suited to the hot, dry northern plains, while sheep prefer the cool slopes of the Himalayas. The lamb available in the West is perfect for Indian dishes traditionally made with the meat of sheep or goats, such as the classic Moghul dish *saag gosht* (lamb with spinach) or the intriguing *masalchi mutton* (meat braised with pepper and fresh herbs), a traditional Passover dish among the small, ancient Jewish community on India's west coast.

The meat that Indians value most is neither lamb nor goat, but chicken. Northern Indians are known for their superb chicken dishes, such as *murgh malai kabab* (spiced chicken kabobs), *tandoori murgh hariali* (tandoori-baked chicken), and *makkhani murgh* (butter chicken). For the last, day-old tandoori chicken is braised in a creamy, ginger gravy until the chicken pieces soak up the sauces and are transformed into perfumed morsels. Many Punjabis make spice-rubbed, yogurt-marinated tandoori chicken just so they can turn it into *makkhani murgh* the next day.

Opposite: A farmer allows his prized buffalo to graze among the rice paddies of southwest China. **Above, left:** Whitewashed buildings and *ghats* line Pushkar Lake, in Rajasthan. According to legend, the lake was created from one of three rose petals that fell from the hand of Brahma. **Above, right:** Elephants make light work of hauling brush in Calicut, Kerala.

Tandoori Chicken

Tandoori Murghi · Delhi · India

This most popular of all Indian dishes takes its name from the *tandoor,* the clay oven in which it is baked. It can, however, be roasted very successfully using a conventional oven. To color the chicken its traditional bright red hue, add 1 teaspoon red food coloring and 2 teaspoons yellow food coloring to the marinade.

1 small chicken, about 3 lb (1.5 kg), cut into serving pieces, skinned, and trimmed of all visible fat

½ cup (4 oz/125 g) plain yogurt

2 tablespoons fresh lemon juice

1 tablespoon *each* minced garlic and peeled and grated fresh ginger

1 tablespoon ground cumin

1 teaspoon ground coriander

½ teaspoon ground cayenne pepper

¼ teaspoon *each* ground cardamom, cloves, and black pepper

2 teaspoons salt, or to taste

Vegetable oil for brushing

Slices of cucumber, red onion, tomato, and lemon

Serves 4

1 Prick the flesh of the chicken all over with a fork, then, using a sharp knife, cut slashes in the flesh to allow the marinade to penetrate. Place the chicken in a large, shallow dish.

2 To make the marinade, in a glass or ceramic bowl, combine the yogurt, lemon juice, garlic, ginger, cumin, coriander, cayenne, cardamom, cloves, black pepper, and salt. Stir until well mixed, then pour the mixture over the chicken and rub it into the flesh, turning the chicken several times. Cover and marinate in the refrigerator for 8 hours or overnight. (Do not marinate for longer than 2 days.) Remove the chicken from the refrigerator at least 30 minutes before cooking.

3 Grill or roast the chicken. If using a charcoal grill, prepare a fire for direct-heat cooking. Position the grill rack 5 inches (13 cm) from the fire. Allow the coals to burn until white ash covers them and the heat is moderate. Remove the chicken from the marinade, pressing lightly to extract excess marinade, and brush with oil. Place the chicken pieces on an oiled grill rack and grill, covered, with the vents open, turning 3 or 4 times, until the juices run clear when a piece is pierced near the bone with a knife, about 45 minutes.

4 If roasting the chicken, preheat the oven to 450°F (230°C). Place the chicken on a rack in a roasting pan, brush with oil, and cook, turning once, until the juices run clear when a piece is pierced near the bone with a knife, 25–30 minutes.

5 Serve with slices of cucumber, red onion, tomato, and lemon.

THE TANDOOR

Traditional Indian kitchens do not have conventional Western ovens. Yet Indians can still bake, broil, and roast their food using a *tandoor,* a clay-lined oven that is shaped like a barrel with a vent at the bottom. Several cultures, including the Syrian Bedouins and the Persians, devised a rudimentary *tandoor,* a clay pit used primarily for baking breads.

The eastern Pachtun tribes of Pakistan refined the basic model to create the *tandoor* of today. In the oven's most common role, meat is marinated in a yogurt-spice mixture that has been colored with an orange-red dye and then threaded onto skewers. The skewers are lowered into the searing heat of the oven where the meat grills, bakes, and smokes simultaneously, producing remarkable flavor and tenderness.

Tandoori chicken and tandoori nan remain two of the most popular dishes served in Indian restaurants. But other foods, including fish and shellfish, vegetables, and cheese, take on the same earthy aroma and delicious flavor when cooked in this ingenious oven.

Chicken in Kaffir Lime Leaf Curry

Ayam Limau Purut • Malaysia

This curry has the citrus scent and taste of lemongrass, the sweet-sour flavor of tamarind, and the fragrance of kaffir lime leaf. The combination results in a light curry sauce ideal for chicken. In the past, Nonyas (women of Chinese and Malay descent) would hand-pound the spice mixture. Nowadays, a blender may be used to grind the ingredients. Tamarind pulp is sold in blocks in Asian markets. Tamarind concentrate, which dissolves instantly in hot water, is also available in Asian markets and can substituted for the tamarind water.

1 To make the spice paste, place the drained dried chiles in a blender with the lemongrass, galangal, turmeric, garlic, shallots, and fresh chiles. Process until a smooth paste forms. If necessary, add a few tablespoons of water to facilitate the blending.

2 Preheat a wok or large, heavy pot over medium-high heat. When hot, add the vegetable oil and the spice paste and fry, stirring frequently, until the oil and paste are emulsified, about 3 minutes. Continue gently frying the paste, stirring often, until tiny oil beads appear on the surface, 5–8 minutes.

3 To make the tamarind water, in a bowl, combine the tamarind pulp and boiling water. Mash the tamarind pulp to separate the fibers and seeds. Let stand for about 15 minutes, stirring 2 or 3 times. Pour the liquid through a fine-mesh sieve placed over a bowl, pushing against the pulp with the back of a spoon and scraping the underside of the sieve to dislodge the clinging purée. Set aside.

4 Add the chicken pieces to the wok and mix to coat with the spice paste. Add the coconut milk, reduce the heat to medium, and cook, stirring occasionally, for 5 minutes. Add the tamarind mixture, lime leaves, coconut cream, and salt, raise the heat to high, and bring to a boil. Immediately reduce the heat to low, cover, and simmer until the chicken is cooked, about 20 minutes.

5 Uncover and raise the heat to medium-high. Cook, stirring, until the sauce thickens slightly, just a few minutes.

6 Transfer to a serving dish and serve at once.

6 dried red chiles, cracked, seeded, soaked in warm water for 15 minutes, and drained

1 lemongrass stalk, tender midsection only, chopped

2 slices fresh galangal, peeled and coarsely chopped

1 small finger of fresh turmeric, 1 inch (2.5 cm) long, peeled and quartered, or 1½ teaspoons ground turmeric

6 cloves garlic, quartered

3 large shallots, about ¼ lb (125 g) total weight, quartered

5 fresh red Fresno or jalapeño chiles, 2–3 oz (60–90 g) total weight, seeded and quartered

⅓ cup (3 fl oz/80 ml) vegetable oil

TAMARIND WATER

1½ oz (45 g) tamarind pulp

⅔ cup (5 fl oz/160 ml) boiling water

1 chicken, 3½ lb (1.75 kg), cut into serving pieces

2 cups (16 fl oz/500 ml) coconut milk (page 224)

6–8 kaffir lime leaves, spines removed

½ cup (4 fl oz/125 ml) coconut cream (page 224)

2 teaspoons salt

Serves 4

Braised Spicy Ginger Chicken

Dong'an Ji • Western • China

Ginger, garlic, hot red chiles, vinegar, and Sichuan pepper are the typically exuberant flavors used in the kitchens of the landlocked province of Hunan. The city of Dong'an, the reputed birthplace of this dish, is on its southern border.

½ cup (4 fl oz/125 ml) chicken stock or water

1½ tablespoons light soy sauce

1 tablespoon black vinegar (page 227)

2 teaspoons chile oil

1 tablespoon superfine (caster) sugar

14 oz (440 g) boneless chicken thighs, cut into ¾-inch (2-cm) cubes

1 tablespoon dark soy sauce

1 tablespoon cornstarch (cornflour)

Peanut or vegetable oil for deep-frying

¾ cup (2½ oz/75 g) chopped green (spring) onion, including tender green tops

1 hot red chile, seeded and sliced

1 tablespoon peeled and grated fresh ginger

1 tablespoon crushed garlic

Salt to taste

Large pinch of ground white or Sichuan pepper

Serves 4

1 To prepare the sauce, in a small bowl, stir together the stock, light soy sauce, vinegar, chile oil, and sugar. Set aside.

2 In a bowl, combine the chicken, dark soy sauce, and cornstarch and mix well. Let stand for at least 15 minutes.

3 Pour the oil to a depth of 1 inch (2.5 cm) into a wok, and heat to 360°F (182°C), or until a small cube of bread dropped into it begins to turn golden within a few seconds. Carefully slide the chicken into the oil and stir with wooden chopsticks or a slotted spoon to separate the pieces. Fry until golden brown, about 1½ minutes. Using a slotted spoon, transfer to a rack placed over a plate to drain.

4 Pour off all but 2 tablespoons of the oil and return the wok to high heat. Add the green onion, chile, ginger, and garlic and stir-fry until partially wilted, about 30 seconds. Return the chicken to the wok and stir-fry over high heat until the ingredients are evenly mixed, about 30 seconds.

5 Pour in the sauce and stir over high heat until well mixed, about 10 seconds. Reduce the heat to medium-low, cover, and simmer gently until the chicken is tender and the flavors are well blended, about 4 minutes. Season with salt and the white pepper.

6 Transfer to a serving plate and serve at once.

Empress Chicken Wings

Guifei Ji • Eastern • China

In the exuberant 1920s, Shanghai was a city of wealth, culture, and flamboyance and its restaurants strove to delight an international clientele with the most creative dishes imaginable. Yang Kueifei had been a celebrated imperial concubine in the Tang dynasty (AD 618–907). In tribute to her legendary beauty and desirability, a Sichuanese chef in Shanghai created this dish, in which he bathed the tenderest of chicken wings in a subtly sweet, ruby red sauce made from imported port wine.

5 large chicken wings, 1–1¼ lb (500–625 g) total weight

⅓ cup (1½ oz/45 g) sliced bamboo shoot

2 large dried black mushrooms, soaked in hot water to cover for 25 minutes and drained

½ cup (4 fl oz/125 ml) plus 2 tablespoons vegetable oil

1¾ teaspoons superfine (caster) sugar

1 thin slice fresh ginger, peeled and finely julienned

1 tablespoon rice wine

1 tablespoon light soy sauce

1½ cups (12 fl oz/375 ml) chicken stock

Scant ½ teaspoon salt, plus salt to taste

¼ cup (2 fl oz/60 ml) port wine

1 green (spring) onion, including tender green tops, cut into 1½-inch (4-cm) lengths and finely julienned

2 teaspoons cornstarch (cornflour) dissolved in 1 tablespoon water

Fresh cilantro (fresh coriander) sprigs

Serves 4

1 Using a cleaver or heavy knife, separate the chicken wings at the joints. Rinse and drain well. Cut the sliced bamboo shoot into julienne. Remove and discard the stems from the mushrooms and thinly slice the caps.

2 In a wok over high heat, warm the ½ cup (4 fl oz/125 ml) oil until smoking. Add 1 teaspoon of the sugar and, using a wok spatula or wooden chopsticks, stir it in the hot oil for about 10 seconds; it will bubble and brown. Add the chicken wings and stir-fry until lightly browned, about 1½ minutes. Using a slotted spoon, transfer the wings to a rack placed over a plate to drain. Pour off the oil from the wok and discard.

3 Rinse the wok, wipe dry, and replace over high heat. Add the remaining 2 tablespoons oil and heat until smoking. Add the bamboo shoot and mushrooms and stir-fry until glazed with the oil, about 20 seconds. Return the chicken wings to the wok and add the ginger, rice wine, and soy sauce. Heat briefly, then pour in the stock and add the salt. Bring to a gentle boil, reduce the heat to low, and simmer until the wings are just tender, about 15 minutes.

4 Add the port and the remaining ¾ teaspoon sugar to the wok and bring to a boil. Reduce the heat to medium, stir in the green onion, and then the cornstarch mixture. Simmer, stirring continuously, until the sauce is lightly thickened and becomes clear, about 20 seconds. Season to taste with salt.

5 Using tongs, lift the chicken wings onto a serving plate. Spoon the sauce evenly over the wings and garnish with cilantro sprigs.

FOOD FOR AN EMPRESS

The Qing dynasty Dowager Empress Cixi enjoyed a gourmet reputation, so in order to remain in her favor the imperial chefs had to constantly please her with innovative creations. Lavish meals were served, even when she dined alone. Much went untasted, and when she found something special, her praise was usually veiled behind a demand for the name of the new dish.

Lamb was not highly regarded at court. One daring dish of lamb tenderloin in a sweet glaze might have cost the chef his head, had he not invited the empress to suggest a name. Her response—"it's like honey"—became the name of the dish, which is still served today in Beijing.

The empress loved sweet and savory snacks—bite-sized corn breads, sesame-flavored buns, and lotus-filled pastries. On a trip to Guangzhou, she proclaimed *xia jiao* (shrimp dumplings) the "food of heaven." Cixi's fondness for sweet flavors was appeased by countless variations on the sweet-and-sour theme, including a dish of fish served over noodles cooked for her in the ancient capital of China, Kaifeng, in Henan province. Chef Fang Shi was something of an alchemist in the kitchen, devising ways to turn simple food into gold for the empress by embellishing his dishes with egg yolks.

Grilled Skewered Chicken and Lamb with Spicy Peanut Sauce

Satay Ayam dan Kambing • Malaysia

Malay cooks judge the quality of peanut sauce by the color of the oil on the surface, although some Westerners will add the prescribed amount and then spoon off the excess.

4½ tablespoons dark brown sugar

2 tablespoons ground coriander

4 teaspoons ground cumin

2 teaspoons peeled and minced fresh ginger plus 2-inch (5-cm) piece fresh ginger, peeled and chopped

1 teaspoon minced garlic, plus 6 cloves garlic, halved

2 teaspoons ground turmeric

3 teaspoons salt

1 lb (500 g) boneless, skinless chicken thigh or breast meat

1 lb (500 g) boneless lamb

8 dried red chiles, cracked, seeded, soaked in warm water for 15 minutes, and drained

2-inch (5-cm) piece fresh galangal, peeled and chopped

5 large shallots, quartered lengthwise

2 lemongrass stalks, tender midsection only, chopped

1 slice dried shrimp paste, ⅛ inch (3 mm) thick

½ teaspoon ground fennel

½ cup (4 fl oz/125 ml) plus 1 tablespoon vegetable oil

⅓ cup (3 fl oz/80 ml) tamarind water (page 74)

1½ cups (7½ oz/235 g) unsalted roasted peanuts, coarsely ground

1½ cups (12 fl oz/375 ml) water

⅓ cup (3 fl oz/80 ml) coconut cream (page 224)

1 English (hothouse) cucumber, peeled and cut into irregular ¼-inch (6-mm) wedges

1 red onion, cut into ¼-inch (6-mm) wedges

Serves 10

1 Soak 20 bamboo skewers in water to cover for 30 minutes.

2 In a mixing bowl, stir together 1½ tablespoons of the brown sugar, 1 tablespoon of the coriander, 1 tablespoon of the cumin, the 2 teaspoons minced ginger, the 1 teaspoon minced garlic, 1 teaspoon of the turmeric, and 1 teaspoon of the salt. Divide the mixture evenly between 2 bowls. Cut the chicken and lamb into ¾-inch (2-cm) cubes. Thread 3 or 4 pieces of chicken onto the pointed end of each bamboo skewer. They can touch but should not press against each other. Repeat with the lamb. Cover and refrigerate for a few hours or preferably overnight.

3 To make the peanut sauce, in a blender or food processor, combine the drained chiles, chopped ginger, galangal, shallots, 6 cloves of halved garlic, lemongrass, and shrimp paste. Process to form a very smooth paste. If needed, add a few tablespoons of water to facilitate the blending. Add the remaining 1 tablespoon coriander, the remaining 1 teaspoon cumin, the remaining 1 teaspoon turmeric, and the fennel and process until well mixed.

4 In a saucepan over medium heat, warm ½ cup of the vegetable oil. Add the spice paste and fry, stirring continuously, until a thick, fragrant, emulsified mixture forms, about 2 minutes. Reduce the heat to medium-low and continue frying, stirring occasionally, until oil beads appear on the surface, about 10 minutes longer. Stir in the tamarind water, peanuts, 2 tablespoons of the brown sugar, the remaining 2 teaspoons salt, and the water, reduce the heat to low, and simmer gently for 45 minutes. The sauce is done when beads of oil dot the surface and it is the consistency of thick cream. (The sauce can be made up to 3 days in advance, covered, and refrigerated, then reheated.)

5 Prepare a fire in a charcoal grill. To make the basting oil, in a bowl, stir together the coconut cream, the remaining 1 tablespoon vegetable oil, and the remaining 1 tablespoon brown sugar.

6 When the coals are white and glowing, place the skewers on the grill rack about 2 inches (5 cm) above the coals. Brush the meats with the basting oil and grill, turning once, to brown both sides and cook the meats through, about 2 minutes on each side.

7 Meanwhile, reheat the peanut sauce over medium-low heat and pour into a serving bowl. Arrange the skewers on a platter and place the cucumber, and onion alongside. Serve at once with the peanut sauce.

Crisp-Fried Chile-and-Garlic Quail

Zha Ganlajiao Anchun • Western • China

In this dish, a technique the Chinese call *peng* is used. The main ingredient is first fried in oil, then the oil is drained and additional ingredients are stir-fried in the same pan.

3 large quail

1 teaspoon chile oil

2 teaspoons dark soy sauce

Vegetable or peanut oil for frying

1 tablespoon sesame oil (optional)

2 teaspoons peeled and finely chopped fresh ginger

2 teaspoons finely chopped garlic

2 teaspoons finely chopped hot red chile

2 teaspoons light soy sauce

Pepper-salt (page 226)

1 tablespoon finely chopped green (spring) onion tops

Serves 3–6

1 To prepare the quail, cut each quail in half along the breastbone. Trim off and discard the necks and wing tips. Rinse under running cold water, drain well, and pat dry with paper towels. In a small dish, stir together the chile oil and soy sauce, and brush evenly over the quail. Set aside for 10 minutes.

2 Pour the vegetable oil to a depth of ½ inch (12 mm) into a large frying pan or wok, and heat over high heat until the oil shimmers and begins to smoke. Add the sesame oil, if using. Pat the quail dry again with paper towels and carefully slide them into the oil. Fry for 1 minute, reduce the heat to medium-high, and continue to fry until golden brown and cooked through, 7–8 minutes. Test by pushing a fine skewer into the thigh or breast of a quail half; if no pink juices flow, the quail are done. Lift them out with a wire skimmer or 2 slotted spoons and set aside on a plate.

3 Pour off all but 1 tablespoon of the oil and return the pan to medium-high heat. Add the ginger, garlic, and chile and stir-fry until very fragrant and beginning to brown, about 30 seconds. Return the quail to the pan and add the soy sauce. Shake the pan over high heat, about 10–20 seconds, so the quail tumble and turn until evenly coated with the seasonings. Add 1 teaspoon of the pepper-salt and the green onion tops and repeat the shaking, tossing action, about 10–20 seconds.

4 Tip the quail onto a serving plate and serve at once with the remaining pepper-salt.

Duck in Red Curry

Gaeng Ped Supparot • Thailand

Traditional Chinese roast duck cooked in a typical Thai red curry paste characterizes the melding of two great cuisines. The duck should be purchased from a Chinese shop selling prepared foods but the curry paste can be found at most well-stocked markets.

½ Chinese roast duck

½ cup (4 fl oz/125 ml) coconut cream (page 224)

3 tablespoons Thai red curry paste (see note)

1–2 tablespoons palm or brown sugar

1–2 tablespoons fish sauce

2½ cups (20 fl oz/625 ml) coconut milk (page 224)

8 kaffir lime leaves, spines removed

1 cup (6 oz/185 g) cubed pineapple (1-inch/2.5-cm cubes)

8 cherry tomatoes, halved

1 cup (1 oz/30 g) fresh Thai basil leaves

Serves 4

1 Chop the duck into small pieces. In a wok or deep saucepan over medium heat, combine the coconut cream and curry paste and cook, stirring, until tiny beads of oil appear on the surface, 5–8 minutes. Add the palm or brown sugar, fish sauce, and duck and stir to mix. Add the coconut milk and lime leaves, bring to a boil, and immediately reduce the heat to medium-low. Simmer gently for about 5 minutes to heat the duck.

2 Add the pineapple, tomatoes, and basil leaves and stir just until the basil leaves are wilted. Transfer to a serving dish. Serve hot or at room temperature.

Butter Chicken

Makkhani Murgh • Punjab • India

While Westerners in an Indian restaurant usually order tandoori chicken, Indians invariably ask for *makkhani murgh.* Indians place a high value on the sauce in a dish, much more than on the main ingredient. The velvety sauce in butter chicken—consisting of tomatoes, cream, and spices—is held in particular esteem.

6 tomatoes, 1½–1¾ lb (750–875 g) total weight, coarsely chopped

1-inch (2.5-cm) piece fresh ginger, peeled and coarsely chopped, plus 1 tablespoon, peeled and finely shredded

4 fresh hot green chiles such as serrano, stemmed

2 teaspoons ground coriander

Salt and freshly ground pepper to taste

½ cup (¾ oz/20 g) chopped fresh cilantro (fresh coriander)

1 recipe day-old Tandoori Chicken (page 73) or Chicken Malai Kabob (page 94)

¼ cup (2 fl oz/60 ml) heavy (double) cream

¼ cup (2 oz/60 g) unsalted butter, softened

Serves 6

1 Working in batches, in a blender or food processor, combine the tomatoes, chopped ginger, chiles, and ground coriander and process until smooth. Transfer the purée to a saucepan and bring to a boil over high heat. Reduce the heat to medium and cook, uncovered, until the sauce is reduced by half, about 10 minutes. Remove from the heat and strain through a fine-mesh sieve into a large frying pan.

2 Add the shredded ginger, salt, pepper, half of the cilantro, and the chicken to the sauce. Cook over medium-low heat, stirring frequently to prevent sticking or burning, until the sauce comes to a boil. Reduce the heat to low, cover, and simmer until the chicken absorbs some of the sauce, about 5 minutes. Remove from the heat. In a small bowl, mix together the cream, butter, and the remaining cilantro. Pour over the chicken. Do not mix; the cream and butter should streak the tomato sauce. Transfer to a shallow serving dish and serve immediately.

TAMARIND

Indians are often surprised to discover that one of their beloved flavorings is not native to India. Introduced from Africa in prehistoric times, tamarind is valued for both its floral aroma and sweet-sour taste. Although popular throughout the country, the pulpy pods are primarily used in the southern kitchen, where they are indispensable in preparations such as lentil stews (*sambar*), soups (*rasam*), and fish dishes. The flavoring is also valued for its cooling properties, and Indians typically sip iced tamarind tea or soda water to beat the summer heat.

Tamarind pods grow on large shade trees, *Tamarindus indica,* that dot the Indian countryside. While the pods are the most commonly used parts of the tree, Indians also employ the leaves and tender stems in cooking. The ripe pods are opened and seeded, and the pulp is pressed into blocks for sale. The soft, sticky brownish pulp is soaked in hot water and its juice extracted before use in cooking. Ready-made tamarind water and concentrated paste are also available in stores. In an emergency, processed or canned paste is an acceptable alternative.

Fried Chicken with Lime and Coconut

Ayam Goreng Kalasan • Indonesia

Kalasan is an ancient Buddhist temple in central Java, located in the same area as the more famous sites of Borobudur and Prambanan. It is a mystery as to why this dish is named after the temple, but it is commonly served during festive occasions. The chicken is first braised in coconut juice and a few spices and then deep-fried until the skin is crisp and flavorful.

1 Rub the chicken pieces with the lime juice and set aside while preparing the spice paste.

2 To make the spice paste, in a mortar, pound the peppercorns. Add the chiles, shallots, and garlic and pound to form a smooth paste. Alternatively, make it in a blender, adding a few tablespoons of water to facilitate the blending.

3 Put the spice paste into a wok or large, heavy pot. Add the chicken pieces, coconut juice, lemongrass, lime leaves, *salam* leaf, 1 teaspoon of the salt, and several grinds of pepper. Bring to a boil over high heat, reduce the heat to medium, cover, and boil gently for about 20 minutes. Using a slotted utensil, transfer the chicken to a plate, draining it well. If you would like to serve a little sauce with the chicken, strain the cooking liquid and spoon off any fat from the surface. Return it to a clean saucepan and boil over medium-high heat until it is reduced to a light sauce consistency. Keep warm over very low heat.

4 Pour the oil to a depth of about 2 inches (5 cm) in a wok or heavy, deep frying pan and heat to 350°F (180°C) on a deep-frying thermometer. Blot the chicken pieces dry with paper towels and sprinkle them with the remaining 1 teaspoon salt. When the oil is ready, add half of the chicken pieces and deep-fry, turning as needed, until golden brown on all sides, about 5 minutes total.

5 Using tongs or a wire skimmer, transfer the chicken pieces to paper towels to drain. Repeat with the remaining chicken pieces.

6 Arrange the chicken pieces on a serving platter and serve immediately. If using the sauce, pour it into a small bowl and pass it at the table.

1 chicken, 3½ lb (1.75 kg), quartered or cut into serving pieces

Juice of 2 limes

SPICE PASTE

6 peppercorns

4 red Fresno or jalapeño chiles, seeded and quartered

2 large shallots, quartered

3 cloves garlic, quartered

2 cups (16 fl oz/500 ml) frozen coconut juice, thawed

1 lemongrass stalk, tender midsection only, smashed

5 kaffir lime leaves, spines removed

1 *salam* leaf (page 226)

2 teaspoons salt

Freshly ground pepper to taste

Vegetable oil for deep-frying

Serves 4

Duck with Bamboo and Mushrooms

Hongshao Ya Qingsun Xianggu • Northern • China

Bamboo shoots are sold salted, ready to use in cans, and fresh in plastic bags packed in water. Salted dried bamboo shoots should be rinsed and blanched before use.

½ large duck, about 1¾ lb (875 g), chopped into 2-inch (5-cm) pieces

½ cup (2 oz/60 g) cornstarch (cornflour)

1 cup (8 fl oz/250 ml) vegetable or peanut oil

6 oz (185 g) bamboo shoot, cut into 1-inch (2.5-cm) chunks

2 green (spring) onions, white part only, cut into ½-inch (12-mm) pieces, plus tender green tops of 1 green onion, thinly sliced

12 large dried black mushrooms, soaked in hot water to cover for 25 minutes

2½-inch (6-cm) piece fresh ginger, cut into chunks

½ cup (4 fl oz/125 ml) dark soy sauce

¼ cup (2 fl oz/60 ml) oyster sauce

1 tablespoon rice wine

3–4 teaspoons superfine (caster) sugar

1¾ oz (50 g) bean thread noodles, soaked in hot water for 15 minutes, drained, and cut into 4-inch (10-cm) lengths

Salt and freshly ground pepper to taste

1 tablespoon chopped fresh cilantro (fresh coriander) (optional)

Serves 4–6

1 Rinse the duck under running cold water and pat dry. Spread the cornstarch in a shallow dish, then dip the duck into the cornstarch, coating lightly and evenly and tapping off the excess.

2 In a wok or frying pan over high heat, warm the oil until smoking. Add half of the duck pieces and fry, turning once or twice, until the surface is lightly browned, about 5 minutes. Using tongs or a wire skimmer, transfer to a heavy saucepan. Fry the remaining duck pieces in the same way and add to the saucepan.

3 Add the bamboo shoot and white part of the green onions to the oil and stir-fry until glazed with the oil, about 30 seconds. Add to the duck.

4 Drain the mushrooms, reserving ¾ cup (6 fl oz/180 ml) of the soaking water. Remove and discard the stems from the mushrooms, if necessary, and add the whole caps to the duck. Add the ginger, soy sauce, oyster sauce, rice wine, 2 teaspoons of the sugar, and the reserved mushroom water. Bring to a boil over medium heat, cover the saucepan tightly, and simmer, turning the duck pieces occasionally, until the duck is almost tender, 1 hour.

5 Add the noodles and simmer briefly to soften and absorb the flavors of the sauce. Taste and season with salt and pepper and with 1–2 teaspoons sugar. Add the green onion tops and the cilantro, if using, and mix briefly. Serve directly from the saucepan, or transfer to a serving bowl.

Chicken Curry with Pumpkin and Eggplant

Gaeng Kiow Wan Gai • Thailand

Thai markets showcase a large assortment of eggplants, from white, green, and yellow to orange and purple. Prepared Thai green curry paste can be found at most grocery stores.

2 cans (13½ fl oz/420 ml each) coconut milk (page 224)

1 lb (500 g) boneless, skinless chicken breasts and thighs

1-lb (500-g) pumpkin, peeled

1 Asian (slender) eggplant

4 slices fresh galangal

3 tablespoons Thai green curry paste (see note)

2 tablespoons fish sauce

1 tablespoon dark brown sugar

8 kaffir lime leaves, spines removed

½ cup (½ oz/15 g) fresh Thai basil leaves

Serves 4–6

1 Do not shake the cans of coconut milk. Open the cans and spoon off 1 cup (8 fl oz/ 250 ml) of cream from the tops. Place the cream in a heavy saucepan and reserve the remaining coconut milk. Place the pan over medium-high heat and bring the cream to a gentle boil. Adjust the heat to maintain a gentle boil and cook, stirring continuously, until tiny beads of oil appear on the surface, 5–8 minutes.

2 Cut the chicken and the pumpkin into ¾-inch (2-cm) pieces. Cut the eggplant into 1-inch (2.5-cm) pieces. Add the galangal and green curry paste and fry, stirring constantly, until the mixture is aromatic and the oil separates from the paste, 8–10 minutes. Add the chicken pieces and fry them in the paste until well coated, about 2 minutes. Raise the heat to high and stir in 2 cups (16 fl oz/500 ml) of the reserved coconut milk (save the rest for another use), the pumpkin, eggplant pieces, fish sauce, brown sugar, and lime leaves. Reduce the heat to a gentle boil and cook until the pumpkin is tender, 10 minutes.

3 Taste and adjust the seasoning with curry paste, fish sauce, or brown sugar. Add the basil leaves and stir just until they begin to wilt. Transfer to a serving dish and serve.

Chicken in Pandanus Leaves

Gai Hor Bai Toey • Thailand

When pandanus leaves, also known as screw pine, are wrapped around chicken, they impart a woody fragrance and flavor to the meat.

1½ lb (750 g) boneless chicken thighs

½ teaspoon peppercorns

2 cloves garlic

2 tablespoons fresh coriander (fresh cilantro) roots or stems

2 lemongrass stalks, tender midsection only, finely minced

2 tablespoons *each* oyster sauce and light soy sauce

2 teaspoons sugar

1½ teaspoons Asian sesame oil

36 pandanus leaves, each about 12 inches (30 cm) by 2 inches (5 cm) wide

Peanut oil or corn oil for deep-frying

Serves 6–8

1 Cut the chicken into 1½-inch (4-cm) pieces. In a mortar, pound the peppercorns to a coarse powder. Add the garlic, coriander roots, and lemongrass and pound together to form a coarse paste. Scrape into a bowl and add the oyster sauce, soy sauce, sugar, and sesame oil. Mix together and add the chicken. Mix well, cover, and refrigerate for 2 hours.

2 Remove the chicken from the refrigerator. To make the chicken bundles, lay a pandanus leaf on a work surface. Make a mound of chicken about 1½ inches (4 cm) high (using 1 or 2 pieces of chicken) about 4 inches (10 cm) from the stem end of the leaf. Bring up the ends, then pull the long end over and around to cover the front of the chicken pieces. Tuck the end under and up to meet at the top with the stem end. Tug a bit to enclose the chicken securely in the tiny bundle.

3 Pour the peanut oil or corn oil to a depth of 2 inches (5 cm) in a deep, heavy frying pan and heat to 350°F (180°C) on a deep-frying thermometer. Working in batches, add the chicken bundles and fry until the meat is firm and cooked through, about 4 minutes. Using a slotted spoon or tongs, transfer the bundles to paper towels to drain.

4 Arrange the chicken bundles on a platter. To eat, unwrap the leaves and discard them.

THE CHINESE ART OF SMOKING

The carving of camphor-wood chests is a respected craft in China. It yields waste chips and shavings of fragrant wood that, in a smoker, impart a rich golden amber coloring and intense yet delicate flavor. Delectable camphor- and tea-smoked duck is now a signature dish of Sichuan cuisine.

Smoking is an ancient cooking method and references to it are dotted throughout Chinese literature. The Qing dynasty author Cao Xueqin (AD 1715–63) wrote on the sensuality of food, particularly citing cypress-smoked Siamese suckling pig. In that same era, pork marinated in wine and garlic was smoked over smoldering bamboo and stored, rather like a confit, in pickling jars. Tang dynasty connoisseurs raved about the black smoked apricots of Hubei, as the Fujianese now do about silver pomfret and smoked amber over black tea leaves and crushed rock sugar.

Smoking in the home kitchen is easy with a heavy wok, a rack, and a fitted lid. Black tea leaves, fragrant green tea, and wood shavings are the smoke fuel, with extra flavor deriving from crystal sugar, tangerine peel, and whole spices. Small items cook as they smoke; large fish or poultry is steamed first. Set them on the rack, cover tightly, and let the smoke perform its magic.

Tea-Smoked Quail

Zhang Cha Anchun • Western • China

Quail have the most delicate taste of all game birds, yet it is emphatic enough to match with strong flavors. They also respond beautifully to smoking. In one Beijing dish, smoke imparts a fragrant, golden brown skin to tender steamed chicken, and Sichuanese chefs vary that recipe for the ubiquitous quail from their rice fields, using full-flavored tea and fragrant *chenpi* (tangerine peel) from the region's plantations to serve as smoke fuel.

3 quail

1 teaspoon rice wine

1 teaspoon salt, plus salt to taste

5–6 teaspoons vegetable oil

3 tablespoons tea leaves such as black, jasmine, litchi, or Lapsang souchong

5 pieces dried tangerine peel, each about ¾ inch (2 cm) square (optional)

½ tablespoon superfine (caster) sugar

5 teaspoons sesame oil

1 small bunch flowering chives or garlic chives, cut into 1½-inch (4-cm) pieces

2 teaspoons light soy sauce

Serves 6

1 To prepare the quail, rinse and dry the birds. Cut off the necks and wing tips, then split each quail in half along the breastbone. In a large, shallow bowl, stir together the wine, 1 teaspoon salt, and 1 tablespoon vegetable oil. Add the quail and turn in the mixture, rubbing the birds with your fingers to coat evenly. Leave for 20 minutes, turning twice.

2 Bring water to a boil in the base of a steamer. Set the quail on the metal steamer rack, cover tightly, reduce the heat so the water continues to simmer, and steam for 5 minutes. Remove the quail on the rack and place the rack over a plate or bowl to drain.

3 Line a large, heavy saucepan or wok with a double thickness of aluminum foil. Place the tea leaves, tangerine peel (if using), and sugar on the foil in the bottom of the pan and set over medium heat. Place the quail on the rack in the pan. Cover the pan (you also may want to line the lid with aluminum foil to prevent discoloration) and smoke-cook until golden brown, about 12 minutes. Remove the quail from the rack and brush them with 2 teaspoons of the sesame oil. Sprinkle lightly with salt.

4 In a wok, warm the remaining 2–3 teaspoons vegetable oil over high heat. When hot, add the chives and stir-fry until they begin to wilt, about 20 seconds. Add the remaining 1 tablespoon sesame oil and soy sauce and continue to stir-fry until softened, about 20 seconds longer.

5 Spread the chives on a platter and arrange the quail on top. Serve at once.

"Strange Flavor" Chicken

Guai Wei Ji • Western • China

The Sichuanese are generally considered to be expressive cooks who create ebullient flavors from robust seasoning and generous spicing. Names reflect the flavor characteristics of their dishes. "Strange flavor" denotes a dish in which sweet, sour, hot, salty, and spicy blend with no single flavor predominating.

1 First, prepare the sauce: In a bowl, using a whisk or fork, beat together the green onion, ginger, garlic, sesame paste, soy sauce, water, sesame oil, vinegar, vegetable oil, chile oil, sugar, and the pepper, if using, until a thin, creamy sauce forms. Set aside.

2 Bring water to a simmer in a steamer base. Place the chicken legs on a metal steamer rack, place over the simmering water, cover, and steam until tender, about 25 minutes. To test for doneness, insert a thin skewer into the thickest part of the thigh; no pink juices should flow. Remove from the steamer and allow to cool and dry for 5 minutes, then brush lightly with the soy sauce and leave uncovered, about 20 minutes, to dry and cool.

3 Pour the oil to a depth of 3 inches (7.5 cm) into a wok and heat to 360°F (182°C), or until a small cube of bread dropped into it turns golden within a few seconds. Carefully slide the chicken legs into the hot oil and fry until the skin is amber and glossy, about 2 minutes. Carefully lift out the chicken, using a broad ladle or a wire skimmer underneath for support and holding it over the pan for a moment to drain. Leave to cool for at least 5 minutes. The chicken is best when served just slightly warmer than room temperature.

4 Cut or tear the meat and the skin from the bones and cut into bite-sized strips. Arrange in a pile on a platter. Spoon half of the sauce over the chicken, and pass the remainder in a bowl at the table.

SAUCE

2 tablespoons very finely minced green (spring) onion, including tender green tops

1 tablespoon peeled and grated fresh ginger

1 tablespoon very finely chopped garlic

1 tablespoon sesame paste

2½ tablespoons light soy sauce

2 tablespoons water

5–6 teaspoons sesame oil

1 tablespoon red vinegar

1 tablespoon vegetable oil

2–3 teaspoons chile oil

2½ teaspoons superfine (caster) sugar

½ teaspoon ground Sichuan pepper (optional)

2 whole chicken legs

1 tablespoon light soy sauce

Vegetable oil for deep-frying

Serves 4

Chicken Chat

Murghi ka Chat · Delhi · India

Marinating diced, cooked tandoori chicken in a tangy dressing of fresh lemon juice, roasted cumin, and cayenne pepper creates this wonderfully smoky and spicy chicken salad. The plump, moist chicken pieces are layered with refreshing yogurt and ginger before serving. You can make the *chat* even more complex by adding a sweet tamarind chutney.

½ recipe day-old Tandoori Chicken (page 73) or Chicken Malai Kabob (page 94) or ¾ lb (375 g) day-old grilled or roasted chicken meat from your favorite recipe, cut into 1-inch (2.5-cm) cubes

1 boiling potato, boiled, peeled, and diced (¾-inch/2-cm dice)

½ cup (2 oz/60 g) diced red onion (¾-inch/2-cm dice)

1 apple, preferably a crisp, tart variety such as Granny Smith, or 1 Bartlett (Williams') pear, peeled, cored, and sliced ¼ inch (6 mm) thick

SOUR DRESSING

¼ cup (2 fl oz/60 ml) water

2 teaspoons fresh lemon juice

1 teaspoon dried mint leaves, crushed

½ teaspoon cumin seeds, roasted and ground (page 225)

¼ teaspoon freshly ground black pepper

¼ teaspoon ground cayenne pepper

¼ teaspoon salt

8 large lettuce leaves, preferably oak leaf or red leaf

½ cup (4 oz/125 g) plain yogurt

1 teaspoon chopped fresh mint

1 tablespoon peeled and finely slivered fresh ginger

½ cup (⅔ oz/20 g) chopped fresh cilantro (fresh coriander)

Serves 4

1 In a large bowl, combine the chicken, potato, onion, and apple or pear.

2 To make the sour dressing, in a cup, combine the water, lemon juice, dried mint leaves, cumin, black pepper, cayenne, and salt. Pour over the chicken. Toss well, cover, and set aside for 30 minutes at room temperature or up to 2 hours in the refrigerator to allow the flavors to blend.

3 When ready to serve, arrange the lettuce leaves on a serving platter or individual plates. In a cup, combine the yogurt and mint. Pour the yogurt mixture over the chicken, tossing carefully to coat the chicken and vegetables lightly with the sauce. Pile the chicken mixture atop the lettuce.

4 Sprinkle with the ginger slivers and cilantro, then serve immediately.

Grilled Chicken with Pepper-Lime Dip

Mouan Ang • Cambodia

As with many Southeast Asian dishes, the condiments and dips used here embellish an already delectable dish. The Cambodian pepper-lime dip known as *tik marij* is a typical table condiment, and it sets off the flavors of this classic chicken dish deliciously.

1 teaspoon *each* peppercorns and coarse salt

6 cloves garlic, quartered

¼ cup (2 fl oz/60 ml) mushroom soy sauce

2 tablespoons sugar

1 tablespoon vegetable oil

2 small chickens, 2½ lb (1.25 kg) each, halved

Fresh cilantro (fresh coriander) sprigs

PEPPER-LIME DIP

1 tablespoon ground peppercorns

1½ teaspoons coarse salt or sea salt

2 limes, halved

Serves 4

1 In a mortar, coarsely grind the peppercorns. Add the garlic and crush to a coarse paste. Transfer the mixture to a bowl and stir in the mushroom soy sauce, sugar, vegetable oil, and coarse salt. Place the chicken halves in a large, shallow baking dish and add the soy sauce mixture. Turn to coat the chicken evenly. Cover and refrigerate for at least 1 hour or up to overnight.

2 Prepare a fire in a charcoal grill. Place the chicken halves, skin side down, on the grill rack about 4 inches (10 cm) from the fire and grill until the skin is nicely charred, about 15 minutes. Turn and grill until nicely charred on the second side and the juices run clear when a thigh is pierced, 10–15 minutes longer. Transfer to a cutting board and cut into serving pieces. Arrange on a platter. Garnish with fresh cilantro sprigs.

3 To make the dip, equally distribute the pepper and salt among 4 dipping saucers. Have each diner squeeze ½ lime into his or her saucer and stir until the salt dissolves. One can either dip the chicken pieces into the dip or slather them with the dip.

THE SPICE PANTRY

Southeast Asian cooks rely on dried whole spices—coriander, cumin, fennel, cinnamon, clove, cardamom—purchased from spice merchants in the many open-air markets and picturesque shops throughout the region. Walk into the sprawling Thein Gyi Zei, the so-called Indian market in central Yangon (Rangoon), and the aroma of exotic spices, mingled with those of dried fish, tropical fruits, and countless other foodstuffs, washes over you. Vendors surrounded by sacks of cinnamon bark and cardamom pods, cumin seeds and nutmeg kernels, weigh out small amounts for their customers, deftly handling simple scales dulled with the patina of age.

On Sabah, which covers the northwest tip of Borneo, the outdoor Sunday markets, or *tamus*, are seas of cattle dealers, betel-nut sellers, cloth merchants, vegetable brokers, and, of course, spice vendors, all shading themselves from a relentless tropical sun.

In the ancient heart of Hanoi, where trades and goods traditionally were confined to streets that bore their names, spice dealers share space with other merchants, thousand-year-old temples, grilled fish restaurants, and small parks. In Singapore on Serangoon Road, called Little India by the locals, spice sellers, tucked into storefronts and booths among sari shops, pot-and-pan emporiums, and jewelry stores, sell the spices for a Malaysian *rempah* or an Indian *masala*. Southeast Asian cooks who buy whole spices nearly always toast them before use to bring out their flavor and eliminate any raw aftertaste. The flavor is further heightened when the seeds are pounded in a mortar to draw out the aromatic oils. A spice grinder does a respectable job as well. To toast whole spices, use a dry (ungreased) cast-iron frying pan over medium-low heat. Add the spice and toast it, stirring frequently, until it exudes a heady bouquet and turns a shade or two darker. Depending upon the spice, this may take anywhere from a minute to five minutes. While the spice is still warm, transfer it to a mortar or spice grinder and pound or grind to a fine powder.

Chicken Malai Kabob

Murgh Malai Kabab • Punjab • India

2 lb (1 kg) skinless, boneless chicken

3 tablespoons fresh lemon juice

2 teaspoons salt

½ cup (4 oz/125 g) plain yogurt

¼ cup (2 oz/60 g) sour cream

2 tablespoons minced fresh cilantro (fresh coriander)

1 tablespoon peeled and grated fresh ginger

2 teaspoons minced garlic

1 tablespoon garam masala (page 225)

1 teaspoon ground cayenne pepper

1 teaspoon minced fresh thyme

4 tablespoons (2 fl oz/60 ml) vegetable oil

Serves 4

1 Cut the chicken meat into 1½-inch (4-cm) pieces. Place the chicken pieces in a bowl and rub them with the lemon juice and 1 teaspoon of the salt. In a small bowl, combine the yogurt, sour cream, cilantro, ginger, garlic, garam masala, cayenne, thyme, and the remaining 1 teaspoon salt. Pour over the chicken and stir well to coat thoroughly. Carefully fold in 2 tablespoons of the oil. Cover and marinate for 1 hour at room temperature or overnight in the refrigerator.

2 Preheat a broiler (grill) to maximum temperature and place the broiler pan 5 inches (13 cm) from the heat. Or, preheat the oven to 500°F (260°C).

3 Thread 4 or 5 pieces of chicken onto each of four 10-inch (25-cm) metal skewers, leaving about ¼ inch (6 mm) space between each piece. Brush with some more of the oil and broil (grill) or roast, turning and brushing occasionally with any remaining marinade, until the chicken is opaque throughout and firm to the touch, 7–9 minutes. Toward the end of the cooking time, and again just before serving, brush the kabobs with some of the remaining oil to give them extra gloss. Transfer to a warmed platter and serve immediately.

Lamb with Spinach

Saag Gosht • Punjab • India

1½ lb (750 g) lamb shoulder or leg meat

4 tablespoons (2 fl oz/60 ml) vegetable oil

3 yellow onions, finely chopped

1 tablespoon *each* peeled and grated fresh ginger and minced garlic

3 tablespoons ground coriander

1 tablespoon paprika

½ teaspoon ground cayenne pepper

½ cup (4 oz/125 g) plain yogurt

2 tomatoes, finely chopped

1½ teaspoons salt, or to taste

1 cup (8 oz/250 g) cooked spinach

2 fresh hot green chiles, minced

2 teaspoons garam masala (page 225)

½ cup (¾ oz/20 g) chopped fresh cilantro (fresh coriander)

Serves 4

1 Trim the lamb of fat and sinew and cut into 1½-inch (4-cm) pieces. In a heavy nonstick pan over high heat, warm 2 tablespoons of the oil. When hot, add a few pieces of meat and sear, turning and tossing, until they are nicely browned all over, about 2 minutes. Transfer the seared meat pieces to a plate. Repeat in batches with the remaining meat pieces.

2 Add the remaining 2 tablespoons oil and the onions to the pan and cook over medium-high heat, stirring often, until they turn caramel brown, about 15 minutes. Stir in the ginger, garlic, ground coriander, paprika, cayenne, and yogurt. Cook, stirring occasionally, until the moisture evaporates and the yogurt begins to fry, about 3 minutes. Return the meat to the pan. Add the tomatoes, 1½ cups (12 fl oz/375 ml) water, and salt and bring to a boil. Reduce the heat to low, cover, and simmer, stirring often, until the meat is cooked and very tender, about 1½ hours. Coarsely purée the cooked spinach. Fold in the chiles, spinach, garam masala, and cilantro. Heat through briefly and serve at once.

DUCKS

Barely a thirty-minute drive from the outskirts of Beijing are the huge duck farms that supply the city's famous Peking duck restaurants. Over a period of just seventy days, thousands of ducks make the transition from fluffy golden ducklings, born and nurtured in heat-controlled indoor runs, to robust birds fast-fattened to their optimum saleable weight of 4½ Chinese katties (6 pounds/3 kg).

Over ten thousand ducks are roasted each week by a process that was perfected over three hundred years ago and refined in the nineteenth century for the gourmet Empress Dowager Cixi. The ducks are cleaned, plucked, and washed. Compressed air forced between skin and meat ensures crisp, dry skin, and a glaze of liquid malt sugar seals the pores, further adding to the crispness. They are then hung to dry. In some restaurants the cavity is filled with water to ensure that the meat will be gently steam-cooked from the inside when the ducks are roasted over the flickering fires of fruit wood.

Beijing kaoya wancan, the multicourse duck dinner, is an experience not to be missed during a visit to Beijing. The duck skin, carved separately, is served first, wrapped in soft wheat-flour pancakes and served with sweet hoisin sauce and green (spring) onions. The breast and leg meat can be served the same way or in a stir-fry. Finally, the carcass is used to make a milky soup.

Duck with Hot-and-Sour Cabbage

Beijing Kaoya Labaicai • Northern • China

There is an art to roasting in the Chinese way that is irresistible. Perhaps it is the startling redness of some of the products that first captures your attention. And the smell! You can't ignore the tantalizing aromas that waft out from a roast meat shop.

HOT-AND-SOUR CABBAGE

10 oz (315 g) napa cabbage

Boiling water to cover, plus 2 tablespoons

2 teaspoons salt

1½ teaspoons superfine (caster) sugar

3 tablespoons rice vinegar

1 hot red chile, seeded and thinly sliced

1 tablespoon vegetable oil

1 tablespoon sesame oil

1 teaspoon chile oil (optional)

½ teaspoon Sichuan peppercorns, lightly crushed (optional)

2 green (spring) onions, white part only, for onion curls, or fresh cilantro (fresh coriander) sprigs

½ Chinese roast duck

Serves 6–8

1 To prepare the cabbage, cut the pale green leaves from their white stems. Cut the leaves into 1½-inch (4-cm) squares, and thinly slice the stems. Place all the cabbage in a heat-proof bowl and add boiling water to cover. Let stand for 3 minutes, then drain in a colander and return to the bowl.

2 In a small bowl, stir together the salt, sugar, vinegar, and the 2 tablespoons boiling water until the sugar and salt are dissolved. Add the chile and pour the mixture over the cabbage. Toss to coat completely.

3 In a small saucepan over low heat, gently warm the vegetable oil and sesame oil, and the chile oil and peppercorns, if using. Pour the mixture over the cabbage and mix well. Cover and marinate for at least several hours at room temperature or for up to 4 days in the refrigerator.

4 If preparing onion curls, trim off the root ends from the green onions. Using a needle, a straight pin, or the tip of a small, sharp knife, shred one end of each onion, leaving a ½-inch (12-mm) base at the opposite end unshredded. Place in a bowl of ice water in the refrigerator for at least 1 hour; the shredded ends will curl.

5 Just before serving, remove the breast meat from the duck half and cut it into strips. Bone the remaining duck and cut or tear the meat into strips. The duck meat can be served at room temperature, or warmed in a steamer set over gently simmering water for 3–4 minutes.

6 To serve, mound the cabbage in the center of a platter. Drape the duck strips over the cabbage. Garnish with the onion curls or cilantro.

Lemongrass Chicken

Ga Xa Ot · Vietnam

It is almost impossible to think of Vietnamese food without lemongrass chicken coming to mind. Indeed, every restaurant menu includes this aromatic mix of chicken, hot chiles, and citrusy lemongrass. The secret ingredient, however, is caramel syrup, which is added near the end of cooking to give the chicken a beautiful sheen and slightly sweet flavor.

1 To make the marinade, in a large bowl, stir together the garlic, fish sauce, sugar, cornstarch, pepper, and the 1 tablespoon of vegetable oil. Mix well. Add the chicken, toss to coat evenly, and let stand at room temperature for 30 minutes.

2 Preheat a wok or large frying pan over medium heat. When the pan is hot, add the 2 tablespoons of vegetable oil and swirl to coat the pan. When the oil is hot, add the garlic, shallots, and lemongrass and stir-fry slowly until they turn a light gold and the shallots smell sweet, 3–5 minutes.

3 Add the chicken with its marinade, the chile, bell pepper, and carrot and stir-fry until the chicken turns opaque and feels firm to the touch, 3–4 minutes.

4 Add the fish sauce and caramel syrup and stir-fry until the chicken is fully cooked, about 1 minute longer. The sauce will be sticky, so add the chicken stock or water to dilute it, mixing well. There should be only a little gravy left at the bottom of the pan.

5 Transfer the chicken to a serving platter and serve immediately.

MARINADE

2 cloves garlic, chopped

1 tablespoon fish sauce

2 teaspoons sugar

1 teaspoon cornstarch (cornflour)

½ teaspoon freshly ground pepper

1 tablespoon vegetable oil

¾ lb (375 g) boneless, skinless chicken thighs, cut into ¾-inch (2-cm) cubes

2 tablespoons vegetable oil

2 cloves garlic

2 large shallots, thinly sliced

3 lemongrass stalks, tender midsection only, finely chopped

1 green jalapeño or serrano chile, seeded and chopped

½ red bell pepper (capsicum), seeded and thinly sliced

¼ cup (1 oz/30 g) julienned carrot (1½ inches/4 cm long)

1 tablespoon fish sauce

1 tablespoon caramel syrup (page 223)

¼ cup (2 fl oz/60 ml) chicken stock or water

Serves 6

Chicken with Chiles and Peanuts

Chengdu Ji · Western · China

Peanuts grow abundantly in the rich Sichuan basin, where boiled and fried peanuts are enjoyed as an appetizer and are often served with sliced meats.

¾ lb (375 g) boneless, skinless chicken thighs, cut into ½-inch (12-mm) cubes

2 teaspoons cornstarch (cornflour)

1 teaspoon rice wine

2 tablespoons light soy sauce

1 cup (8 fl oz/250 ml) peanut oil or vegetable oil

⅓ cup (1½ oz/45 g) raw peanuts

½ cup (2½ oz/75 g) cubed bamboo shoot (⅓-inch/9-mm cubes)

⅓ cup (1½ oz/45 g) diced green bell pepper (capsicum)

2 green (spring) onions, including tender green tops, thickly sliced

1 large, hot red chile, seeded and sliced

2 teaspoons peeled and finely chopped fresh ginger

2 teaspoons finely chopped garlic

1 teaspoon hot bean sauce or garlic-chile sauce (page 223)

½ teaspoon superfine (caster) sugar

2 teaspoons cornstarch (cornflour) dissolved in ¼ cup (2 fl oz/60 ml) chicken stock

¼ teaspoon ground Sichuan pepper (optional)

Serves 4–6

1 In a bowl, combine the chicken, cornstarch, rice wine, and 1 tablespoon of the soy sauce and mix well. Let stand for 15 minutes.

2 In a wok over high heat, warm the oil. When hot, add the peanuts and fry until golden, about 1 minute. Using a slotted spoon, transfer to paper towels to drain. Set aside.

3 Return the wok to high heat. When the oil is smoking, add the chicken and stir-fry, keeping the chicken pieces constantly moving and turning so they cook quickly and evenly, until lightly colored and almost cooked, about 1½ minutes. Using a slotted spoon, transfer to a plate.

4 Pour off all but 2 tablespoons of the oil from the wok and reheat over high heat until smoking. Add the bamboo shoot, bell pepper, green onions, chile, ginger, and garlic and stir-fry until beginning to soften, about 40 seconds. Add the hot bean or garlic-chile sauce, the remaining 1 tablespoon soy sauce, and the sugar and stir-fry for 10 seconds until well mixed and aromatic. Return the chicken to the wok and continue to stir-fry until cooked, about 30 seconds.

5 Add the cornstarch mixture and stir until the sauce is lightly thickened and glazes the ingredients, about 30 seconds. Stir in the peanuts and transfer to a serving dish. Sprinkle on the pepper, if using, and serve at once.

Pork in Hot-and-Sour Sauce

Sorpotel · Goa · India

This intensely flavored preparation tastes best when made with fatty, tender shoulder meat. If you enjoy very hot dishes, double the amount of cayenne pepper.

1½ lb (750 g) pork shoulder meat

2 cloves garlic, unpeeled, bruised, plus 2 teaspoons minced garlic

2 cassia leaves (page 224)

5 tablespoons (2½ fl oz/75 ml) olive oil

2 cups (10 oz/315 g) finely chopped yellow onion

1 tablespoon peeled and grated or crushed fresh ginger

2 teaspoons ground cayenne pepper

1 teaspoon ground turmeric

½ teaspoon *each* ground black pepper, ground cumin, cinnamon, and cloves

6 serrano chiles, seeded and sliced

¼ cup (2 fl oz/60 ml) coconut milk (page 224) or red wine vinegar

⅓ cup (3 fl oz/80 ml) tamarind water (page 74)

2 tablespoons maple syrup

1¼ teaspoons salt, or to taste

Serves 4–6

1 Cut the pork into 1-inch (2.5-cm) cubes and place in a deep pot. Add the unpeeled garlic, cassia leaves, and 3 cups (24 fl oz/750 ml) water and bring to a boil over high heat. Reduce the heat to low and simmer gently, uncovered, occasionally skimming the froth off the top with a skimmer, until the meat is partially cooked, about 20 minutes. Using tongs or a slotted spoon, transfer the meat to a cutting board.

2 Strain the stock, return it to the pot, bring to a boil over high heat, and boil until reduced in volume to about 1 cup (8 fl oz/250 ml). Set aside.

3 In a large, heavy frying pan over high heat, warm 2 tablespoons of the olive oil. When hot, add a few of the meat pieces and sear quickly until lightly browned, about 2 minutes. Using a slotted spoon, transfer the seared meat pieces to a bowl. Repeat in batches with the remaining meat pieces.

4 Add the remaining oil and the onion, ginger, and minced garlic to the pan. Cook, stirring, until the onion is lightly browned, about 8 minutes. Stir in the cayenne, turmeric, black pepper, cumin, cinnamon, and cloves. Mix well. Return the cooked meat, with its juices, to the pan. Add the chiles, coconut milk or vinegar, tamarind water, maple syrup, salt, and reserved pork stock. Bring to a boil over high heat, reduce the heat to medium-low, cover, and simmer until the meat absorbs much of the liquid and the sauce is thickened, about 30 minutes. Transfer to a warmed serving dish and serve at once.

CHILES

Today, India is the world's largest producer of hot chiles, which makes it difficult to believe that they were unknown there until the end of the fifteenth century, when the Portuguese colonized the country. It took until the late seventeenth century for chiles to be cultivated in the region. Nowadays, the addiction to their heat is so widespread that many Indians travel with a small bottle of the spice in case they're confronted with a "bland" meal.

Chiles are appreciated for the flavor they add to a dish as well as for their heat. For example, the taste of the milder árbol variety is often preferred over that of the very hot bird's eye chile. Capsaicin, the chemical that gives chiles their characteristic heat, can cause painful burns if not handled properly. It is a good idea to wear kitchen gloves when chopping and seeding them, being sure to avoid contact with your eyes or any sensitive skin.

Red Roast Pork

Cha Shao Rou • Southern • China

Chinese cooks find many uses for versatile roast pork: tossed in a stir-fry, chopped into soups, served over steamed rice, rolled in steamed rice sheets, or minced into dumplings.

1 or 2 pork tenderloins, ¾–1 lb (375–500 g) total weight

MARINADE

2 tablespoons light soy sauce

1½ teaspoons dark soy sauce

1½ tablespoons superfine (caster) sugar

1½ teaspoons five-spice powder

¾ teaspoon baking soda (bicarbonate of soda)

1 teaspoon crushed garlic

1½ tablespoons vegetable oil

1 cup (8 fl oz/250 ml) water

Serves 4–8

1 Trim the pork tenderloin(s) to remove any sinew, skin, and fat. Cut in half lengthwise, and then cut the halves crosswise into 6-inch (15-cm) pieces.

2 To prepare the marinade, in a wide, flat dish, combine the light and dark soy sauces, sugar, five-spice powder, baking soda, garlic, and oil, mixing well. One by one, dunk the pork strips into the marinade, turning to coat evenly, then arrange them in a single layer in the dish. Cover and refrigerate for at least 1½ hours, turning every 20 minutes, or for up to overnight, turning occasionally.

3 Position a rack in the second highest level in the oven. Pour the water into a drip pan and place it on a rack below. Preheat the oven to 400°F (200°C).

4 Arrange the marinated pork on the rack, allowing space between the strips, and roast for 12 minutes. Turn and roast for 5 minutes longer. The surface should be glazed and slightly charred at the edges, and the meat inside still pink and tender.

5 Remove from the oven and allow the pork to rest for 6 minutes before slicing. If cooking in advance, let cool completely on the rack, wrap loosely in waxed paper, and refrigerate until needed or for up to 4 days.

Pork Ribs with Black Beans and Chile

Dou Shi Pai Gu • Eastern • China

The distinctive, earthy saltiness of black beans is showcased in this dish, where it's paired with meaty, fat-layered pork ribs and seasoned with a bit of red chile.

2 lb (1 kg) thickly sliced meaty pork ribs

1 cup (3 oz/90 g) chopped green (spring) onion, including half the tender green tops, plus remaining chopped green tops for garnish

2 tablespoons peeled and chopped fresh ginger

1½ tablespoons chopped garlic

1 tablespoon seeded and chopped fresh or dried red chile

2 tablespoons thick black bean sauce

1 tablespoon light brown sugar

¾ cup (6 fl oz/180 ml) water

⅓ cup (3 fl oz/80 ml) rice wine

¼ cup (2 fl oz/60 ml) light soy sauce

Chopped fresh cilantro (fresh coriander)

Serves 4–6

1 Cut the pork ribs into 2-by-3-by-1-inch (5-by-7.5-cm-by-2.5-cm) pieces. Spread the pork pieces in a single layer in a baking dish, scatter the 1 cup (3 oz/90 g) green onion, ginger, garlic, and chile evenly over the top. In a bowl, stir together the black bean sauce with the brown sugar, water, rice wine, and soy sauce. Pour over the pork. Cover and refrigerate for at least 1 hour or for up to 4 hours, turning the pork pieces several times.

2 Preheat the oven to 325°F (165°C). Place the covered dish in the preheated oven and braise, turning the pork occasionally, for 1¼ hours. Uncover, raise the heat to 375°F (190°C), and cook until the pork has crisped in places and the liquid is partially reduced, about 20 minutes longer.

3 Remove the dish from the oven, uncover, and skim off the excess fat from the surface. Garnish with the green onion tops and cilantro and serve directly from the dish.

Grilled Five-Spice Pork Chops

Thit Heo Nuong Vi • Vietnam

Five-spice powder, a highly fragrant Chinese spice blend, is frequently used by Vietnamese cooks, as in this pork dish, which is excellent served with a crisp cucumber-carrot salad.

4 bone-in pork loin chops

½ teaspoon peppercorns

1 whole star anise

1 lemongrass stalk, tender midsection only, finely chopped

4 cloves garlic, halved

1 shallot, quartered

1 tablespoon fish sauce

1½ teaspoons light soy sauce

1 teaspoon Asian sesame oil

1 tablespoon sugar

½ teaspoon five-spice powder

Nuoc cham dipping sauce (page 113)

Serves 4

1 Place the pork chops on a flat work surface and, using a meat pounder, pound to ½–¾ inch (12 mm–2 cm) thick.

2 In a mortar or blender, pound or grind the peppercorns and star anise to a fine powder. Add the lemongrass, garlic, and shallot and pound or blend until a purée forms. Add the fish sauce, soy sauce, sesame oil, sugar, and five-spice powder and mix well.

3 Put the pork chops in a shallow bowl, add the marinade, and turn to coat. Cover and refrigerate for at least 2 hours or overnight.

4 Prepare a fire in a charcoal grill. Bring the pork chops to room temperature.

5 Scrape the marinade off the chops and place on the grill rack 4 inches (10 cm) above the fire. Grill, turning once, until nicely charred on both sides, about 8 minutes total.

6 Transfer to a cutting board and cut each chop into several strips, leaving the bone attached. Reassemble the strips on individual plates to look like whole chops. Serve with the dipping sauce.

Stewed Pork with Coconut Juice

Thit Heo Kho Nuoc Dua • Vietnam

Coconut juice is the liquid trapped inside a coconut and should not be confused with coconut milk, which is made from the meat of a mature coconut.

2 tablespoons vegetable oil

3 cloves garlic, chopped

2 shallots, chopped

2 lemongrass stalks, tender midsection only, finely minced

2 lb (1 kg) boneless pork butt, cut into 1-inch (2.5-cm) cubes

2 tablespoons caramel syrup (page 223)

⅓ cup (3 fl oz/80 ml) fish sauce, or to taste

2 tablespoons sugar, or to taste

1 teaspoon five-spice powder

½ teaspoon ground black pepper

½ teaspoon ground white pepper

2 cups (16 fl oz/500 ml) frozen coconut juice, thawed

1–2 cups (8–16 fl oz/250–500 ml) chicken stock or water

3 hard-boiled eggs, peeled

Serves 6

1 Preheat a saucepan over medium-high heat. When the pan is hot, add the vegetable oil and swirl to coat the bottom of the pan. When the oil is hot, add the garlic, shallots, and lemongrass and stir-fry until golden brown, about 30 seconds. Raise the heat to high and add a small batch of the pork. Brown evenly on all sides and transfer to a dish. Repeat until all the pork is browned.

2 Return all the pork to the pan and add the caramel syrup, fish sauce, sugar, five-spice powder, black pepper, and white pepper. Stir well and cook over medium heat, stirring occasionally, until bubbly and fragrant, about 2 minutes. Add the coconut juice and enough chicken stock or water just to cover the pork. Bring to a boil and skim off any foam or other impurities that rise to the surface. Reduce the heat to medium-low, cover, and simmer until tender, about 1½ hours.

3 Starting 1 inch (2.5 cm) from the end of a hard-boiled egg and stopping within 1 inch (2.5 cm) of the opposite end, make 4 evenly spaced lengthwise scores around the egg. Repeat with the remaining eggs. Add the eggs to the stew and simmer until the meat is tender, about 15 minutes longer.

4 Transfer the contents of the saucepan to a serving dish and serve immediately.

ROAST SUCKLING PIG

Ru zhu (roast suckling pig) has been called the Peking duck of the south. It, too, has glassy amber-red skin, featherlight and crisp as a wafer, over meat that is pink-tender and as soft as butter. These attributes make it the star of banquet menus in Guangdong, Hong Kong, and nearby southern regions. Suckling pig is regarded as one of the ultimate symbols of good fortune, and is served at all celebratory occasions.

A young pig, slaughtered at two months of age and weighing around twelve pounds (6 kg), is considered ideal for a banquet, yet pigs of all sizes are selected for the occasion.

The skills of roasting have been handed down from father to son over generations. The pigs, suspended on chains over glowing wood embers, are roasted in tall brick ovens. Alternatively, they are slowly turned on a spit over a pit of coals to produce a crisp, bubbled crackling over sweetly succulent meat.

The Chinese of the far west also enjoy pork when they can. Eating houses in remote Lanzhou in Gansu province, once a strategic town on the ancient Silk Road, offer a succulent specialty meal of baby roast suckling pig, even though mutton is the favored meat of the region.

Twice-Cooked Pork

Hui Guo Rou · Western · China

Hui guo rou translates as "return to the pot," giving the dish its name: twice cooked. These dishes began as a kitchen practicality, in the days before refrigeration. Boiled meat keeps better than fresh, so large cuts were cooked and then carved as needed for other dishes.

PORK

1½ lb (750 g) pork belly or pork loin with thick fat layer, in one piece

2 teaspoons salt

¾-inch (2-cm) piece fresh ginger, peeled and thickly sliced

1 green (spring) onion, trimmed

2½ tablespoons vegetable oil

½ red bell pepper (capsicum), about 2½ oz (75 g), seeded and cut into 1-inch (2.5-cm) diamonds

½ green bell pepper (capsicum), about 2½ oz (75 g), seeded and cut into 1-inch (2.5-cm) diamonds

Pinch of salt, plus salt to taste

1½ teaspoons chopped garlic

1½–3 teaspoons hot bean sauce

2 tablespoons hoisin sauce

¼ cup (1¼ oz/40 g) sliced bamboo shoot

1 green (spring) onion, including tender green tops, cut into 1-inch (2.5-cm) lengths

1 small, hot red chile, seeded and sliced

¾ cup (1½ oz/45 g) bean sprouts

1 tablespoon light soy sauce

2 teaspoons rice wine

Ground white pepper to taste

Serves 4

1 To prepare the pork, bring a saucepan three-fourths full of water to a boil. Add the pork, blanch for 10 seconds, and pour into a colander in the sink to drain. Place the pork under gently running cold water until cool.

2 Return the pork to the saucepan, add fresh water to cover, and add the salt, ginger, and green onion. Bring to a boil over high heat, reduce the heat to medium, and simmer, uncovered, skimming the surface occasionally to remove froth, until the pork is barely cooked, about 25 minutes. It will be a pink-gray and a hint of blood will seep if the meat is pierced with a thin skewer.

3 Leave the pork in the liquid to cool partially, about 15 minutes, then transfer to a plate and let air-dry for 20 minutes. Using a sharp knife or cleaver, thinly slice the pork. Cut the slices into 2-by-1-inch (5-by-2.5-cm) pieces. (If desired, strain the stock and freeze for use in soups or other dishes.)

4 In a wok over high heat, warm half of the oil. When the oil is hot, add the red and green bell peppers and the pinch of salt and stir-fry until barely softened, about 40 seconds. Transfer to a plate.

5 Add the remaining oil to the wok and return to high heat. Add the pork and stir-fry for 20 seconds. Add the garlic, hot bean sauce to taste, and hoisin sauce and stir-fry until the pork is well coated, about 20 seconds longer. Return the bell peppers to the wok and add the bamboo shoot, green onion, and chile and stir-fry for 20 seconds. Add the bean sprouts, soy sauce, and rice wine and stir-fry just until well mixed. Season to taste with salt and white pepper.

6 Transfer to a warmed serving plate and serve immediately.

Shaking Beef with Garlic Sauce

Bo Luc Lac • Vietnam

Although the sound of the sizzling oil coupled with the rapid shaking of the pan gave birth to the name of this dish, it may be more appropriate to call it sautéed beef with lots of sweet garlic sauce.

¾ lb (375 g) beef sirloin, cut into 1-inch (2.5-cm) cubes

6 cloves garlic, chopped (about 2 tablespoons)

1 tablespoon fish sauce

1 tablespoon sugar

¼ teaspoon salt

3 tablespoons vegetable oil

SALAD

1 small red onion, thinly sliced

1½ teaspoons distilled white vinegar

1½ teaspoons Japanese-style soy sauce

1½ teaspoons olive oil

½ teaspoon sugar

¼ teaspoon *each* salt and ground pepper

1 bunch watercress, tough stems removed

Serves 4–6

1 In a bowl, combine the beef with half of the garlic, the fish sauce, sugar, salt, and 1 tablespoon of the vegetable oil. Turn the beef to coat well, cover, and let stand for at least 30 minutes at room temperature or refrigerate for as long as 2 hours.

2 To make the salad, in a bowl, toss together the onion and vinegar and set aside for about 5 minutes. In a small bowl, stir together the soy sauce, olive oil, sugar, salt, and pepper. Add to the onion and mix well. Add the watercress, toss, and arrange on a platter.

3 Preheat a wok or frying pan over high heat. When hot, add the remaining 2 tablespoons vegetable oil and swirl to coat the pan. When the oil is hot, add the remaining garlic and stir-fry until lightly browned, about 1 minute. Add the beef in a single layer and let sit, undisturbed, until seared, about 1 minute. Give the pan handle a quick shake to flip the meat over to brown and sear on the second side, about 1 minute, then cook for about 3 minutes longer. The meat should be cooked to medium-rare.

4 Arrange the beef on top of the watercress salad and serve immediately.

Cocktail Kabobs

Kabab • Uttar Pradesh • India

This kabob recipe comes from the Muslim community in Agra, the home of the beautiful Taj Mahal. The kabobs may be made larger and served as a main dish. Either way they are delicious with tamarind or fresh mint chutney

2 tablespoons vegetable oil

1 cup (5 oz/155 g) finely chopped yellow onion

1 lb (500 g) ground (minced) beef or lamb

1½ teaspoons garam masala (page 225) or ground cumin

1 teaspoon salt, or to taste

⅛ teaspoon ground cloves

¼ cup (⅓ oz/10 g) finely chopped fresh cilantro (fresh coriander)

4 fresh mild green chiles such as Anaheim, minced

1 egg

1 slice white bread, crusts removed

2 tablespoons milk

Makes 32; serves 8

1 In a large nonstick frying pan over medium-high heat, warm the oil. When hot, add the onion and cook, stirring often, until it turns caramel brown, about 9 minutes. Transfer to a bowl and add the meat, garam masala or cumin, salt, cloves, cilantro, chiles, and egg.

2 In a small bowl, soak the bread in the milk for 1 minute, mash it to a pulp, and add it to the meat mixture. Mix thoroughly, preferably with your hands, kneading the mixture until it is uniformly smooth and silky. Divide the mixture into 4 equal portions, then make 8 balls with each portion. (If necessary, dip your fingers in water to prevent the meat from sticking to them while you make the kabobs.)

3 Heat 2 large nonstick frying pans over high heat until hot. Place 16 kabobs in each pan. Reduce the heat to medium-high and fry, shaking and turning, until they are cooked through and browned all over, about 8 minutes. If necessary, reduce the heat to medium during the last few minutes of cooking.

4 Serve hot, warm, or at room temperature.

Stir-Fried Beef with Ginger and Celery

Cong Bao Niu Rou • Southern • China

Speed, heat, and movement are the essentials of stir-frying—high heat so the food does not stew and constant turning to expose every surface briefly to the hot oil.

10 oz (315 g) well-trimmed boneless beef steak such as rump or sirloin

4 teaspoons light soy sauce

2½ teaspoons cornstarch (cornflour)

¼ teaspoon baking soda (bicarbonate of soda)

¼ cup (2 fl oz/60 ml) chicken or beef stock

2 teaspoons rice wine

½ teaspoon superfine (caster) sugar

⅓ cup (3 fl oz/80 ml) vegetable oil

8 thin slices fresh ginger, peeled and finely julienned

3 green (spring) onions, including tender green tops, thinly sliced on the diagonal

2 celery stalks, thinly sliced on the diagonal

Salt and ground white pepper to taste

Serves 3 or 4

1 Cut the beef across the grain into paper-thin slices, then cut each slice into pieces about 1½ inches (4 cm) long. Place in a dish, add 2 teaspoons of the soy sauce, 1 teaspoon of the cornstarch, the baking soda, and 1 tablespoon water, and mix well. Set aside to marinate and tenderize for about 20 minutes.

2 To prepare the sauce, in a small bowl, slowly stir together the stock, rice wine, the remaining 2 teaspoons soy sauce, the remaining 1½ teaspoons cornstarch, and the sugar.

3 In a wok over high heat, warm the oil until it shimmers and begins to smoke. Add the ginger, green onions, and celery and stir-fry until beginning to soften, about 30 seconds. Using a slotted spoon, transfer the vegetables to a plate and set aside.

4 With the wok still over high heat, add the beef and stir-fry, keeping the meat moving and turning in the wok constantly, until barely cooked, about 1 minute. Return the vegetables to the wok and stir-fry for about 20 seconds to mix well with the beef.

5 Pour the sauce mixture into the wok and stir until it is lightly thickened and glazes all the ingredients, about 30 seconds. Season with salt and white pepper.

6 Transfer to a serving plate and serve at once.

Beef Fondue with Vinegar

Bo Nhung Dam • Vietnam

Table-top cooking is popular in Vietnamese restaurants and homes. For a special occasion, a Chinese clay brazier, fired by glowing charcoal, is set in the middle of the dining table, and one of Vietnam's signature dishes, beef fondue with vinegar, is served. The ingredients are prepared in advance, while the actual cooking is done at the table.

BEEF PLATTER

1 lb (500 g) boneless lean beef loin, round, or chuck from the top blade, wrapped in plastic wrap and placed in the freezer for 1 hour

Ground pepper to taste

1 white onion, thinly sliced

BROTH

1 tablespoon vegetable oil

1 tablespoon chopped garlic

2 lemongrass stalks, tender midsection only, halved and smashed

2 cups (16 fl oz/500 ml) frozen coconut juice, thawed, or 1½ cups (12 fl oz/ 375 ml) water

1½ cups (12 fl oz/375 ml) distilled white vinegar

4 teaspoons sugar

2 teaspoons salt, or to taste

TABLE SALAD AND ACCOMPANIMENTS

Nuoc cham dipping sauce (right)

½ lb (250 g) bean sprouts

1 carrot, peeled and finely julienned

1 English (hothouse) cucumber, halved lengthwise and thinly sliced crosswise

1 cup (1 oz/30 g) fresh mint leaves

1 cup (1 oz/30 g) fresh cilantro (fresh coriander) leaves

1 cup (1 oz/30 g) fresh Thai basil leaves

12 dried round rice papers, 12 inches (30 cm) in diameter

Serves 4

1 Remove the partially frozen beef from the freezer and cut across the grain into paper-thin slices. Arrange the slices attractively on a serving platter. Sprinkle with the pepper and scatter the onion slices on top. Cover and refrigerate.

2 Next, make the broth: In a saucepan over medium-high heat, warm the oil. When the oil is hot, add the garlic and lemongrass and sauté until fragrant, about 1 minute. Add the coconut juice or water, vinegar, sugar, and 2 teaspoons salt and bring to a boil. Reduce the heat to medium and simmer for 10 minutes. Transfer the broth to a fondue pot or small Chinese clay pot. Bring to the table and place on a table-top burner.

3 To prepare the table salad and accompaniments, pour the dipping sauce into individual saucers. Arrange the bean sprouts, carrot, cucumber, mint, cilantro, and basil in serving plates surrounding the broth pot. Set a large shallow bowl of warm water on the table for rice-paper dipping, or bring rehydrated rice papers, covered with a damp cloth, to the table. Remove the beef platter from the refrigerator and place it on the table.

4 To eat the fondue, take a round of rice paper and, if still dry, dip it into the water, set it on a dinner plate, and allow it to soften for about 30 seconds until it feels like a wet tissue. Place a little of each vegetable and herb in a mound on the paper. With chopsticks, pick up a slice of beef with a few onion slices and submerge in the hot broth. Cook until medium-rare, about 1 minute. Put the beef on top of the vegetable-covered rice paper. Roll up the rice paper into a log and, holding it in your hand, dip into the dipping sauce and eat.

NUOC CHAM

Every Vietnamese cook has his or her recipe for nuoc cham, *a sauce eaten with nearly every meal and snack. Adjust the ingredient amounts to suit your taste.*

1 large clove garlic

1 fresh red chile, seeded

¼ cup (2 fl oz/60 ml) fresh lime juice

5 tablespoons (2½ fl oz/75 ml) fish sauce

3 tablespoons sugar

6 tablespoons (3 fl oz/90 ml) water

2 tablespoons grated carrot

In a mortar, using a pestle, pound together the garlic and fresh red chile until the mixture is puréed (or pass the garlic clove through a garlic press). Stir in the lime juice, fish sauce, sugar, and water. Pour into a dipping saucer, add the carrot, and serve as directed in the recipe. Any leftover *nuoc cham* should be stored in a tightly covered container and kept in the refrigerator.

Makes about 1 cup (8 fl oz/250 ml)

Tangerine Peel Beef

Chenpi Niurou • Western • China

Next time you peel a tangerine, scrape the white pith away and place the peeling in a sunny place or low oven. Some Chinese markets also sell peels to take home and dry.

10 oz (315 g) trimmed, boneless beef steak such as rump or sirloin

2 teaspoons peeled and grated fresh ginger

1 teaspoon superfine (caster) sugar, plus sugar to taste

2 tablespoons dark soy sauce

3 tablespoons vegetable oil

½ yellow onion, cut into narrow wedges and layers separated

1 hot red chile, seeded and sliced

6 pieces dried tangerine peel, each about ¾ inch (2 cm) square, soaked in hot water for 20 minutes and drained

½ teaspoon Sichuan peppercorns

2½ teaspoons hoisin sauce

1–2 teaspoons hot bean sauce or garlic-chile sauce (page 223)

Salt to taste

Serves 3 or 4

1 Cut the beef across the grain into paper-thin slices, then cut the slices into pieces about 1½ inches (4 cm) long. Place in a dish and add the ginger, 1 teaspoon sugar, and 1 tablespoon of the soy sauce and mix well. Set aside to marinate for about 20 minutes.

2 In a wok over high heat, warm 2 tablespoons of the oil until it shimmers and begins to smoke. Add the onion and stir-fry until it begins to soften and color, about 40 seconds. Push to the side of the wok or, using a slotted spoon, transfer to a plate.

3 With the wok still over high heat, add the beef and stir-fry, keeping the meat moving and turning in the wok constantly, until lightly cooked, about 1½ minutes. Using the slotted spoon, transfer to a plate (with the onion, if it has been removed) and set aside.

4 Add the remaining 1 tablespoon oil to the wok, reduce the heat to medium-high, and add the chile, tangerine peel, and Sichuan peppercorns. Stir-fry until the chiles and tangerine peel are crisp and the peppercorns are very fragrant, about 1½ minutes. Transfer to a separate plate and set aside.

5 Raise the heat to high and return the beef and onion to the wok. Add the remaining 1 tablespoon soy sauce, the hoisin sauce, and the hot bean or garlic-chile sauce to taste, reduce the heat to medium-high, and stir-fry until the meat and onion are cooked and glazed with the sauce, about 40 seconds. Raise the heat to high again, return the chile, tangerine peel, and peppercorns to the wok, and mix with the beef and onion for about 20 seconds. Season to taste with salt and sugar.

6 Transfer to a serving plate and serve at once.

Honey-Glazed Beef and Walnuts

Fengmi Niulijirou Hetaoren • Northern • China

This version of honey-glazed beef may have derived from a dish created for Emperor Qianlong, after he bagged three deer while hunting north of the Great Wall. He entrusted the deer to his head chef, who created a dish the emperor declared "sweeter than honey."

10 oz (315 g) lean beef round, partially frozen

3 tablespoons cornstarch (cornflour) or tapioca starch

1 tablespoon water

1 small egg

1 tablespoon light soy sauce

2 teaspoons five-spice powder

Vegetable or peanut oil for deep-frying

¾ cup (3 oz/90 g) walnut halves

¼ cup (3 oz/90 g) honey

1 tablespoon rice wine

1 tablespoon light soy sauce

1 tablespoon ginger juice (page 225)

¾ teaspoon black vinegar (page 227)

½ teaspoon salt

1½ teaspoons sesame seeds (optional)

Serves 4–6

1 Using a very sharp knife, cut the meat across the grain into paper-thin slices, then stack the slices and cut into long strips no wider than a matchstick.

2 In a bowl, stir together 2½ tablespoons of the cornstarch or tapioca starch, the water, egg, soy sauce, and five-spice powder. Add the meat strips and, using chopsticks to separate the strips, mix thoroughly.

3 Pour the oil to a depth of 1¾ inches (4 cm) into a wok, and heat to 360°F (182°C), or until a small cube of bread dropped into it begins to turn golden within a few seconds. Carefully add the marinated meat and, using long wooden or metal chopsticks, quickly stir the meat to separate the strips. Stir-fry until lightly browned, about 2 minutes. Using a wire skimmer or slotted spoon, lift out the beef, holding it over the oil for a few moments to drain, then tip onto a plate.

4 Add the walnuts to the hot oil and fry until lightly crisped, about 1 minute. Using the skimmer or spoon, transfer to the plate with the beef. Pour the oil into a heatproof container. Rinse out the wok and dry carefully. In a small bowl, stir together the honey, rice wine, soy sauce, ginger juice, vinegar, and salt.

5 Return the wok to high heat and add 2 tablespoons of the reserved oil. When it is hot, add the wine mixture and simmer for 15–20 seconds to make a glaze. Add the meat and walnuts, reduce the heat to medium-high, and stir until each piece is evenly glazed and dry enough on the surface so that the pieces do not stick together, 3–5 minutes.

6 Pile the beef and walnuts on a serving plate, sprinkle with the sesame seeds, if using, and serve at once.

Mongolian Sesame Lamb

Mengu Zhima Yangrou • Northern • China

Lamb has historically found favor in China only with the nomadic people of the far north and west and in the cuisine of resident Muslims. But lamb dishes are now an integral part of the dining experience in Beijing and other northern cities. In the south, a lamb dish needs a gimmick, and the sizzling hot plate provides it. A cast-iron plate is preheated in the oven, then the stir-fry is half cooked, tipped onto the hot plate, and brought to the table, preceded by a theatrical crackle of sizzling sounds and wafts of enticing aromas.

MARINADE

¼ cup (2 fl oz/60 ml) light soy sauce

1½ tablespoons hoisin sauce

1 tablespoon sesame oil

1 tablespoon rice wine

2 teaspoons cornstarch (cornflour)

1½ teaspoons superfine (caster) sugar or honey

½ teaspoon five-spice powder

1 lb (500 g) boneless lean lamb from leg or shoulder, sliced paper-thin, then cut into pieces 2 inches (5 cm) long by ¼ inch (2 cm) wide

1 tablespoon sesame seeds

2 tablespoons vegetable oil

1 tablespoon sesame oil

1 large yellow onion, cut into narrow wedges and the layers separated

⅓ cup (3 fl oz/80 ml) lamb stock, chicken stock, or water

1½ teaspoons cornstarch (cornflour) dissolved in 1 tablespoon water

Ground Sichuan or white pepper to taste

Finely julienned hot red or green chile to taste (optional)

Serves 2–4

1 To prepare the marinade, in a large, flat dish, stir together the soy sauce, hoisin sauce, sesame oil, rice wine, cornstarch, sugar, and five-spice powder. Add the lamb and turn to coat evenly with the marinade. Cover and marinate for at least 30 minutes at room temperature or for up to overnight in the refrigerator.

2 Heat a dry wok over medium heat. Add the sesame seeds and toast briefly, stirring, until golden. Pour onto a small dish and set aside.

3 Add the vegetable and sesame oils to the wok and heat over high heat. When the oils are hot, add the onion and stir-fry until softened, about 3 minutes. Transfer to a plate.

4 Return the wok to high heat. When it is very hot, add the lamb and its marinade and stir-fry until cooked, about 1 minute. Using a slotted spoon, transfer the lamb to the plate holding the onion.

5 Pour the stock, and the cornstarch mixture into the wok and cook, stirring, until lightly thickened, about 1 minute. Return the lamb and onion to the pan, mix in lightly, and heat through. Season with pepper. Transfer to a warmed serving plate and sprinkle with the sesame seeds and the chile, if using.

6 To serve on a hot iron plate, preheat the iron plate in a 400°F (200°C) oven. Stir-fry the onion only until half cooked. Cook the lamb as directed and set aside separately from the onion. Cook the sauce as directed and return the lamb to it. To serve, remove the hot plate from the oven, spread the onion over it, and carry it to the table. Pour the lamb and sauce onto the plate at the table. Top with the sesame seeds and the chile, if using.

MONGOLIA

The Mongolians are a tough, nomadic sheep- and cattle-herding people who retain many of their old traditions. Their history of war-mongering saw a Mongol emperor, Kublai Khan, installed in the imperial palace in Beijing during the thirteenth-century Yuan dynasty. The Great Wall of China was dramatically extended in the Ming dynasty, which followed, to keep the Mongols out of China. Mongolia can be credited with only one notable contribution to China's culinary traditions: the introduction of mutton and lamb. In the Yuan court, mutton was the staple food of the Mongol rulers, who had the kitchens altered to accommodate huge cauldrons for boiling sheep whole. This inelegant fare was carved at the table with the same sharp knives the Mongol warriors used on the battlefield, and was washed down with stupefying quantities of *koumiss,* an alcoholic beverage usually made from fermented mare's milk. Marco Polo described it as similar in color and quality to a good grape wine.

Today, Mongolian restaurants in the major northern cities feature many lamb dishes, including the famous three—*shuan yangrou,* the tabletop firepot in which thin-sliced lamb is swished to cook, the Mongolian barbecue of lamb cooked on a drum-style iron barbecue, and flaming lamb *shashliks.*

Madras-Style Lamb with Coconut

Kurma • Tamil Nadu • India

You can make a vegetarian version of *kurma* by replacing the meat with the same weight of potato, eggplant (aubergine), cauliflower, okra, or Brussels sprouts, in any combination.

2 tablespoons poppy seeds

2 tablespoons coriander seeds

1 teaspoon aniseeds

¾ teaspoon ground turmeric

5 tablespoons (3 fl oz/80 ml) vegetable oil

2 lb (1 kg) lean lamb shoulder meat or beef, trimmed of fat and sinew and cut into 1-inch (2.5-cm) cubes

4 dried red chiles

1 cinnamon stick

3 green cardamom pods, lightly crushed

6 whole cloves

1 cup (4 oz/125 g) chopped yellow onion

1 teaspoon *each* minced garlic and peeled and minced fresh ginger

2 cups (16 fl oz/500 ml) coconut milk (page 224)

1½ teaspoons salt, or to taste

Serves 4

1 In a small, dry frying pan over medium-high heat, dry-roast the poppy seeds, coriander seeds, and aniseeds, shaking and tossing, until the spices are fragrant and turn a few shades darker, about 5 minutes. Transfer to a small bowl so that the spices are not cooked further by residual heat. Let cool, then transfer to a blender, mortar, grinding stone, or a coffee grinder reserved solely for spices and pound or process to a fine powder. Transfer to a small bowl and add the turmeric. Set aside.

2 In a large, heavy nonstick frying pan over high heat, warm 2 tablespoons of the oil. When the oil is hot, add a few of the meat pieces and sear until they are lightly browned but not cooked through, about 2 minutes. With a slotted spoon, transfer to a bowl. Repeat in batches with the remaining meat pieces.

3 To the same pan over medium-high heat, add the the remaining 3 tablespoons oil and the chiles, cinnamon, cardamom, and cloves. Cook until they are fragrant and look puffed, about 2 minutes. Add the onion and cook, stirring often, until it is light brown, about 7 minutes. Stir in the garlic, ginger, and reserved spice mixture. Mix well.

4 Return the browned meat to the pan, add the coconut milk and salt, and bring to a boil over high heat. Reduce the heat to low, cover, and simmer until the meat is tender enough to be broken apart with a fork, about 1½ hours. Adjust the seasonings and serve.

Lamb Curry with Pumpkin

Gosht • Delhi and Uttar Pradesh • India

This is the quintessential dish of India, particularly in the north, where meat eating is more prevalent. Every family in northern India boasts a special way of cooking or seasoning *gosht,* the secret of which is passed on from one generation to another with great fanfare. Like any braised dish, *gosht* tastes even better the next day.

4 tablespoons (2 fl oz/60 ml) vegetable oil

1 lb (500 g) lean lamb shoulder meat, trimmed and cut into 1-inch (2.5-cm) cubes

1 cup (4 oz/125 g) chopped yellow onion

3 black or green cardamom pods

2 cassia leaves (page 224)

1 tablespoon peeled and grated fresh ginger

2 teaspoons minced garlic

2 tablespoons ground coriander

½ teaspoon ground turmeric

1 cup (6 oz/185 g) chopped tomato

1 tablespoon tomato paste

2 cups (16 fl oz/500 ml) chicken stock or water

1½ teaspoons salt, or to taste

1-lb (500-g) piece pumpkin or butternut squash, peeled, seeded, and cut into 1-inch (2.5-cm) pieces

1 tablespoon garam masala (page 225)

¼ cup (⅓ oz/10 g) chopped fresh cilantro (fresh coriander)

Serves 2–4

1 In a large, heavy, flameproof baking dish over high heat, warm 2 tablespoons of the vegetable oil. When hot, add a few of the meat pieces and sear until they are lightly browned all over but not cooked through, about 3 minutes. Transfer to a bowl. Repeat with the remaining meat pieces.

2 Add the remaining 2 tablespoons oil to the baking dish over medium-high heat. When hot, add the onion, cardamom, and cassia leaves and cook, stirring occasionally, until the onion is browned, about 8 minutes. Stir in the ginger, garlic, coriander, and turmeric.

3 Return the browned meat to the baking dish along with the tomato, tomato paste, stock or water, and salt. Bring to a boil, then reduce the heat to low, cover, and cook until the meat is tender when pierced with a fork, about 2 hours. Alternatively, place the covered baking dish in an oven preheated to 350°F (180°C) for 2½ hours.

4 About 20 minutes before the meat is done, stir in the pumpkin, re-cover, and continue cooking until the meat and pumpkin are tender and cooked through. Check and correct the seasoning. Transfer the curry to a warmed platter, taking care not to crush the pumpkin. Sprinkle with the garam masala and cilantro and serve.

Lamb Braised with Pepper and Herbs

Masalchi Mutton • Maharashtra • India

On India's tropical west coast, amid the Hindus and Christians, is a tiny community of Jews. Known as Bene Israel, they are believed to be the descendants of the original Jews in India who arrived at this region in the second century BC. The Bene Israel possess a cuisine that is a wonderful amalgam of Indo-Jewish flavors. One delectable example, *masalchi mutton,* is traditionally made for the Passover Seder using only freshly harvested spices. It tastes best when made with goat meat but lamb makes a fine substitute.

1½ cups (1½ oz/45 g) packed fresh cilantro (fresh coriander), leaves and tender stems

6–12 fresh hot green chiles such as serrano, stemmed

6 large cloves garlic

2-inch (5-cm) piece fresh ginger, peeled and coarsely chopped

2–3 tablespoons water, if needed

8 green cardamom pods

1 cinnamon stick, broken into bits

6 whole cloves

1 tablespoon ground coriander

1 teaspoon ground turmeric

1 teaspoon ground cayenne pepper

2 teaspoons cracked black peppercorns

2 cassia leaves (page 224)

4 tablespoons (2 fl oz/60 ml) peanut oil

2 lb (1 kg) lamb or goat shoulder meat, trimmed of fat and sinew and cut into 1-inch (2.5-cm) pieces

3 yellow onions, finely chopped

3 tomatoes, chopped

2 teaspoons salt, or to taste

Serves 6

1 In a food processor or blender, combine 1 cup (1 oz/30 g) of the cilantro, the chiles, garlic, and ginger and process until finely puréed. If necessary, add the water to speed up the process. Set aside.

2 With the base of a heavy pan, lightly crush the cardamom pods to open them and release the seeds. Do not discard the skins. In a small, dry frying pan over medium-high heat, combine the cardamom seeds and skins, cinnamon, and cloves. Roast the spices, shaking and tossing constantly, until fragrant, about 4 minutes. Let cool, then transfer the spices to a grinding stone, mortar, blender, or a coffee grinder reserved solely for spices and pound or process them to a fine powder. Transfer to a small bowl and add the ground coriander, turmeric, cayenne, black peppercorns, and cassia leaves. Set aside.

3 In a large, shallow nonstick frying pan over high heat, warm 1 tablespoon of the oil. When hot, add a few pieces of the meat and cook, turning and tossing, until it loses its red color but is only lightly fried, about 3 minutes. (Do not overbrown the meat, as this will make the sauce very dark.) Using a slotted spoon, transfer the seared meat pieces to a bowl. Repeat in batches with the remaining meat.

4 To the same pan, add the remaining 3 tablespoons oil and the onions. Reduce the heat to medium-high and cook, stirring occasionally, until the onions are golden brown, about 10 minutes. Add the cilantro paste and cook, stirring, until it loses its raw aroma, about 2 minutes.

5 Add the tomatoes and cook, stirring occasionally, until they look soft, about 5 minutes. Return the meat with its juices to the pan. Add the spice mixture and salt and mix well. Reduce the heat to low, cover, and simmer gently until the meat is fully cooked and very tender, about 1½ hours. Check and stir often to ensure that the meat is not sticking and burning. Turn off the heat and let the dish rest for 5 minutes, covered, before serving. Check and adjust the seasonings to taste. Transfer to a warmed platter, sprinkle with the remaining cilantro, and serve.

FRANCE

T*he fundamental components of meat dishes in France are, in many ways, the same from region to region. Poultry, lamb, beef, pork, variety meats, cheeses, cream, vegetables, wine, brandy, herbs, butter, olive oil, and goose or duck fat are the sustaining ingredients. They are made into stews, braised, roasted, grilled, or sautéed. But there the similarities end, for each corner of France has its indigenous* produits du terroir, *which, along with seasonal ingredients, personalize basic preparations, making them unique.*

To gaze into the window of a French butcher shop is to see luxury and frugality displayed, with nearly every edible part of the animal shown off with care. There are the famous Bresse chickens neatly stacked with their long necks and heads tucked beneath their breasts. Large, fattened capons, preferred for their succulence and flavor, await their transformation into a traditional *coq au vin.* If the shop doubles as a charcuterie, there may be housemade pâtés and terrines, some coarse and country-style, others smooth and suave, perhaps enriched with silky foie gras or pungent black truffle. Carefully dressed rabbits, their livers, kidneys, and hearts still attached, are displayed next to partridges, pigeons, and quail, reminiscent of a time when "barnyard animals" and seasonally hunted game were common additions to the rural larder. Plump sausages, pork and beef roasts—rolled, larded, and artfully tied—and thick slices of veal shank brimming with luscious marrow inspire visions of rib-sticking *choucroutes,* rabbit a dozen ways, and veal shanks simmering in sauce.

Such stews and braises are central to French cooking, and they take many forms. Wine is a crucial addition, its complexity of flavors rounding out the stew and helping to create the final amalgamation of savory tastes. A stew made with stock differs from one that includes wine. And depending upon what wine was used, the flavor of the stew varies. In Provence, for example, the menus of some restaurants list which wine was used in making the daube, and every home cook will have a wine that he or she insists is necessary for the ideal result.

Wine is not the only defining component, however. Stews in different regions and during different seasons show off the local specialties. In Provence, a stew, whether of rabbit, chicken, beef, or fish, is likely to include olives, garlic, and perhaps a branch or two of aromatic local thyme, sage, or marjoram. In Normandy, the additions are apples or cream, thanks to the area's abundant orchards and dairy herds, while in the north and in Alsace, potatoes and cabbage are popular. The stew might marinate in red wine and *eau-de-vie* in Provence, in cider plus a little Calvados in Normandy, in white wine or beer in Alsace. Locally gathered wild mushrooms might be added to stews in Provence, Languedoc, the Périgord, and the Alps, while Belgian endive might be chosen in the north.

When it comes to braising, cream and cider appear again in Normandy and Brittany. However, the pork, sausages, and sauerkraut that make up *choucroute,* the signature dish of Alsace, are all treated to a long braise in a regional white wine. In Burgundy, local red wines define *boeuf bourguignon* and *coq au vin,* but in rugged Corsica a beef stew is made with a robust island wine. In the south, fleshy red tomatoes and fragrant olive oil set the pattern.

Grilled steak—especially when served with a pile of crisp, well-salted *frites*—lamb, and pork chops are always popular choices both in restaurants and when cooking at home. When pan grilling, French cooks will often make a sauce by deglazing the pan with a little wine or vinegar, perhaps then enriching the pan juices with a quick swirl of butter and then pouring the tasty results over the steak or chops.

French cooks have proved to be very creative with roasted main dishes: A pork roast cooked in a Provençal kitchen will be well seasoned with the region's tastiest herbs before being ringed with whole heads of garlic, while a roast duck is likely to be glazed to a glistening amber color with locally harvested lavender honey. In Alsace, the pork roast or duck might be seasoned with juniper and surrounded by thick wedges of cabbage. Birds stuffed and then roasted, such as guinea fowl, chicken, pheasant, and turkey, are filled with local bread crumbled and mixed with prunes and walnuts in Gascony, dried apricots in the south, or truffles in the Périgord and Haute Provence. Especially in Provence, where the sheep gain a special flavor as they range over the craggy scrubland and undulating hills, there is no Easter without lamb, and the *gigot* (leg) is the preferred dish of the traditional wedding banquet. Older, more muscular sheep, 12 to 18 months old, are seasoned with thyme and garlic and braised to flavorful tenderness in the classic preparation known as *le gigot de sept heures,* or 7-hour lamb. Food is of the land in France, and people undoubtedly eat better for understanding that.

Opposite: A faded wall shows the effects of time and the weather in Carpentras, an important market town of the Vaucluse. **Above, left:** Aix-en-Provence's fashionable cours Mirabeau is lined by seventeenth- and eighteenth-century buildings on one side and elegant cafés on the other. **Above, right:** In the area around Charolles, in Burgundy, the prized Charollais beef cattle are raised. They are slaughtered at age six rather than five, the common age for many other breeds, in the belief that the extra year delivers extra flavor.

Chicken with Apricot-Fig Stuffing

Poussins Farcis aux Abricots et Figues Sèches • Languedoc • France

Apricots and figs, fresh or dried, are beloved fruits of the Mediterranean. They go well with the regional herbs, as you will see here. Rubbing the chickens inside and out with resinous rosemary and sage before roasting subtly flavors the meat and makes a good companion to the savory sweetness of the stuffing, which is also flavored by herbs.

4 young chickens or Cornish hens, 1–1¼ lb (500–625 g) each

1 teaspoon salt

2 teaspoons freshly ground pepper

¼ cup (⅓ oz/10 g) minced fresh sage

¼ cup (⅓ oz/10 g) minced fresh rosemary

STUFFING

4–5 cups (8–10 oz/250–315 g) sliced or cubed two-day-old baguette, *pain au levain,* or any combination of coarse country breads

1 tablespoon unsalted butter

½ large yellow onion, minced (about 1 cup/6 oz/185 g)

1 clove garlic, minced

2 cups (16 fl oz/500 ml) boiling water

½ cup (3 oz/90 g) chopped dried figs

½ cup (3 oz/90 g) chopped dried apricots

3 tablespoons minced fresh rosemary

3 tablespoons minced fresh thyme

1 teaspoon salt

2 teaspoons freshly ground pepper

GLAZE

½ cup (5 oz/155 g) apricot jam

2 tablespoons Banyuls vinegar or balsamic vinegar

Fresh rosemary sprigs

Serves 4

1 Preheat the oven to 400°F (200°C).

2 Rinse the birds and pat dry. Rub inside and out with the salt and pepper, then with the sage and rosemary. Discard the herbs, or for a stronger flavor, leave some of the herbs clinging to the skin or tucked under the skin.

3 To make the stuffing, place the bread in a large bowl and set aside. In a small saucepan over medium heat, melt the butter. Add the onion and garlic and sauté until translucent, 3–4 minutes. Add the boiling water and pour the mixture over the bread. Turn the bread to soak all the pieces. Let stand until the bread is cool enough to handle and the water has been absorbed, 10–15 minutes. Using your hands, squeeze the bread, breaking it down until a thick paste forms. Add the dried figs and apricots, rosemary, thyme, salt, and pepper, and continue squeezing to incorporate them into the paste.

4 Spoon the stuffing into the cavities using ⅓–½ cup (3–4 oz/90–125 g) per bird. Do not pack the cavities too full. Gently slip your fingers between the skin and the meat of the breast to make a pocket, and tuck some of the stuffing under the skin as well. Tie the legs together with kitchen string and tuck the wings under the breasts.

5 Place the birds, breast sides up, on a rack in a roasting pan. Roast the birds for about 25 minutes.

6 While the birds are roasting, prepare the glaze: In a small saucepan over low heat, combine the jam and the vinegar and heat, stirring occasionally, until a syrup forms, 3–4 minutes.

7 Remove the birds from the oven and, using a pastry brush, coat them with the glaze. Return to the oven and roast until the juices run clear when the thickest part of the thigh is pierced with the tip of a knife, about 25 minutes longer.

8 Remove the birds from the oven, garnish with rosemary sprigs, and serve.

Chicken Breasts with Asparagus

Suprêmes de Volaille aux Asperges • Provence • France

Near the ramparts of Avignon, just through a gateway into the old city from the banks of the Rhône River, is the restaurant Le Jardin de la Tour. This simple dish was inspired by the restaurant's chef, Jean-Marc, who makes an unbeatable springtime lunch, handling two pans at once and deftly transferring the flavorful liquid from cooking the asparagus to the chicken, to marry the two with a light sauce.

1 Rinse the chicken breasts and pat dry with paper towels.

2 Combine the parsley, cilantro, mint, and thyme or savory on a cutting board or large platter. Mix well, then roll the chicken breasts in the herbs and let stand for about 1 hour before cooking. (They can be left longer but must be refrigerated and then returned to room temperature before cooking.)

3 Meanwhile, if the asparagus stalks are thick, peel them to within about 2 inches (5 cm) of the tips and snap off the tough ends. Place the asparagus in a frying pan, add the butter, season lightly with salt and pepper, and pour in the water. Cover and set the pan aside.

4 In a large frying pan over high heat, warm the olive oil. When the pan is hot enough to sear the chicken, add the chicken breasts, and cook until browned on the first side, about 3 minutes.

5 Turn the chicken breasts, season with salt and pepper, reduce the heat to medium-low, and cook until the second side is browned and the chicken is opaque throughout, about 3 minutes longer.

6 When the chicken is half cooked, place the pan holding the asparagus over high heat and bring to a boil. Move the lid slightly ajar and boil until the water is reduced by half and the asparagus is cooked, about 3 minutes. Using tongs or a slotted utensil, transfer the asparagus to warmed individual plates, reserving the pan juices.

7 Transfer the chicken breasts to the plates, placing them alongside the asparagus, and keep warm. Place the pan used to cook the chicken over medium-high heat, add the asparagus water, and boil, stirring constantly and scraping up any browned bits from the pan bottom, until the liquid is reduced to a light sauce consistency. Taste and adjust the seasoning. Spoon the sauce over the chicken and serve immediately.

4 skinless, boneless chicken breasts

3 tablespoons chopped fresh flat-leaf (Italian) parsley

2 tablespoons chopped fresh cilantro (fresh coriander)

2 tablespoons chopped fresh mint

1 tablespoon chopped fresh thyme or winter savory

20 asparagus spears

¼ cup (2 oz/60 g) unsalted butter

Salt and freshly ground pepper to taste

1 cup (8 fl oz/250 ml) water

3 tablespoons olive oil

Serves 4

Chicken Braised in Wine

Coq au Vin • Burgundy and Lyon • France

Today, one still finds restaurants and homes that prepare this farmhouse dish the traditional way with a rooster or a capon, but more often a young chicken is used.

3 oz (90 g) lean bacon, cut into strips ¼ inch (6 mm) thick and 1 inch (2.5 cm) long

12 pearl onions

4 tablespoons (2 oz/60 g) unsalted butter

1 chicken, 3½ lb (1.75 g), cut into serving pieces

1 tablespoon all-purpose (plain) flour

2 tablespoons brandy

1 bottle (24 fl oz/750 ml) red Burgundy or other full-bodied red wine

3 fresh thyme sprigs

3 fresh flat-leaf (Italian) parsley sprigs

1 dried bay leaf

1 teaspoon freshly ground pepper

½ teaspoon salt

½ lb (250 g) fresh white mushrooms, brushed clean

Serves 4 or 5

1 In a saucepan over medium-high heat, combine the bacon strips with cold water to cover. Bring to a boil, reduce the heat to low, and simmer, uncovered, for 10 minutes. Drain, then rinse the bacon under cold water, and pat dry. Fill a saucepan three-fourths full with water and bring to a boil. Add the pearl onions and boil for 10 minutes. Drain, cut off the root ends, slip off the skins, and trim off the stems if you like.

2 In a deep, heavy pan with a lid, melt 3 tablespoons of the butter over medium heat. When it foams, reduce the heat to medium-low, add the bacon and onions, and cook, stirring, until lightly browned, about 10 minutes. Using a slotted spoon, transfer the bacon and onions to a plate. Add the chicken and raise the heat to medium. Cook, turning as needed, until the chicken begins to brown, about 10 minutes. Sprinkle with the flour and, turning from time to time, continue to cook until the chicken and the flour are browned, about 5 minutes. Pour the brandy over the chicken, ignite with a long match to burn off the alcohol, and let the flames subside. Return the bacon and onions to the pan. Pour in a little of the wine and deglaze the pan, stirring to dislodge any bits clinging to the bottom. Pour in the remaining wine and add the thyme, parsley, bay leaf, pepper, and salt. Cover and simmer, stirring occasionally, until the chicken is cooked through, 45–60 minutes.

3 Meanwhile, in a frying pan over medium-high heat, melt the remaining 1 tablespoon butter. When it foams, add the mushrooms and sauté until lightly golden, 3–4 minutes. Remove from the heat and set aside. About 15 minutes before the chicken is done, add the mushrooms to the chicken. When the chicken is finished cooking, using a slotted spoon, transfer the chicken, onions, mushrooms, herb sprigs, and bacon to a bowl. Skim off and discard the fat from the pan juices. Raise the heat to high and boil until the liquid is reduced by nearly half, about 5 minutes. Return the chicken, onions, and mushrooms to the pan (and the bacon, if you wish). Reduce the heat to low and cook, stirring, until heated through, 3–4 minutes. Transfer to a warmed dish or serve directly from the pan.

WILD MUSHROOMS

France is a nation possessed by a love for wild mushrooms, or *champignons sauvages,* and both the eating of the beloved fungi and the hunt itself causes a near frenzy with many enthusiasts. Fall is the primary season, and from September until the first freeze, when you see cars parked helter-skelter alongside roadsides, you can be virtually certain the owners are hunting mushrooms.

There is a subtle competition among the people in some villages to see who gets the first mushrooms. As the season approaches, more and more residents can be seen taking seemingly innocent walks after lunch or in the late afternoon. But close observation will reveal a

plastic bag peeking out of a pocket, in discreet preparation for a possible find.

Once the mushrooms are found, the women sit in front of their doors, cleaning them for everyone to see. Of course, no one asks where they were found—that piece of information is a secret.

In local markets, *épiceries,* and even supermarkets, cèpes, *sanguins,* chanterelles or *girolles, pieds de mouton,* and *trompettes de mort* are proudly displayed. Restaurants and home cooks alike present dishes that celebrate the *terroir* and the season, including wild mushroom omelets, gratins, sauces, and grills. It is one of the best times of the year to sit down to a meal in France.

Guinea Fowl with Cabbage and Chestnuts

Pintade aux Choux et Marrons • Central • France

Guinea fowl, or *pintade,* and pheasant are commonly cooked with cabbage and chestnuts in the chestnut country of the Berry, south of Paris, an area also renowned for its abundance of wild game. The wild boars that roam the forests feed on the fallen chestnuts, and in years past, the farmers used to take their pigs out into the chestnut forests to forage for their food, a custom rarely practiced today. If you don't have guinea fowl, you can prepare this dish with chicken or duck with equal success.

2 guinea fowl or pheasants, about 2 lb (1 kg) each

1½ teaspoons salt

1¼ teaspoons freshly ground pepper

4 celery stalks, halved

2 carrots, peeled and halved

4 cloves garlic, minced

6 fresh thyme sprigs

8 slices bacon

3 cups (24 fl oz/750 ml) dry white wine

2 lb (1 kg) fresh chestnuts

6 tablespoons (3 oz/90 g) unsalted butter

1 lb (500 g) fresh chanterelle mushrooms, brushed clean and halved or quartered if large

1 small head cabbage, cored and cut lengthwise into slices ½ inch (12 mm) thick

½ cup (4 fl oz/125 ml) water

Serves 4

1 Preheat the oven to 350°F (180°C).

2 Rub the guinea fowl or pheasants with 1 teaspoon each of the salt and pepper. In a roasting pan, combine the celery, carrots, garlic, and thyme. Place the guinea fowl or pheasants on top of the vegetables, then top with the bacon slices. Pour 2 cups (16 fl oz/ 500 ml) of the wine over all and cover the pan.

3 Roast until the birds are tender and the juices run clear when the thickest part of the breast is pierced with a knife, 1¼–1½ hours. The timing will depend on the age of the birds and whether they were wild or farm raised. Older or wild birds may be slightly tougher and take longer to cook. Overcooking, however, will result in a dry bird.

4 While the birds are cooking, prepare the chestnuts: Using a sharp knife, cut an X on the flat side of each chestnut. Place them on a baking sheet and roast along with the birds until the cut edges begin to lift slightly, about 30 minutes. Remove from the oven, let cool slightly, then peel away the hard shells. With the knife, remove the soft, furry skin surrounding each nut. Cut the chestnut meats into ½-inch (12-mm) cubes. Set aside.

5 In a frying pan over medium heat, melt 4 tablespoons (2 oz/60 g) of the butter. When it foams, add the mushrooms and sauté until some juices are released, 6–7 minutes. Add the cubed chestnuts and the remaining 2 tablespoons butter, reduce the heat to low, and cook, stirring often, until the chestnuts soften, 3–4 minutes. Sprinkle with ¼ teaspoon of the salt and the remaining ¼ teaspoon pepper and set aside. Keep warm.

6 Just before serving, place the cabbage slices on a rack in a steamer over boiling water, cover, and steam just until translucent, about 5 minutes. Remove from the heat, sprinkle with the remaining ¼ teaspoon salt, and set aside. Keep warm.

7 Remove the birds from the roasting pan. If you prefer to carve them before serving, discard the bacon. Slice off the breast meat and the legs, and keep warm. Remove the carcasses and discard. Otherwise, set the birds aside and keep warm.

8 Using a slotted spoon, remove the vegetables from the roasting pan and discard. Place the pan on the stove top over high heat and add the remaining 1 cup (8 fl oz/250 ml) wine and the water. Bring to a boil and deglaze the pan, stirring to scrape up any bits clinging to the bottom. Boil until the liquid is reduced to 1 cup (8 fl oz/250 ml).

9 On a warmed platter, make a bed of the cabbage. Spread the mushroom-chestnut mixture over the cabbage and top with either the breast meat and legs, if carved, or the whole birds. Pour the sauce over all and serve immediately. To carve the whole birds, remove them to another platter.

Roast Chicken with Zucchini Stuffing

Poulet Rôti Farci aux Courgettes • Provence • France

Slipping a stuffing under the skin of a chicken rather than into the cavity marvelously perfumes the breast. Here a stuffing of grated zucchini and herbs imparts flavor to the meat and to keeps the breast succulent while the remainder of the chicken cooks.

2 large or 3 small zucchini (courgettes), cut or grated into a fine julienne to yield 2 cups (10 oz/315 g)

2 green (spring) onions, including tender green tops, sliced

2 tablespoons white bread crumbs from day-old bread

2 tablespoons grated Parmesan cheese

1 tablespoon chopped fresh oregano

1 teaspoon chopped fresh thyme

Salt and freshly ground pepper to taste

1 roasting chicken, 4 lb (2 kg)

About 3 tablespoons olive oil

JUS (OPTIONAL)

1 cup (8 fl oz/250 ml) light chicken stock or water

½ chicken bouillon cube if using water

Salt and freshly ground pepper to taste

About ½ teaspoon tomato paste (optional)

1 tablespoon sherry or Madeira (optional)

Serves 4

1 Preheat the oven to 425°F (220°C). Oil a roasting pan. In a bowl, combine the zucchini, green onions, bread crumbs, Parmesan cheese, oregano, and thyme. Season with salt and pepper and mix thoroughly.

2 Rinse the chicken and pat dry. Make sure that the flesh around the cavity end of the bird is not exposed to the breastbone. If it is, carefully sew up loosely with a needle and kitchen string. Turn the bird and carefully open the skin that protrudes from where the neck has been removed. Slip your fingers between the skin and the flesh of the bird, easing away any membrane that holds the skin to the flesh and being careful not to tear the skin. There should now be a wide passageway between the skin and the breast into which the stuffing can be spooned.

3 Carefully fill the cavity between the skin and the breast with the stuffing, pressing it toward the cavity end of the bird and plumping it into a rounded shape as you go. The cavity should be large enough to accommodate all the stuffing.

4 Smooth the neck skin back over the opening and close the opening by pressing the neck skin around to the underside of the bird. This may be secured with a needle and kitchen string, but if the skin is long enough and has been firmly pressed, it should hold in place.

5 Lay the bird, breast side up, in the prepared roasting pan. Season the top of the bird with salt and pepper and smear with the olive oil.

6 Roast the chicken, rotating the pan at the midway point, until the juices run clear when a knife tip is inserted into the thigh joint, about 1¼ hours. An instant-read thermometer inserted into the thickest part of the thigh away from the bone should register 180°F (82°C). If the bird begins to overbrown, reduce the oven temperature to 400°F (200°C).

7 Transfer the chicken to a cutting board, tent loosely with aluminum foil, and let rest for 10–15 minutes. Use poultry shears or sturdy kitchen scissors to cut the chicken into 4 pieces. First, carefully cut alongside the breastbone, then gently force the bird open a little and cut down along either side of the backbone. Remove the backbone and discard. Then cut each bird half in half again, following the rounded line of the leg bones so that each person getting a wing section also gets a little extra breast.

8 If making the jus, add the stock or water and the bouillon cube to the roasting pan and place over high heat. Bring to a boil and deglaze the pan, stirring to scrape up any browned bits from the pan bottom. Boil down to a light, syrupy consistency and season with salt and pepper. If the sauce lacks flavor, add the tomato paste or the sherry or Madeira. Strain into a warmed serving bowl.

9 Arrange the chicken and stuffing on warmed individual plates and serve. Pass the sauce at the table.

Duck with Lavender Honey

Canard au Miel de Lavande • Provence • France

Lavender honey speaks distinctly of Haute Provence and the Drôme, where fields of lavender create shimmering waves on the plateaus. The honey doesn't taste like lavender, but it has its faint aroma. Used in sweets and certainly for tartines, it also makes a fragrant glaze for duck or chicken. Added near the end of the cooking, it quickly lacquers a duck to a deep mahogany, or a chicken to a deep gold. Here, the liver of the duck roasts inside the cavity. Spread it on toasts for eating along with the carved bird.

1 Preheat the oven to 350°F (180°C).

2 In a mortar or a spice grinder, grind together 2 teaspoons of the fresh lavender blossoms (or 1 teaspoon of the dried), the thyme, winter savory, peppercorns, and salt.

3 Remove all the inner fat and the giblets from the cavity of the duck. Rinse and pat dry. Using a sharp knife, cut crisscrosses through the fat—but not into the meat—of the breast. Rub the duck inside and out with the herb mixture. Replace the liver, heart, and gizzard in the cavity. Discard the neck. Place the duck, breast side up, on a rack in a roasting pan.

4 Roast for 2 hours. Remove from the oven and pour off all but 1 tablespoon of the collected fat from the pan. Spread the duck breast with 2 tablespoons of the honey and return to the oven for another 10 minutes. Once again, remove from the oven and, using a large spoon, baste with the pan juices, now mingled with the honey. Return to the oven and roast for another 10 minutes. Remove the duck again, spread with the remaining 2 tablespoons honey and sprinkle with 1 teaspoon of the remaining fresh lavender (or ½ teaspoon of the dried). Roast for 10 minutes longer, then baste again with the pan juices. Cook for 5 minutes longer and remove from the oven. When done, the juices should run pinkish clear when the breast is pierced with the tip of a knife at its thickest part, or an instant-read thermometer inserted into the thickest part registers 165°F (74°C). The duck skin should be crisp and deeply browned.

5 Transfer the duck to a platter, cover loosely with aluminum foil, and let stand for 10 minutes while you prepare the sauce. Pour off the collected fat, leaving the pan juices, which should measure about 3 tablespoons, in the pan. Put the roasting pan over medium heat and add the remaining 1 teaspoon fresh lavender (or ½ teaspoon dried) and the red wine. Deglaze the pan, stirring with a wooden spoon to remove any browned bits from the pan bottom. Cook until well blended and slightly reduced, 3–4 minutes. Keep warm.

6 Remove the giblets from the duck cavity. Carve the duck, separating the wings, legs, and thighs from the body and slicing the breast. Arrange the duck pieces and giblets on a warmed platter. Drizzle with the sauce and serve immediately.

4 teaspoons fresh lavender blossoms or 2 teaspoons dried blossoms

2 teaspoons fresh thyme leaves or ½ teaspoon dried thyme

2 teaspoons fresh winter savory or 1 teaspoon dried savory

12 peppercorns

1½ teaspoons salt

1 duck, about 5½ lb (2.75 kg), with giblets

4 tablespoons (3 oz/90 g) lavender, acacia, or other strong-flavored honey

3 tablespoons red wine

Serves 2–4

Rabbit Roasted with Prunes

Lapin aux Pruneaux · The Pyrenees and Gascony · France

Throughout France, rabbit, part of the *basse-cour* (barnyard) along with chickens, guinea hens, and other small animals, plays a big part in the simple, home-style country cooking. The lean, firm white meat is suited to a number of preparations, and cooks in each region vary the dishes according to the local *terroir*. Thus, rabbit with prunes in Gascony, with cream in Normandy, with mustard in Burgundy, and with olives in Provence.

½ teaspoon minced fresh thyme

½ teaspoon minced fresh sage

½ teaspoon minced fresh rosemary

½ teaspoon pepper

1 young rabbit, about 2½ lb (1.25 kg), cut into 8–10 serving pieces

8–10 pitted prunes

8–10 slices bacon

Serves 4

1 Preheat the oven to 350°F (180°C).

2 In a small bowl, combine the thyme, sage, rosemary, and pepper and mix well. Rub each piece of rabbit with the mixture. Place a prune alongside each piece of rabbit, wrap them together with the bacon, and fasten the bacon in place with a toothpick. Put the wrapped rabbit pieces in a shallow roasting pan just large enough to accommodate them.

3 Roast, basting from time to time with the pan juices, until the thickest rabbit pieces are tender when pierced with the tip of a sharp knife and the meat is opaque to the bone, 1–1¼ hours. Transfer to a warmed platter and serve at once.

Sautéed Foie Gras with Grapes

Foie Gras aux Raisins • Southwestern • France

Fresh foie gras cut into slices and then sautéed is a great delicacy. It forms a thin crust on the outside, leaving the inside creamy. Freshly squeezed grape juice and Armagnac or Cognac are combined with the rich pan juices to make a light sauce. Classically, large, sweet Muscat grapes are used in this specialty of Bordeaux.

1 fresh foie gras of duck, about 1 lb (500 g), chilled

1 teaspoon salt

1 teaspoon freshly ground pepper

2–3 tablespoons fresh grape juice, strained

2 tablespoons Armagnac or Cognac

1 cup (6 oz/185 g) Muscat or other sweet grapes, peeled and seeded if desired

Serves 3 or 4

1 Separate the small and large lobes of the liver by slicing between them with a sharp knife. Cut the lobes lengthwise into slices ½ inch (12 mm) thick. Remove the exposed nerves with your fingers or the tip of the knife. Place the slices in a single layer between sheets of waxed paper and refrigerate until thoroughly chilled and hard, about 1 hour.

2 Place a large frying pan over high heat. Sprinkle the foie gras slices on both sides with the salt and pepper. When the pan is very hot, add the slices and cook just until a crust forms on the first side, 30–40 seconds. Turn and cook for another 30–40 seconds. The pan must be very hot for this step so that a crust quickly forms; overcooking will result in melted foie gras. Transfer the slices to a platter and cover loosely with aluminum foil to keep warm.

3 Pour off any fat from the pan and return the pan to high heat. Add the grape juice and Armagnac or Cognac and deglaze the pan, stirring with a wooden spoon to dislodge any browned bits from the pan bottom. Continue to stir over high heat until the liquid is reduced by about half. Stir in the grapes and cook, stirring, until just warmed through, about 1 minute.

4 Arrange the grapes around the foie gras on the platter and pour the hot pan juices over them. Alternatively, arrange the foie gras and grapes on individual plates and top each serving with the pan juices.

FOIE GRAS

Although most people think of geese when they think of foie gras, ducks are equally fine sources of the fattened liver. Of course, such a bold statement only fuels the continuing argument among gourmands about whether the more intensely flavored duck liver is preferable to the mild, subtly flavored goose liver.

In both cases, the prized oversized organ is achieved by force-feeding the animals an excessive amount of ground corn during the *gavage,* or fattening period.

In the region of Périgord Noir, where foie gras is a specialty, the summer months are quite hot, and many *éleveurs* choose to raise ducks instead of geese because they are thought to better tolerate the heat. But fattened duck livers are smaller than those of geese, weighing only about a pound (500 g) each, while a goose liver might weigh as much as a pound and a half (750 g), a fact that goose partisans are quick to point out. The debate continues.

Little Parcels of Saddle of Rabbit

Râble de Lapin en Paupiettes • Provence • France

The saddle, that is, the loin and fillets that sit between the front and back legs of the rabbit, is the animal's most tender meat. The animal, however, is quite lean, particularly if it is wild and has run the fields, and thus the meat can dry out easily. For this reason, it is typically braised rather than roasted. Here, the moist pork stuffing and air-cured ham deliver additional succulence to the finished dish. Few vendors sell only the saddles, but the remainder of the rabbit can be set aside, or frozen, for use in any ragout recipe.

2 large rabbits, about 3½ lb (1.75 kg) each

STUFFING

¼ lb (125 g) ground (minced) pork

¼ lb (125 g) ground (minced) veal

1 shallot, finely chopped

1 clove garlic, finely chopped

Grated zest of 1 small lemon

2 fresh sage leaves, finely chopped

3 tablespoons chopped black olives

1 egg, lightly beaten

Salt and freshly ground pepper to taste

8 spinach leaves, stems removed (optional)

8 thin slices air-cured ham (page 225) or prosciutto

3 tablespoons olive oil

1 cup (8 fl oz/250 ml) dry white wine

2 fresh sage leaves

1 fresh thyme sprig

Salt and freshly ground pepper to taste

2 tablespoons water

Serves 4

1 Place each rabbit, belly side down, on a cutting board. Run a sharp knife around the outline of each leg, slice away from the tail area of the carcass, then remove the legs. Using a cleaver or heavy knife, sever the front legs from the saddle (loin) section. Reserve the 4 legs for another recipe (see note).

2 Turn the saddles belly side up and remove the kidneys and their fat. Discard the fat. Chop the kidneys and reserve for the stuffing. Working with 1 saddle at a time, and using a sharp, pointed knife, release the meaty section along the stomach side of the carcass and, without cutting it off, turn the carcass and continue around onto the back of the saddle, continuing to release the fleshy part of the meat from the carcass. When finished, you should have 2 pieces of meat from each saddle. Trim off any fleshy remains from each carcass and chop finely for the stuffing.

3 To make the stuffing, in a bowl, combine the ground meats, shallot, garlic, lemon zest, sage, olives, and reserved kidneys and rabbit trimmings. Mix well, then add the egg and mix well again. Season with salt and pepper.

4 Lay the meat flat on a work surface. Using a meat pounder, shape each piece into a rough oval about 7 inches (18 cm) long and 3½–4 inches (9–10 cm) wide. Line each piece with 2 spinach leaves, if using, and then spread with the stuffing, dividing it evenly among the 4 pieces. Working from a narrow end, roll up each piece into a cylinder and wrap with 2 pieces of the ham. Tie each parcel with kitchen string at 3 intervals along its length.

5 In a deep frying pan, warm the olive oil. Add the parcels, neatest side down, and brown, turning once, until lightly browned on both sides, 5–8 minutes. Add the white wine, sage, and thyme and bring to a boil. Season lightly with salt and pepper, then reduce the heat to low, cover, and simmer slowly until tender when pierced with the point of a sharp knife, 15–20 minutes. Transfer the parcels to a cutting board, tent loosely with aluminum foil, and let rest for 5 minutes.

6 Cut the parcels into slices ½ inch (12 mm) thick. Slide a spatula under the slices of each parcel and transfer to warmed individual plates. Return the pan to high heat, add the water, bring to a boil, and deglaze the pan, stirring to scrape up any browned bits from the pan bottom. Boil until reduced slightly, then taste and adjust the seasoning with salt and pepper. Spoon the sauce over the slices and serve.

Roast Pork Loin with Sage

Carré de Porc aux Feuilles de Sauge • Provence • France

Both the standing rack of lamb and that of pork are often served *persillé* style in Provence. Lines are scored across the back of the rack, and the classic *persillade* mixture of olive oil, garlic, and parsley is pressed against the scored surface. Throughout Provence, you will find the same enthusiasm for adding fruits to pork found elsewhere in the world. Roast pork might be surrounded by panfried figs or orange sections, or sprinkled with cinnamon and served with grapes, but a simple farmhouse recipe with apples and sage is still the best.

1 pork loin, about 2½ lb (1.25 kg) and with 6 or more chops

3 large fresh sage sprigs, each with 12–14 leaves

1 yellow onion, cut into wedges

3 cloves garlic, crushed

3 tablespoons olive oil

2 tablespoons lavender honey or other honey

3 tablespoons unsalted butter

2 Granny Smith apples, peeled, halved, cored, and cut into medium-thick slices

Salt and freshly ground pepper to taste

¾ cup (6 fl oz/180 ml) water

Serves 6

1 The night before serving, run a sharp, thin-bladed knife along the lower part of the bone behind the base of the chop meat. Remove 2 or 3 sage leaves from 1 of the sprigs and push them into the cavity from each side of the loin. Stand the loin in a roasting pan. Press 2 of the sage sprigs across the top and back of the pork, splaying them out to cover the surface. Place the third sprig on the bottom of the pan. In a bowl, toss the onion wedges and garlic with the oil and then spill the contents of the bowl over the meat. Cover and refrigerate overnight. Bring to room temperature before proceeding.

2 Preheat the oven to 400°F (200°C).

3 Place the roasting pan in the oven and roast for 15 minutes. Reduce the oven temperature to 375°F (190°C) and continue to roast the pork, without basting, until the juices are no longer pink when the pork is pierced, about 45 minutes longer. An instant-read thermometer inserted into the pork should register 160°F (71°C). About 10 minutes before the end of the cooking time, raise the oven temperature again to 400°F (200°C), remove the pan from the oven, and drizzle the honey over the pork. Return the loin to the oven for 10 minutes to glaze the meat. Transfer the pork loin to a warmed serving platter and keep warm. Set the pan aside, unwashed.

4 In a large frying pan over high heat, melt the butter. Just as the butter begins to brown, add the apple slices in a single layer and fry until well browned on the first side, about 3 minutes. Turn the slices and brown on the second side, about 2 minutes longer. Season with salt and pepper and transfer the slices to the platter, arranging them around the pork. Keep warm in a low (225°F/110°C) oven with the door ajar.

5 Place the roasting pan with the onion wedges and honey flavoring on the stove top over high heat. Add the water to the pan, bring to a boil, and deglaze the pan, stirring to scrape up any browned bits from the pan bottom. Season with salt and pepper.

6 Spoon 2 tablespoons of the sauce over the apples, and pour the remainder into a warmed serving bowl. Carve the pork loin at the table. Serve accompanied with the sauce.

Country-Style Pâté with Armagnac

Pâté de Campagne à l'Armagnac • Normandy • France

Hand chopping the ingredients for this pâté results in an interesting and varied texture, while a meat grinder makes a more uniform pâté. You may need to special order the caul fat or fatback from your butcher. Order a fresh pork liver at the same time. The final texture and flavor of your pâté will be better than if a frozen one is used. Cornichons are classic accompaniments for this pâté and for others of all kinds.

1 Preheat the oven to 325°F (165°C).

2 For a more varied texture, finely chop the liver, pork butt, and fatback separately and set them aside. For a finer, more even texture, cut the meats and fat into chunks, then pass through a meat grinder fitted with a ⅜-inch (1-cm) disk; set aside.

3 In a small saucepan over medium heat, bring the Armagnac just to a simmer. Immediately light it with a match to burn off the alcohol, let the flames subside, then cool.

4 In a large bowl, using your hands, mix together the chopped meats and fatback, garlic, salt, pepper, ground juniper berries, and Armagnac until thoroughly blended. Fry a tiny nugget of the mixture in a small frying pan, taste, and adjust the seasonings of the mixture, remembering that over time the seasonings will become more pronounced.

5 Line a 10-by-3-by-3-inch (25-by-7.5-by-7.5-cm) terrine or loaf pan (with a cover) with the caul fat, allowing the edges to overhang the sides. If you are using fatback, line the inside of the container with overlapping pieces, reserving enough to cover the top. Pack the pâté mixture into the pan and cover with the overhang of caul fat or the reserved pieces of fatback. In a small cup, stir together the flour and water to make a paste, then spread it along the edge of the pan where the cover sits. Set the cover on the pan and press it into the paste to create a seal during cooking. Place the terrine in a larger baking pan and pour hot water into the larger pan to reach halfway up the sides of the terrine.

6 Bake until the juices run clear when the pâté is pierced with a fork, about 2½ hours. Remove from the oven and lift the terrine from the water bath. Uncover the terrine. Cut a piece of aluminum foil slightly larger than the surface of the terrine and place it on top of the cooked meat, pressing it down and into the corners to make a snug fit. Wrap a brick or similar weight with foil and place it on top.

7 The weight should rest directly on the pâté to compact it; this is an important step. Let cool to room temperature.

8 Pour off any accumulated juices. Refrigerate the pâté, with the weight still in place, for at least 12 hours but preferably 24 hours. Remove the weight and cover the pâté with the lid or plastic wrap and store for up to 10 days.

9 To serve, cut the pâté into slices ¼–½ inch (6–12 mm) thick.

2 lb (1 kg) pork liver

2 lb (1 kg) pork butt

¼ lb (250 g) fatback

¼ cup (2 fl oz/60 ml) Armagnac

1 small head garlic, minced

¼ cup (2 oz/60 g) salt

2 tablespoons coarsely ground pepper

2 tablespoons juniper berries, ground in a spice mill

1 piece caul fat, about 10 by 12 inches (25 by 30 cm), or an equivalent amount of fatback, sliced ¼ inch (6 mm) thick (page 224)

2 tablespoons all-purpose (plain) flour

½–1 tablespoon water

Makes one 3- to 4-lb (1.5- to 2-kg) pâté

Veal Chop Ragout

Côtelettes de Veau en Petit Ragoût • Provence • France

In Provence, veal cutlets and chops are often pot-roasted. Here, their aromatic quality is enhanced with the addition of fresh lemon juice and mint.

3 tablespoons unsalted butter

1 tablespoon olive oil, plus more if needed

6 thick-cut young veal chops

1 yellow onion, cut into 8 thin wedges

¾ cup (6 fl oz/180 ml) dry white wine

4 slender carrots, peeled and sliced

3 large fresh mint sprigs, tied with kitchen string

Salt and freshly ground pepper to taste

1¼ lb (625 g) young fava (broad) beans, shelled and peeled (page 225)

½ cup (4 fl oz/125 ml) water

½ cup (4 fl oz/125 ml) heavy (double) cream

About 1 teaspoon fresh lemon juice, or to taste

2 tablespoons shredded fresh mint leaves

Serves 6

1 In a deep sauté pan over high heat, melt the butter with the 1 tablespoon olive oil. Add the veal and brown on both sides, 10–12 minutes total. Transfer to a plate. Reduce the heat to medium, add the onion, and sauté for 1½–2 minutes, adding more oil if needed. Add the wine, raise the heat to high, and deglaze the pan, scraping up any bits from the bottom. Return the chops to the pan, add the carrots and tied mint, season with salt and pepper, cover, reduce the heat to low, and cook for 20 minutes.

2 Turn the chops, add the fava beans, and stir once. Add the water, re-cover, and simmer until the veal is tender, about 20 minutes longer.

3 Transfer the chops and vegetables to individual plates and keep warm. Discard the tied mint. Add the cream to the pan, raise the heat to high, and boil, stirring, to reduce to a sauce consistency. Adjust the seasoning. Add the lemon juice, stir in the shredded mint, and spoon the sauce over the chops.

Sauerkraut with Pork, Sausages, and Potatoes

Choucroute Garnie • Alsace-Lorraine • France

Alsace, with its strong German influence, has a regional enthusiasm for sauerkraut, finely shredded fermented cabbage. In this classic version of the traditional Alsatian *choucroute garniç*, sauerkraut is slowly braised in white wine, and assorted meats are buried in it as it simmers. Sauerkraut is sold both cooked and *cru*, or "raw." If you use the cooked variety the end result will have a more souplike texture.

3 lb (1.5 kg) raw or cooked sauerkraut (see note)

1 clove garlic, minced

10 juniper berries

1 dried bay leaf

2 whole cloves

6 peppercorns

¼ cup (2 oz/60 g) pork lard or rendered goose fat

1 large yellow onion, minced

4 smoked ham hocks, about 2 lb (1 kg) total weight

2 cups (16 fl oz/500 ml) dry Riesling, Sylvaner, or other dry white wine

About 1 cup (8 fl oz/250 ml) water

½ teaspoon freshly ground pepper

¼-lb (125-g) piece slab bacon

¼-lb (125-g) piece lean fresh pork belly (optional)

8 firm-fleshed potatoes, peeled

6 pure pork frankfurters

Serves 6–8

1 Preheat the oven to 325°F (165°C).

2 If using raw sauerkraut, in a large bowl, soak the sauerkraut in cold water to cover for 15 minutes to remove some of its saltiness, then taste it. If it is still too salty, soak again. Drain. Put the raw sauerkraut in a clean, dry kitchen towel, gather up the ends, and wring out the excess water. Cooked sauerkraut does not need to be rinsed.

3 Place the sauerkraut in a bowl, then, using a fork, fluff it to rid it of any clumps.

4 Place the garlic, juniper berries, bay leaf, cloves, and peppercorns on a square of cheesecloth (muslin), bring the corners together, and tie securely with kitchen string.

5 In a deep, heavy pan with a lid, warm the lard or goose fat over medium heat. When it melts, add the onion and sauté slowly, reducing the heat if necessary, until the onion is translucent but not browned, about 5 minutes. Add half of the sauerkraut, the cheesecloth bag of seasonings, and the ham hocks, then top with the remaining sauerkraut. Pour over the wine and then add the water nearly to cover. Add the ground pepper and bring to a boil, uncovered.

6 Cover, place in the oven, and cook for 1 hour. At the end of the hour, stir the sauerkraut, pushing some to the side. Add the bacon and the fresh pork belly, if using, re-cover, and cook for 1 hour longer.

7 Remove the pan from the oven and stir the sauerkraut. Place the potatoes on the top. Cover and return to the oven to cook until the potatoes soften, about 30 minutes longer.

8 Just before the sauerkraut is ready, bring a saucepan three-fourths full of water to a boil over high heat. Add the frankfurters, reduce the heat to medium, and cook until hot, 6–8 minutes. Drain and add to the sauerkraut, turning once or twice.

9 To serve, transfer the sauerkraut to a warmed large, shallow bowl or deep platter. Top with the ham hocks and frankfurters. Cut the bacon and the fresh pork belly, if used, into slices and add them as well. Surround the sauerkraut with the potatoes and serve hot.

Sweetbreads with Mushrooms

Ris de Veau aux Champignons · Champagne · France

Sweetbreads, really thymus glands, are considered a delicacy by the French, who have a wonderful way with *les abats,* the innards of animals. Indeed, some of the most beloved dishes of the French table are made from kidneys, livers, and sweetbreads. The sauce created in this dish is especially succulent, so serve it with rice, noodles, or toast.

2 lb (1 kg) veal or calf sweetbreads

¼ cup (2 fl oz/60 ml) white wine vinegar

3 tablespoons unsalted butter

2 carrots, peeled and diced

2 shallots, minced

2 celery stalks, diced

2 tablespoons minced fresh flat-leaf (Italian) parsley

1 teaspoon minced fresh thyme

1 dried bay leaf

½ teaspoon freshly ground pepper

½ cup (4 fl oz/125 ml) dry white wine

½ teaspoon salt

16 white onions, each 1–1½ inches (2.5–4 cm) in diameter, peeled

½ lb (250 g) fresh mushrooms, brushed clean and quartered

Serves 4

1 In a bowl, combine the sweetbreads with cold water to cover. Cover the bowl and refrigerate for 2 hours, changing the water several times. If the sweetbreads were purchased whole, they will need trimming. With the sweetbreads still in the water, using a knife, separate the two lobes, which are connected by a tube, and discard the tube. Drain the sweetbreads and return them to the bowl with fresh water to cover. Add the vinegar and let the sweetbreads soak for another 30 minutes. Then remove as much of the remaining filament as possible without the sweetbreads losing their shape.

2 In a frying pan over medium heat, melt the butter. When it foams, add the carrots, shallots, celery, parsley, thyme, bay leaf, and ¼ teaspoon of the pepper. Reduce the heat to low and cook, stirring, until the vegetables are soft but not browned, about 10 minutes. Add the wine, raise the heat to high, and boil until reduced by half, 3–4 minutes.

3 Sprinkle the sweetbreads with the salt and the remaining ¼ teaspoon pepper and place them in the frying pan, arranging them snugly in a single layer atop the vegetables. Baste them with the butter and vegetables, cover tightly, and cook, still over low heat, until they turn opaque and begin to release their juices, about 5 minutes. Turn the sweetbreads and baste them again. Replace the cover and cook for another 5 minutes to release the juices further. The sweetbreads will reduce considerably in size as they render their juices.

4 Add the onions to the pan. Butter a sheet of parchment (baking) paper and place, buttered side down, over the sweetbreads and onions. Cover and cook over very low heat until the onions are tender and nearly translucent, about 30 minutes. Remove the cover and lift the paper. Turn the sweetbreads and add the mushrooms. Replace the paper and the cover and cook until the sweetbreads are tender when pierced with the tip of a sharp knife, about 15 minutes.

5 Using a slotted spoon, transfer the sweetbreads and vegetables to a platter. Discard the bay leaf. Raise the heat to high and boil to reduce the pan juices by half, 2–3 minutes. Meanwhile, cut the sweetbreads into slices ½ inch (12 mm) thick. Return the slices and the vegetables to the pan and cook just to warm them through, 1–2 minutes.

6 Transfer the sweetbreads and cooked vegetables and their juices to a warmed platter or shallow bowl and serve immediately.

COOKING WITH WINE

Wine is a deeply treasured part of the French patrimony, and people are profoundly proud of the wines that each region, each village, and each vineyard produce. Wines—red, white, sweet, dry, and fortified—are part of every cook's pantry, like salt, pepper, herbs, butter, cream, and olive oil, and they are added with a practiced hand. What wine is used generally depends upon what is locally produced, and the taste of a dish will reflect the regional wine. You'll find wine is an essential ingredient in the making of soups, stews, and sauces. It is employed to deglaze pans, to poach fruit, and to make homemade aperitifs and digestifs. Distilled spirits—brandy, Cognac, Armagnac, and Calvados—are used with equal aplomb for the same purposes, although in lesser quantities. The spirits have the additional quality of being flammable because of their high alcohol content. The flaming burns off the alcohol, leaving behind the complex flavors of the spirits.

Beef Cheeks Braised in Red Wine

Joue de Boeuf · Corsica · France

This dish uses beef cheeks—the thick meat of the face—whose flavor and tenderness are revealed only after long, slow cooking in a regional red wine, such as a hearty red from the Mediterranean island of Corsica or from Languedoc-Roussillon in Southern France.

1 calf's foot, cut into several pieces

2 lb (1 kg) beef cheeks, cut into 1-inch (2.5-cm) cubes

1 bottle (24 fl oz/750 ml) hearty red wine

3 tablespoons extra-virgin olive oil

2 yellow or white onions, chopped

3 shallots, chopped

2 celery stalks

¼ cup (⅓ oz/10 g) chopped fresh flat-leaf (Italian) parsley

2 teaspoons fresh thyme leaves

1 teaspoon chopped fresh marjoram

1 orange zest strip, 3 inches (7.5 cm) long

½ teaspoon salt

½ teaspoon freshly ground pepper

2 cups (16 fl oz/500 ml) water

Serves 4

1 Put the calf's foot and beef pieces in a bowl, add the wine, cover, and refrigerate for 24 hours.

2 In a heavy saucepan over medium heat, warm the olive oil. Add the onions and shallots and sauté just until translucent, 2–3 minutes. Drain the meat, reserving the marinade, and pat dry. Working in batches, add the meat to the saucepan and cook, turning as needed, just until lightly browned, 3–4 minutes. Transfer to a plate.

3 When all of the meat is browned, return it to the pan. Add the celery stalks, parsley, thyme, marjoram, orange zest, salt, pepper, the marinade, and the water. Stir well, cover, reduce the heat to low, and cook until the meat is easily separated with a fork, 3–4 hours.

4 Discard the celery stalks, then discard the calf's foot, if desired. To serve, spoon into a deep platter.

Seared Steaks with Fresh Herbs

Côtes de Boeuf aux Herbes • Provence • France

The top sirloin or rib-eye steak is a great luxury in France and, like the leg of lamb, is often featured at wedding banquets and other festive occasions.

2 tablespoons *each* unsalted butter and olive oil

2 thick-cut, bone-in top sirloin steaks, each about 1½ lb (750 g)

Sea salt and freshly ground pepper to taste

SAUCE

3 tablespoons unsalted butter

4 shallots, finely chopped

¾ cup (6 fl oz/180 ml) beef stock

2 tablespoons green mustard with herbs or Dijon mustard

3 tablespoons chopped mixed fresh flat-leaf (Italian) parsley, chervil, and tarragon

Salt and freshly ground coarse pepper to taste

Serves 6

1 In a cast-iron frying pan over high heat, melt the butter with the olive oil until the mixture turns a light brown. Add the steaks and sear, about 1 minute. Turn, sprinkle with sea salt, and brown on the second side for 1 minute longer. Turn again, reduce the heat slightly, and cook, turning once, for about 6 minutes on each side for rare, or until done to your liking. Transfer to a platter, tent with aluminum foil, and let rest for 5–8 minutes before carving.

2 Meanwhile, make the sauce: In a saucepan over medium heat, melt 2 tablespoons of the butter. Add the shallots and sauté until softened but not colored, about 30 seconds. Add the stock, bring to a boil, and cook until reduced by half. Remove from the heat and stir in the mustard, the remaining 1 tablespoon butter, and the herbs. Stir in any juice that has collected on the platter holding the beef. Season with salt and pepper. Pour the sauce into a warmed serving bowl.

3 Transfer the steaks to an attractive cutting board and sprinkle them with pepper, then carry the board to the table. Cut along the bone to free the meat, then carve into slices diagonally across the grain. Pass the sauce at the table.

Roasted Veal with Whole Garlic

Rôti di Veau à l'Ail • Provence • France

Veal is frequently used in France, where a wide variety of cuts is available. Roasting transforms the whole garlic from sharp and pungent to tender and sweet.

1 boneless veal loin or rib roast, about 3½ lb (1.75 kg)

3 tablespoons extra-virgin olive oil

1 teaspoon salt

1 teaspoon freshly ground pepper

2 bay leaves

4 fresh thyme sprigs

¼ lb (125 g) fatback, sliced ¼ inch (6 mm) thick

6 heads garlic

6 cloves garlic

1 cup (8 fl oz/250 ml) dry white wine

½ cup (4 fl oz/125 ml) water

Serves 6

1 Preheat the oven to 425°F (220°C).

2 Rub the roast with 1 tablespoon of the olive oil and ¾ teaspoon each of the salt and pepper. Put the bay leaves and thyme sprigs on top, then lay the sliced fatback along the top. Tie into a neat roll with kitchen string. Cut the upper ¼ inch (6 mm) off the top of each garlic head. Rub the heads with the remaining 2 tablespoons olive oil and sprinkle with the remaining ¼ teaspoon each salt and pepper. Put the roast, fat side up, on a rack in a roasting pan. Place the garlic heads and the garlic cloves in the pan around the rack.

3 Roast, occasionally basting the garlic heads with the pan juices, until an instant-read thermometer inserted into the thickest part of the roast registers 145°F (63°C), about 1 hour. Transfer the roast and the garlic to a platter, cover loosely, and let rest for 10 minutes before carving.

4 Meanwhile, put the pan on the stove top over medium-low heat. Add the white wine and deglaze, stirring to dislodge any bits on the bottom. Add the water and stir until reduced a bit, 1–2 minutes.

5 Cut the roast into slices about ½ inch (12 mm) thick, remove the fatback and kitchen string, and arrange on a serving platter with the garlic heads. Drizzle a little of the sauce over the roast and pass the remaining sauce at the table.

Steak with Shallot–Red Wine Sauce

Bifteck Marchand de Vin • Southwestern • France

With a luxurious red wine and shallot sauce, these simple seared steaks are right at home in an upscale Parisian bistro. Serve with *frites* and a glass of velvety Bordeaux.

2 rib steaks, ½–¾ inch (12 mm–2 cm) thick

½ teaspoon salt

1 teaspoon freshly ground pepper

2 teaspoons minced fresh thyme

2 tablespoons unsalted butter

¼ cup (1½ oz/45 g) minced shallots

⅓–½ cup (3–4 fl oz/80–125 ml) dry red wine

Fresh flat-leaf (Italian) parsley

Serves 2

1 Trim the steaks of excess fat. Pat them dry and sprinkle with the salt, pepper, and thyme, pressing the seasonings into both sides. Heat a heavy, nonstick frying pan over medium-high heat. Add 1 tablespoon of the butter. When it has melted and is near sizzling, put the steaks in the pan and sear them, turning once, for 3–4 minutes on each side for medium rare; the timing will depend upon the thickness of the steaks and the desired amount of doneness. Keep the heat high, but do not let the fat burn. Test for doneness by cutting into one of the steaks. When they are ready, transfer them to a warmed platter and cover loosely with aluminum foil while you prepare the sauce.

2 Pour off all but 1 tablespoon of the pan juices. Return the pan to medium heat and add the shallots. Sauté until translucent, 2–3 minutes. Add the wine and deglaze the pan, stirring to dislodge any browned bits on the bottom. Cook until the wine is reduced by half and the mixture has thickened, 2–3 minutes. Stir in the remaining 1 tablespoon butter.

3 Pour the hot sauce over the steaks, garnish with the parsley, and serve immediately.

Braised Provençal Beef

Nougat de Boeuf • Provence • France

The name of this recipe comes from the layering of different cuts of meat, giving the dish a look similar to that of fruit-and-nut-studded nougat candy, a Provençal specialty.

1 oxtail, about 2 lb (1 kg), cut into several pieces

2 lb (1 kg) beef brisket or rump

2 lb (1 kg) chuck steak

1½ lb (750 g) boneless beef shank

1 calf's foot, split lengthwise (optional)

½ lb (250 g) salt pork

1 piece fresh pork rind, 6 by 4 inches (15 by 10 cm)

2 large tomatoes, peeled, seeded, and chopped

4 cloves garlic, finely chopped

1–2 teaspoons finely chopped orange zest

1 tablespoon tomato paste, or as needed

3 tablespoons salt-packed capers, rinsed

1 teaspoon peppercorns

Salt and freshly ground pepper to taste

3 yellow onions studded with 6 whole cloves, cut into wedges

2 carrots, peeled and cut into thick slices

3 leeks, including tender green tops, cut into large chunks

Large bouquet garni (page 223)

1 bottle (24 fl oz/750 ml) full-bodied dry red wine such as Cabernet Sauvignon

¼ cup (2 fl oz/60 ml) brandy

5 tablespoons (2½ fl oz/75 ml) *each* red wine vinegar and olive oil

2 salt-packed anchovies, filleted and rinsed (page 223), or 4 olive oil–packed anchovy fillets

Serves 8–10

1 The day before serving, trim the excess fat and membrane from the oxtail, the 3 beef cuts, and the calf's foot, if using. Cut the beef into pieces about ¼ lb (125 g) each. Cut the salt pork into thick slices about 2 inches (5 cm) long. Place the pork rind, skin side up, on the bottom of a large, preferably oval, heavy Dutch oven.

2 In a bowl, mix together the tomatoes, the garlic, the zest, the 1 tablespoon tomato paste, 1 tablespoon of the capers, and the peppercorns. Pour one-third of the tomato mixture over the pork rind. As you layer the ingredients, sprinkle with salt and pepper. Scatter one-third of the meats over the top, along with one-third of the onions, carrots, and leeks. Top with about half of the remaining tomato mixture, the bouquet garni, and then half of the remaining meats and vegetables. Repeat using the remaining tomato mixture, meats, and vegetables. Pour in the wine, brandy, vinegar, and oil. Cover and refrigerate overnight.

3 The following day, bring the pot slowly to a boil over medium heat. Reduce the heat to very low, cover tightly, and simmer for 4–4½ hours. The meat will be tender and almost melted into a syrupy sauce. About 20 minutes before the end of cooking, crush the anchovies in a mortar. Add 2 tablespoons of the cooking liquid, stir to blend, and then stir the mixture into the stew. Re-cover and continue cooking for the final 20 minutes or so.

4 Using a slotted utensil, transfer the meat to a warmed platter. Discard the bouquet garni. Taste the cooking liquid for salt and, if it is not too salty, boil it down over high heat to a syrupy sauce consistency. Spoon off some of the fat from the surface, if desired, then adjust the seasoning with salt, pepper, and more tomato paste, if necessary

5 Sprinkle the meat with the remaining 2 tablespoons capers and spoon some of the sauce over all. Pass the remaining sauce at the table.

DAUBES

Some culinary observers believe that the French word *daube* is from the Spanish *dabar,* meaning "to cook in a closed environment," linking the adoption to the longtime Catalan community that populated the port of Marseilles. But most Provençaux trace the name of their favorite braised dish to the *daubière,* the tight-lidded, potbellied vessel in which it has been traditionally cooked. Nowadays, the term is applied to any braised dish that is first marinated in wine and then slowly stewed in it. Daubes are most often of beef, and the wine is most often red, but versions based on lamb, pork, venison, rabbit, poultry, and other birds, and even on fleshy monkfish, tuna, or other fish that will not disintegrate during long cooking, can be found as well.

Daubes call for long cooking in a minimum of liquid to soften the fibers of lesser cuts of meats fully, so a heavy, tight-fitting lid is essential to ensure a minimum of evaporation. Characteristically, these hearty dishes are perfumed with herbs and orange peel and simmered over very low heat until the meat can be cut with a spoon and the rendered juices have combined with the wine to become thick and syrupy. Leftover daube, refrigerated, turns into a potted meat, the reduced juices setting into a natural jelly.

Beef Daube

Daube de Boeuf • Provence • France

There are probably as many versions of the daube as there are Provençal cooks, but the common thread is the use of a marinade of red wine and spices and the long, slow cooking time, resulting in meat that is so soft and tender that it can be cut with a spoon. A finished daube is often garnished with a *persillade,* a mixture of finely chopped garlic and parsley.

3 lb (1.5 kg) boneless beef cheek, beef shank, or beef chuck

3 yellow onions, cut into large wedges

3 carrots, peeled and sliced into 1½-inch (4-cm) lengths or batons

5 cloves garlic, chopped

2 or 3 fresh flat-leaf (Italian) parsley sprigs

1 celery stalk, halved crosswise

5 peppercorns, lightly crushed

4 juniper berries, lightly crushed

4 whole cloves

Pinch of freshly grated nutmeg

2 bay leaves

1 large fresh thyme sprig

1 bottle (24 fl oz/750 ml) Bandol red wine or other tannic red such as Cabernet Sauvignon

2 tablespoons red wine vinegar

2 orange zest strips, about ½ inch (12 mm) wide

½ lb (250 g) salt pork

2 oz (60 g) lard

2 tablespoons olive oil

2 tomatoes, peeled, seeded, and coarsely chopped

1 piece fresh pork rind, 6 by 3 inches (15 by 7.5 cm)

Salt to taste

3 tablespoons all-purpose (plain) flour (optional)

Freshly ground pepper to taste

Serves 8

1 Cut the beef into 3 roughly equal pieces. Place the beef in a large dish and add 1 of the onions and the carrots, garlic, parsley, celery, peppercorns, juniper berries, cloves, nutmeg, bay leaves, and thyme. Add the wine and vinegar, cover, and allow to marinate overnight in the refrigerator.

2 The next day, remove the beef from the refrigerator. Pass the marinade mixture through a sieve placed over a bowl to capture the liquid. Remove the onion and carrots from the sieve. Pat the beef and vegetables dry on paper towels. Pick out the herbs, spices, and celery from the sieve and place on a small piece of cheesecloth (muslin). Add the orange zest strips, bring the corners of the cheesecloth together, and tie with kitchen string to form a small parcel.

3 Rinse the salt pork and cut into 2-inch (5-cm) cubes. In a large, heavy dutch oven or sauté pan, melt the lard over medium heat. Add the salt pork and brown on all sides, about 5 minutes. Add the olive oil and the onion from the marinade. Working in batches, add the beef and brown on all sides, 10–15 minutes. Return all the beef to the pan. Add the reserved liquid and carrots from the marinade, the remaining onion wedges, the tomatoes, and the parcel of herbs. Pour in enough water just to reach to the top of the meat, then cover the beef with the piece of pork rind, skin side up. Salt lightly.

4 Bring to a boil, reduce the heat to very low, and simmer, skimming off foam once after 5 minutes. Cover and cook slowly for 4 hours. If desired, to reduce evaporation, mix the flour with enough water to form a paste and rub the paste into the crevice between the pan rim and the lid, to seal the lid.

5 After 4 hours, use a knife to free the flour paste, if used, then remove the lid and check that the beef is very tender by piercing it with a knife. It will probably need to cook for another 30–60 minutes. Return the lid to its place (this time without sealing paste) and simmer slowly until the beef is so soft that it can be broken up with a spoon. When the daube is ready to serve, lift out the beef and vegetables with a slotted utensil and place on a warmed platter. Discard the parcel of herbs. The pork rind can be cut into strips and served with the meat or discarded. Keep the meat and vegetables warm.

6 Spoon off the rendered fat, then return the pot to the stove. Taste the liquid for salt, and if it is not too salty, boil it down over high heat to a fluid sauce consistency. Season with salt and pepper, then spoon the sauce over the meat and serve immediately.

Steak and French Fries

Steak-frites • Ile-de-France • France

Steak-frites is found all over France, from the humblest café to the most elegant restaurant. Various cuts of meat are used but one of the most popular is the *entrecôte,* or rib-eye steak.

4 or 5 russet or other baking potatoes

Vegetable oil for deep-frying

1½ teaspoons salt, plus salt to taste

4 rib or rib-eye steaks, each about ½ inch (12 mm) thick

2 tablespoons minced fresh thyme

1 teaspoon freshly ground pepper

⅓–½ cup (3–4 fl oz/80–125 ml) water

Serves 4

1 Peel the potatoes and slice them lengthwise ¼ inch (6 mm) thick. Stack the slices and cut again lengthwise to form sticks ¼ inch (6 mm) wide. As the potatoes are cut, slip them into a large bowl of cold water. When all of them are cut, let stand in the water for 30–60 minutes. Just before cooking, drain the potatoes and pat dry thoroughly.

2 In a deep-fryer or heavy, deep saucepan, pour in vegetable oil to a depth of 4 inches (10 cm) and heat to 350°F (180°C), or until a potato dropped into it sizzles upon contact.

3 When the oil is ready, put about one-fourth of the potatoes in a deep-frying basket and fry until the potatoes develop a white crust but do not brown, about 2 minutes. Transfer to paper towels to drain. Repeat until all the potatoes are cooked. The second frying can take place as much as 3–4 hours later, but the potatoes should rest a minimum of 5 minutes between the fryings. Do the second frying in batches also, but cook slightly longer, up to 3 minutes, allowing the potatoes to form a golden crust slowly. Transfer to paper towels to drain and sprinkle each batch with a little salt.

4 While the French fries are cooking, sprinkle the steaks with the thyme and the pepper. Sprinkle the 1½ teaspoons salt over the bottom of a large frying pan, and place over high heat for 1–2 minutes, or until a drop of water sizzles upon contact. Place the steaks in the pan and cook, turning once, for about 2 minutes on each side for medium-rare. Transfer to a warmed platter. Still over high heat, pour in the water and deglaze the pan, stirring to dislodge any browned bits from the pan bottom.

5 Pour the pan juices over the steaks and serve immediately with the hot fries.

Beef with Carrots

Boeuf aux Carottes • Provence • France

In restaurants, *boeuf aux carottes* is served on its own, but at home, it is typically served accompanied with a platter or bowl of fresh egg noodles. The sauce from the stew is ladled over the noodles, and then Gruyère cheese is passed around to sprinkle on top of individual servings. Serve with a glass of red Côtes.

2 tablespoons extra-virgin olive oil

1 large yellow onion, chopped

3 cloves garlic, chopped

3 lb (1.5 kg) boneless beef chuck or a combination of boneless beef chuck and beef shank, cut into 2-inch (5-cm) cubes

2 cups (16 fl oz/500 ml) dry red wine

4 fresh thyme sprigs

1 dried bay leaf

1 teaspoon salt

½ teaspoon freshly ground pepper

2 lb (1 kg) carrots, peeled and cut into 1-inch (2.5-cm) lengths

Serves 6

1 In a heavy pot over medium heat, warm the olive oil. Add the onion and garlic and sauté until the onion is nearly translucent, 2–3 minutes. Using a slotted spoon, transfer the onion and garlic to a large plate. Raise the heat to medium-high, add the meat, a few pieces at a time, and turn them to brown on all sides, about 5 minutes. As they are ready, transfer them to the plate holding the onion and garlic.

2 When all the meat is browned and removed from the pot, pour in 1 cup (8 fl oz/ 250 ml) of the wine and deglaze the pan, stirring to scrape up any bits on the bottom. Add the thyme, bay leaf, salt, pepper, and the remaining 1 cup (8 fl oz/250 ml) wine.

3 Return the meat, onion, and garlic and any collected juices to the pan. Reduce the heat to low, cover tightly, and cook for 1 hour, stirring from time to time. Add the carrots, cover, and cook, stirring occasionally, until the meat is tender enough to cut with a fork and the sauce has thickened, 1½–2 hours longer. Taste and adjust the seasonings.

4 Remove the thyme sprigs and the bay leaf and discard. Transfer to a warmed serving bowl or serve directly from the pot.

Rack of Lamb Colette

Carré d'Agneau Colette • Provence • France

This recipe employs a common Provençal technique: a large amount of garlic is boiled, puréed, and then used to thicken the sauce. Garlic loses much of its pungency and strength when boiled, and you will be amazed to find that the two cloves studding the meat are more evident than the twenty cloves cooked and puréed for the sauce. The purée goes well with other lamb dishes and is used in sauces for roast lamb, too. To make the job easier, ask the butcher to french the rib chops for you.

2 large lamb racks, with 9 chops each, or 6 individual racks, with 3 chops each

22 cloves garlic

Salt to taste

¼ cup (2 oz/60 g) unsalted butter, cut into small pieces

2 fresh rosemary sprigs, each broken into several small pieces

6 tablespoons (3 fl oz/90 ml) dry white wine

½ cup (4 fl oz/125 ml) water

1 cup (8 fl oz/250 ml) chicken stock

2 tablespoons chopped fresh flat-leaf (Italian) parsley

Freshly ground pepper to taste

2 teaspoons brandy

Serves 6

1 Preheat the oven to 475°F (245°C). Ideally, your butcher will have frenched the rib chops (trimmed away the meat from the end of each chop). If not, then trim the racks as needed for them to stand without toppling. Protect the stripped tips of the bones from burning by folding aluminum foil across the top. Cut 2 of the garlic cloves into slivers. Using a sharp knife, make shallow slits in the meatiest part of the chops and slip a garlic sliver into each slit. Stand the racks in a roasting pan and rub salt into the fattier side of the meat. Dot the butter over the surface and place the rosemary sprigs here and there.

2 Roast the lamb for 10 minutes. Add the wine to the pan and continue to roast until an instant-read thermometer inserted into the thickest part of the lamb registers 145°F (63°C) for medium-rare, about 20 minutes longer for larger racks and 10–15 minutes for smaller ones. The lamb should remain pink in the center. If the pan dries out before the lamb is ready, add a few spoonfuls of water.

3 Meanwhile, in a saucepan, combine the remaining 20 garlic cloves with salted water to cover and bring to a boil. Boil until very soft, about 15 minutes. Drain, then push through a sieve or purée in a small food processor. Set aside.

4 Transfer the racks to a warmed platter and keep warm. Spoon off any fat from the pan juices and place the pan over high heat.

5 Add the water to the pan, bring to a boil, and deglaze the pan, scraping up any browned bits from the pan bottom. Continue to boil until the juices are reduced to the point that they begin to fry onto the bottom of the pan. (This step reinforces the browning of the sauce, because well-seared meats that are eaten rare exude few juices into the pan.)

6 Add the stock to the pan and bring to a boil, scraping up the browned bits from the pan bottom. Mix in the puréed garlic and the parsley. Season with salt and pepper and stir in the brandy. Pour the sauce into a warmed bowl.

7 Serve the small racks on warmed individual plates, or carve the larger racks and divide among warmed plates. Pass the sauce at the table.

Grilled Lamb Chops with Fresh Thyme

Côtelettes d'Agneau Grillées · Provence · France

One of the definitive aspects of the food of Provence is the use of wild herbs. Sometimes they are used in combination, as in the case of herbes de Provence, but they are often used individually as well. In spring, when the wild thyme flowers create veritable carpets of purple and lamb is in season, grilled lamb chops with thyme are cooked for at least one midday Sunday meal, preferably eaten outside.

4 lamb sirloin chops, each ½ inch (12 mm) thick

2 teaspoons fresh thyme leaves and blossoms, if possible, finely minced, plus whole blossoms or sprigs for garnish

Scant ½ teaspoon salt

½ teaspoon freshly ground pepper

Serves 4

1 Prepare a fire in a grill.

2 Rub each chop with ½ teaspoon of the thyme, firmly pressing it into the flesh.

3 Place the chops on the grill rack. Cook on the first side until browned, 4–5 minutes. Turn and cook until the meat springs back when touched with your finger, 4–5 minutes longer for medium-rare.

4 Transfer to a warmed platter, season with the salt and pepper, and garnish with whole thyme blossoms or sprigs.

Seven-Hour Leg of Lamb

Le Gigot de Sept Heures • Provence • France

The nearer you get to a lamb-producing community—in this case the foothills of the Alps, near Sisteron—the more you find the people talking about the virtues of eating older lamb. These sheep, twelve to eighteen months old, are considered more succulent and richer in flavor than their younger counterparts, making them the ideal choice for use in this classic Provençal recipe.

1 leg of lamb, 5–5½ lb (2.5–2.75 kg) (see note)

2 tablespoons unsalted butter

1 tablespoon olive oil

3 tablespoons brandy

2 heads garlic, separated into cloves and peeled (about 40 cloves)

⅔ cup (5 fl oz/160 ml) dry red wine

⅔ cup (5 fl oz/160 ml) chicken stock

4 large fresh thyme sprigs

Salt and freshly ground pepper to taste

Serves 6

1 Fill a large stockpot three-fourths full of water and bring to a boil. Plunge the lamb into the boiling water and allow the water to return to a boil. Then reduce the heat to medium and simmer for 15 minutes. Drain and pat dry.

2 Preheat the oven to 250°F (120°C).

3 In a heavy dutch oven over high heat, melt the butter with the olive oil. Add the lamb and brown on all sides, about 15 minutes. Add the brandy and ignite it with a long match. When the flames subside, add the garlic cloves, wine, stock, and thyme. Season lightly with salt and pepper. Cover, place in the oven, and cook, turning twice, until the lamb is tender, about 7 hours.

4 Remove the pan from the oven and, using a slotted utensil and balancing the leg with a fork, transfer to a warmed platter and keep warm. Pass the contents of the pan through a sieve, pressing firmly on the garlic to extract the cooked flesh. Return the liquid to the pan over high heat and bring to a boil, scraping up any browned bits from the pan bottom. Reduce the liquid to a sauce consistency. Taste and adjust the seasoning. Strain into a small warmed bowl. Carve the lamb, then pass the sauce at the table.

Grilled Lamb Shoulder with Pesto

Paillard d'Agneau au Pistou • Provence • France

The word *paillard* literally means "bawdy," but when used to describe meat, it refers to a cut that has been butterflied to provide a thin, flat surface, a necessary procedure to bring a thick cut to the grill. Ask your butcher to bone and butterfly the lamb for you.

5 lb (2.5 kg) lamb shoulder, boned and butterflied

½ cup (4 fl oz/125 g) good-quality basil pesto, homemade or purchased

2 cloves garlic, finely chopped

1 tablespoon freshly cracked pepper

5 tablespoons (2½ fl oz/75 ml) olive oil

Salt to taste

Serves 6

1 The night before grilling, using a sharp knife, trim any excess fat from the butterflied shoulder. Slice any thicker parts open horizontally without cutting them completely free, and lay them open to achieve a similar thickness at all points. A meat pounder helps to thin out any remaining thicker areas. The meat should measure about 12-by-6-by-2-inches (30-by-15-by-5-cm). Lay in a large, shallow dish and brush both sides with the pesto. Sprinkle both sides with the garlic and pepper and drizzle with the olive oil. Cover with plastic wrap and refrigerate overnight.

2 Prepare a fire in a grill.

3 Spoon any liquid that has collected in the bottom of the dish over the meat, making sure the surface of the meat is oily. Place the meat on the grill rack over a hot fire and grill, turning once, for 20–25 minutes total for medium-rare. It is best to cook the meat more than halfway through on the first side, which later becomes the side that faces up when carving. Be sure to salt the meat only after it is turned, to prevent the loss of juices.

4 Transfer the lamb to a cutting board, tent loosely with aluminum foil, and let stand for 5 minutes before carving. Carve the meat on the diagonal across the grain and serve directly from the board, or place on warmed individual plates and serve.

Leg of Lamb with Potatoes and Onions

Gigot d'Agneau à la Boulangère • Provence • France

The most treasured lambs in France are those that have grazed either on salt marshes (thus becoming *pré salé,* or "salt meadow" lamb) or on wild herbs, like the famous lamb of Sisteron in the Basses-Alpes. The meat is full of the flavors of the *terroir.*

1 tablespoon unsalted butter

2½ lb (1.25 kg) baking potatoes, very thinly sliced

2½ lb (1.25 kg) large yellow onions, very thinly sliced

1½ cups (12 fl oz/375 ml) beef stock

1 bone-in leg of lamb, 5½–6 lb (2.75–3 kg)

1 tablespoon extra-virgin olive oil

1½ teaspoons dried *herbes de Provence*

½ teaspoon salt

¾ teaspoon freshly ground pepper

3 cloves garlic, cut into fine slivers

Serves 6–8

1 Preheat the oven to 400°F (200°C). Using the butter, grease a baking dish large enough to hold the lamb and vegetables. Set aside.

2 In a large saucepan over medium-high heat, combine the potatoes, onions, and beef stock and bring to a boil. Reduce the heat to low and simmer, uncovered, for 10 minutes to soften the potatoes. Using a slotted spoon, transfer the potatoes and onions to the prepared baking dish, spreading them evenly. Pour the stock over the vegetables and bake for 20 minutes.

3 Meanwhile, prepare the lamb: Using a sharp knife, make 20–25 slits, each 1 inch (2.5 cm) deep, all over the meat. Rub the lamb all over with the olive oil, *herbes de Provence,* salt, and pepper. Insert the garlic slivers into the slits.

4 When the vegetables have cooked for 20 minutes, remove from the oven and place the lamb on top of them. Reduce the oven temperature to 375°F (190°C) and bake until an instant-read thermometer inserted into thickest part of the leg away from the bone registers 125°–130°F (52°–54°C) for medium-rare, about 1 hour. If medium is desired, roast for another 15 minutes, or until the thermometer registers 135°–145°F (57°–63°C). Remove from the oven, cover loosely, and let stand for 15–20 minutes.

5 To serve, transfer the lamb to a cutting board and carve into thin slices. Arrange the potatoes and onions on a warmed serving platter and top with the lamb slices. Pour any juices captured during cooking over the lamb. Scoop up some of the potatoes and lamb slices for each serving.

THE MEDITERRANEAN

Preceding pages: At Lisbon's Monument to the Discoveries, an elaborate mosaic depicts a compass. **Top:** Falorni's butcher shop in Italy specializes in salt-cured *salumi* and other high-quality meats. **Above:** Soft, fresh, and sweet, these Italian pork sausages might be simmered with cannellini beans for *salsice con fagioli*. **Right:** Contemporary Italian life bumps against treasures of antiquity, like these modern scooters set against centuries-old sculptures.

A t a luxurious Italian feast prepared for Pope Pius V by the great chef Bartolomeo Scappi in 1570, the highlights of the meal were skylarks with lemon sauce, pastries filled with veal sweetbreads, spit-roasted veal and kid, and a soup of almond cream with the flesh of pigeons. Extravagant and whimsical, this feast would have been typical of aristocratic cooking at a time when meat was a rare luxury for the vast majority of the rural peasantry.

Until the 1800s, beef or veal was a nearly unattainable luxury for anyone but the bourgeoisie and those above them. *Animali di cortile* (animals of the courtyard)— chickens, guinea hens, and rabbits—were the meats of the common people, and even then were usually saved for holidays or special occasions. Farmers raised pigs to be butchered in the fall, and although some of the meat was eaten fresh, much of it was salted, flavored, or smoked and thus transformed into the region's beloved prosciutti, salamis, and *salsicce*. Because of the scarcity and expense of meat, every scrap was used, with the result that the less choice cuts, often the most flavorful, have come to be preferred. Tuscans adore *fegatini* (chicken livers), using them to enrich pasta sauces, to top crostini, and as a popular main course all on their own. Romans savor every type of

offal, as well as feet, tails, and snouts. These parts are called the *quinto quarto*, the "fifth quarter," referring to the fact that butchered animals are divided into quarters.

Pork is especially delicious in Italy, whether roasted, grilled, or made into one of the country's vast array of cured meats and sausages. A feature of every market and festival throughout Lazio and Umbria is *la porchetta*, a whole pig stuffed with a mix of rosemary, wild fennel, mint, garlic, and pepper and roasted on a spit. Less grand but equally delicious (and more manageable for home cooks) is Tuscany's *arista*, a crispy, rosemary-scented roast loin of pork.

But of all Italy's meat dishes, *bistecca alla fiorentina* is the one for which Tuscany is most famous. A well-prepared *bistecca*, or beefsteak, is a wondrous thing, crusty brown on the outside, red and juicy on the inside,

and abundant enough to satisfy even the heartiest appetite. Veal is also popular in the north in such preparations as *ossobuco* (braised veal shanks) and veal scallopini, thanks to the flat, fertile pasturelands around the flood plains of the Po River. Southerners eat beef, too, although typically it is served cut into thin slices and rolled around a tasty filling, or ground and seasoned to make meatballs, often in combination with other meats such as veal and pork.

In its own category are Tuscan recipes for *cacciagione,* or game. These are throwbacks to a time, centuries ago, when hunting parties canvassed vast private landholdings on the hunt for deer, wild boar, partridge, quail, pheasant, and hare. The intense flavor and scent of wild game were tempered by cooking it in a heady mixture of red wine seasoned with potent, fragrant herbs such as rosemary, sage, and juniper.

Although Iberia is not known for its beef, the Portuguese are addicted to steak, usually frying it and topping it with onions, a fried egg, or ham. In Spain, the finest beef is raised around Avila, in the Basque country, in Galicia, and in Andalusia. The Galician provinces of Lugo and Orense, where rugged *vaqueros* (cowboys) tend their herds, are renowned for their flavorful beef.

Both Muslims and Jews are prohibited from eating pork, so sheep have been raised in Portugal and Spain for centuries, especially in Trás-os-Montes and on the plains of Castile. Baby lamb is usually cooked whole on a spit, and more mature meat is braised in various styles, including with peppers or lemon in Spain and in red wine in Portugal. Kid or goat is popular in the three Beiras and in Ribatejo, where it is usually spit-roasted or braised.

But Iberian cooks revere the pig. In Portugal, aficionados of *leitão assado* (roast suckling pig) travel to the town of Mealhada, where restaurants specializing in crisp-skinned piglets spit-roasted over hardwood fires line both sides of the road. In rural Spain, *la matanza,* the ritual pig slaughter, is held every November 11 to commemorate the beast's culinary versatility. Every part of the animal is eaten—ears, snout, feet, tail, and blood—and the fat is rendered for lard.

Chicken eggs were traditionally more valuable than chicken meat, resulting in a greater repertoire of egg dishes than poultry dishes. However, spit-roasted whole birds and cut-up hens cooked with tomatoes and peppers in earthenware pans were common. For the Spanish Christmas Eve meal, chicken is often the centerpiece, stuffed with fruits and nuts and served it on a silver platter. Spain and Portugal are on the migratory routes of fowl flying south in the winter, so game birds such as quail and partridge, pheasant and goose, woodcock and pigeon also land in cooking pots, as do duck and turkey, again illustrating the wide variety at the heart of the Mediterranean meal.

Opposite: In Lucca, the church of San Michele in Foro displays the ambition and invention that characterized the Pisan Romanesque style. Although construction of the church began in the eleventh century, the completion of the ornate arcading was the pride of fourteenth century *lucchesi.* **Above:** Tuscany abounds in *belle viste*—"beautiful views"—unrolling in almost every direction.

Grilled Chicken on a Spit

Frango no Espeto • Estremadura • Portugal

Portuguese who have worked in Brazil and eaten at the local *churrascarias* usually return to their homeland with a taste for meat cooked on a spit or grill, and many eateries have opened to cater to them. This recipe is a specialty of Bonjardein, a popular restaurant in Lisbon. Traditionally, the meat is basted with a mixture of one part melted butter and two parts *piri-piri* sauce, accented with extra garlic. For those who do not have the fiery chile condiment in their pantry, the quick marinade listed here can be used with great success.

QUICK *PIRI-PIRI* MARINADE

2 cups (16 fl oz/500 ml) olive oil

1 tablespoon red pepper flakes

½ cup (4 fl oz/125 ml) fresh lemon juice

3 cloves garlic, smashed

4 poussins, Cornish hens, or broiler chicken halves, about 1 lb (500 g) each

3 tablespoons unsalted butter

1 tablespoon minced garlic

Sea salt and freshly ground black pepper to taste

Serves 4

1 To make the quick *piri-piri* marinade, in a saucepan over medium heat, heat the olive oil until it is very hot but not boiling. Drop in a red pepper flake. If it skips to the surface of the oil and bubbles but doesn't turn brown or black, add all of the pepper flakes. If the oil is too hot, the flakes will burn and you will have to start all over, as you don't want the oil to taste bitter. If the oil is not hot enough, the pepper flake will sink but not bubble. Keep heating and testing with a few random flakes. They should sizzle and bubble and stay on the surface of the oil for a few minutes. Then the action will subside and the oil will become a pale orange. Remove from the heat. Add the lemon juice and smashed garlic, then let the marinade cool completely. Pour off 6 tablespoons (3 fl oz/90 ml) and reserve for basting.

2 If using poussins or Cornish hens, first butterfly them: Rinse the birds. Insert a sharp knife through the cavity of a bird and split the bird down the back. Then carefully cut along the backbone to remove it entirely. Bend the bird until it lies flat. Tuck the wings under. Remove the excess neck skin. The bird will have the shape of a butterfly. Repeat with the remaining birds. Place the birds in a shallow container and pour the cooled marinade over them. If you are using broiler halves, combine them with the marinade. Cover and refrigerate overnight.

3 The next day, prepare a fire in a charcoal grill. Bring the birds to room temperature.

4 To make the basting sauce, in a small frying pan, melt the butter. Add the reserved *piri-piri* marinade and the minced garlic and simmer for 2–3 minutes. Season with salt and black pepper.

5 Remove the birds from the marinade and sprinkle them with salt and black pepper. Place on the grill rack, skin side up, and grill, basting with the *piri-piri*–butter mixture, 5–6 minutes. Turn and cook, continuing to baste, until the juices run clear when a thigh is pierced, about 5 minutes longer. The timing will depend upon the intensity of the fire.

6 Transfer to a warmed platter and serve.

Fried Chicken with Almond Sauce

Pollo en Pepitoria • Old Castile • Spain

This old Castilian recipe is described in Hispano-Arab documents that date as far back as the thirteenth century. In Spanish, a *pepita* is a seed. Pine nuts were used in the original Moorish-inspired recipes, and the mashed yolks of hard-boiled eggs were added to thicken the sauce. Today, almonds are used but you could use a combination of the two. A pinch of ground cinnamon and cloves may be used instead of the nutmeg.

½ cup (4 fl oz/125 ml) olive oil

½ cup (2½ oz/75 g) blanched almonds

3 cloves garlic, chopped

1 slice coarse country bread, crust removed

1 chicken, 3–4 lb (1.5–2 kg), cut into serving pieces

Salt and freshly ground pepper to taste

¾ cup (6 fl oz/180 ml) chicken stock

¼ teaspoon saffron threads, crushed

½ cup (4 fl oz/125 ml) fino sherry

1 bay leaf

1 teaspoon chopped fresh thyme

2 hard-boiled egg yolks, mashed

Freshly ground nutmeg to taste

3 tablespoons finely minced fresh flat-leaf (Italian) parsley

Serves 4

1 In a frying pan over medium heat, warm a few tablespoons of the olive oil. Add the blanched almonds and sauté until pale gold, 3–5 minutes. Using a slotted spoon, transfer the almonds to a blender, food processor, or mortar. Add the garlic to the oil remaining in the pan and sauté over medium heat for a minute or two until lightly browned. Using the slotted spoon, add the garlic to the almonds. Now fry the bread in the same oil, turning as necessary, until golden, about 5 minutes. Remove from the pan, break up into several pieces, and add to the almonds and garlic.

2 Rinse the chicken pieces, pat dry with paper towels, and sprinkle with salt and pepper.

3 In a large frying pan over high heat, warm the remaining olive oil. Add the chicken pieces and sauté, turning often, until golden, 8–10 minutes. Using tongs or the slotted spoon, transfer to a plate.

4 Measure out 2 tablespoons of the chicken stock and place in a small pan. Add the crushed saffron, heat gently, and set aside. Add the remaining stock to the frying pan used for the chicken along with the sherry. Bring to a boil over high heat and deglaze the pan, stirring to dislodge any browned bits from the pan bottom. Return the chicken to the pan, add the bay leaf and thyme, reduce the heat to low, cover, and simmer gently until the juices run clear when a chicken thigh is pierced, about 10 minutes longer.

5 Meanwhile, add the saffron and its liquid to the almond mixture along with the egg yolks and grind finely to form a *picada*. When the chicken is ready, add the *picada*, stir well, and simmer for a few minutes to thicken the pan sauce.

6 Season with salt, pepper, and nutmeg and transfer to a warmed deep platter. Sprinkle with the parsley and serve immediately.

Chicken Livers with Sage

Fegatini alla Salvia • Tuscany • Italy

In Tuscany, chicken livers are traditionally cooked quickly in olive oil. This recipe, however, calls for cooking the livers slowly in butter, turning them a deep, rich brown on the outside while keeping them softly pink inside. Soaking the livers in milk gives them a sweet, fresh flavor. Sage is commonly paired with all types of meat in Tuscany, particularly liver. Accompany the livers with sautéed spinach, chard, or broccoli rabe.

1 lb (500 g) chicken livers

About 2 cups (16 fl oz/500 ml) milk

⅓ cup (3 oz/90 g) unsalted butter

Handful of fresh sage leaves

Salt and freshly ground pepper to taste

Serves 4

1 Trim away the membranes and connective tissue from the livers, and rinse the livers in running cold water. Place them in a small bowl and add milk to cover. Cover and refrigerate overnight. When ready to use the livers, drain them and wipe dry with paper towels.

2 In a large frying pan over very low heat, melt the butter. Add the livers and sage and cook gently, turning occasionally, until the meat is a deep, rich brown on the outside and tender pink on the inside, 8–10 minutes.

3 Using a slotted spoon, lift the livers and sage leaves out of the butter and distribute them evenly among warmed individual plates. Serve immediately.

Partridge with Cabbage

Perdiz con Coles • Catalonia • Spain

The combination of partridge and cabbage is popular throughout both Spain and Portugal. In Portugal, where the dish is called *perdizes com repolho,* a mixture of tawny port and beef stock might be used in place of the red wine. In the absence of partridges, poussins or Cornish hens can be used. To give the stuffed packets in this Catalan version a heartier filling, mix in ½ pound (250 g) ground (minced) pork with the soaked bread.

4 partridges, about 1 lb (500 g) each

¾ cup (6 fl oz/180 ml) olive oil or lard

1 lb (500 g) *butifarra* or other cured pork sausage

4 slices bacon, chopped

2 large yellow onions, chopped

12 cloves garlic, minced

1 lb (500 g) tomatoes, peeled, seeded, and diced

2 carrots, peeled and sliced

1 teaspoon *each* chopped fresh thyme and marjoram

Pinch of ground cinnamon or cloves

1 strip orange zest

1 cup (8 fl oz/250 ml) dry red wine

¼ cup (2 fl oz/60 ml) brandy

Salt and freshly ground pepper to taste

1 head savoy cabbage

½ teaspoon freshly grated nutmeg, or more to taste

3 slices white bread, soaked in milk to cover and squeezed dry

1 cup (5 oz/155 g) all-purpose (plain) flour

1 egg

Serves 4

1 Preheat the oven to 375°F (190°C).

2 Rinse the birds and pat dry. In a large roasting pan placed over medium-high heat on the stove top, warm half of the olive oil or lard. Add the birds and turn to brown on all sides, about 10 minutes. Add the sausage and bacon and cook for a few minutes to color. Add the onions, garlic, tomatoes, carrots, thyme, marjoram, cinnamon or cloves, and orange zest. Mix together the wine and brandy in a cup and baste the birds with the mixture. Transfer the pan to the oven and roast until the birds are tender and cooked through, about 1 hour. Transfer the birds and sausages to a large *cazuela* or other large baking dish, cover, and set aside. Taste the sauce remaining in the pan and adjust with salt and pepper. Reserve.

3 Meanwhile, bring a large pot two-thirds full of salted water to a boil. Add the cabbage and parboil for 10 minutes. Drain well and let cool.

4 When the cabbage is cool enough to handle, carefully separate the leaves, reserving 8 perfect large outer leaves. Chop the rest of the cabbage, discarding the tough core and any tough ribs. Lay the 8 leaves out on a work surface. Sprinkle with salt, pepper, and the nutmeg. In a bowl, combine the soaked bread and about 2 cups (6 oz/185 g) of the chopped cabbage. Divide the mixture evenly among the cabbage leaves, placing it in the middle of each leaf. Working with 1 leaf at a time, fold the top end over the filling, fold in the sides, and then fold in the stem end and roll up into a cylindrical packet.

5 Spread the flour on a plate, and lightly beat the egg in a shallow bowl. In a large frying pan over high heat, warm the remaining oil or lard. Dip each packet first in the flour, tapping off the excess, and then in the egg and slip them into the hot oil or lard. Fry, turning once, until golden and crusty on both sides, 3–5 minutes. Transfer to paper towels to drain briefly.

6 Slice the pork sausages. Place the cabbage packets between the birds and evenly distribute the sausage slices between the birds and the packets. Spoon the sauce over the packets and sausages.

7 Cover the *cazuela* and place it in the oven. Roast, basting one more time with the sauce, for 15–20 minutes. Serve hot directly from the dish.

SAUSAGES

Two reasons to visit Vich, a Catalan town perched in the foothills of the Pyrenees, are its neoclassical cathedral's golden murals by Josep María Sért and its large, twice-weekly market, a tradition since the tenth century. Perhaps the best reason to stop at Vich, however, is to sample the locally made *butifarra*, a cooked and dried sausage of pork, pork blood, and seasonings that is produced all over Catalonia but is arguably at its finest in this mountain town.

But the *butifarra* is a bit player in Spain, a country whose citizenry is crazy for sausages. The chorizo, in contrast, is the star. At its simplest it is a cured pork sausage flavored with garlic and paprika. But every region has its own version of this ubiquitous *salchicha:*

sometimes the meat is coarsely ground; some mixtures will include heavy doses of spicy chile, while others are sweetened with the addition of cinnamon or nutmeg. They are all tucked into natural pig casings, however, and can turn up thinly sliced as a *tapa* or tucked in among other ingredients in their common role as assertive seasonings.

The Portuguese make a similar pork sausage, which they call *chouriço*. Hefty and deep, rich red, it too carries a sizable measure of paprika and garlic, as does its slimmer cousin, the *linguiça*. *Piri-piri* and red wine usually flavor both sausages, which are standard bar fare—generally grilled and sliced—as well as flavorful additions to *cozidos* and other dishes.

Franca's Lemon Chicken

Pollo al Limone alla Franca · Tuscany · Italy

This recipe is named after the cook at a little *caffè* between Florence and Bologna, where this delicious roast chicken might be served under a grape arbor in the back. If you like, you can vary the recipe by adding 1 cup (5 oz/155 g) of black olives to the pan 10 minutes before the chicken is done and garnishing the finished dish with grated lemon zest.

1 chicken, about 3½ lb (1.75 kg), cut into 8 serving pieces

¼ cup (2 fl oz/60 ml) fresh lemon juice

2 tablespoons olive oil

1 clove garlic, minced

1 tablespoon chopped fresh oregano or 1 teaspoon dried

Salt and freshly ground pepper to taste

Serves 4

1 Arrange the chicken pieces, skin sides down, in a baking dish. In a small bowl, whisk together the lemon juice, olive oil, garlic, oregano, salt, and pepper. Pour over the chicken. Let stand for 1 hour.

2 Preheat the oven to 400°F (200°C). Roast the chicken for 30 minutes. Turn the pieces skin sides up and continue to roast until browned and the juices run clear when a thigh is pierced, 30–45 minutes.

3 Transfer the chicken to a platter, cover loosely with aluminum foil, and keep warm. Pour the pan juices through a fine-mesh sieve into a bowl and skim off the fat. Pour the juices over the chicken and serve.

Chicken with Eggplant, Peppers, and Tomatoes

Pollo en Samfaina • Catalonia • Spain

Catalan *samfaina*, like Provençal ratatouille, is a mixture of onions, garlic, eggplant, peppers, and tomatoes, cooked down to a fragrant and unctuous stew.

1 chicken, about 4 lb (2 kg), cut into pieces

Salt and freshly ground pepper to taste

¼ cup (2 fl oz/60 ml) olive oil

¼ lb (125 g) diced serrano ham (optional)

2 large yellow onions, sliced or coarsely chopped

3 cloves garlic, minced

1 lb (500 g) Asian (slender) eggplants (aubergines), cut into 1-inch (2.5-cm) pieces

¾ lb (375 g) zucchini (courgettes), cut into ½-inch (12-mm) chunks

2 green or red bell peppers (capsicums), seeded and cut into large dice

1½ lb (750 g) tomatoes, peeled, seeded, and chopped

1 bay leaf

2 tablespoons chopped fresh thyme or marjoram

½ cup (4 fl oz/125 ml) dry white wine

Serves 4

1 Rinse the chicken pieces, pat dry, and sprinkle with salt and pepper. In a large, heavy frying pan over high heat, warm the olive oil. Working in batches, brown the chicken pieces on all sides, 8–10 minutes. Using tongs, transfer to a plate; set aside. Add the ham, if using, to the oil remaining in the pan over medium heat and sauté for 1 minute. Add the onions and sauté until soft, about 10 minutes. Add the garlic, eggplants, zucchini, and bell peppers and cook, stirring often, until they begin to soften, about 5 minutes.

2 Add the tomatoes, bay leaf, thyme or marjoram, and wine, then return the chicken to the pan and toss well with the vegetables. Cover and simmer over low heat until the chicken is tender, 25–35 minutes. Season with salt and pepper and serve immediately.

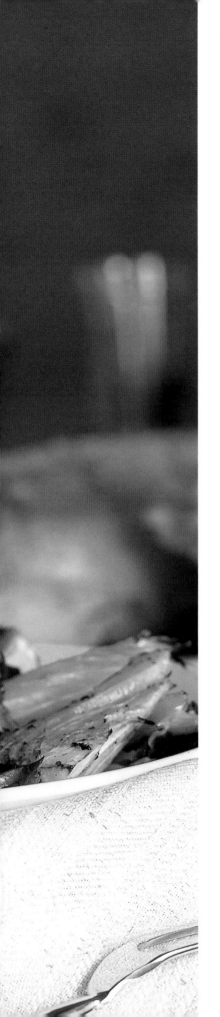

Roast Chicken with Fennel Seed

Pollo al Finocchietto • Tuscany • Italy

Wild fennel, with its bright green, feathery leaves, clusters of sunny yellow flowers, and ribbed aromatic seeds, is one of the Mediterranean's oldest herbs. In ancient times, it was popularly known as *l'erba buona,* or "the good herb," and was prized for its medicinal qualities. This centuries-old recipe is still served all over Tuscany, and for good reason: the chicken is beautiful to look at and the anise-scented fennel seed wonderfully fragrant.

1 chicken, 3½ lb (1.75 kg)

Salt and freshly ground pepper to taste

6 fresh sage leaves, torn into small pieces

2 tablespoons extra-virgin olive oil, plus extra for drizzling

2 oz (60 g) pancetta, cut into small cubes

2 teaspoons fennel seed, crushed

2 large cloves garlic, sliced

Serves 4

1 Preheat the oven to 375°F (190°C).

2 Rinse the chicken and pat dry with paper towels. Sprinkle the cavity with salt, pepper, and the sage. Set aside.

3 In a frying pan over medium-high heat, warm the 2 tablespoons olive oil. Add the pancetta, 1 teaspoon of the fennel seed, and the garlic and sauté gently until the mixture is fragrant but not brown, about 3 minutes.

4 Using a slotted spoon, transfer the pancetta mixture to the chicken cavity. Set aside the oil from the pan for basting the chicken as it roasts. Tuck the wings behind the back, so they stay close to the body. Draw the drumsticks together and tie securely with kitchen string. Place the chicken, breast side up, in a roasting pan. Drizzle with olive oil and sprinkle with the remaining 1 teaspoon fennel seed.

5 Roast, basting occasionally with the reserved oil, until the exterior is a deep golden brown, the juices run clear when a thigh is pricked with a fork, and an instant-read thermometer inserted into the thigh registers 180°F (82°C), about 1 hour.

6 Transfer the chicken to a cutting board, tent loosely with aluminum foil, and let rest for 10 minutes. Transfer to a warmed platter, cut into serving pieces, and serve.

Quail with Grapes and Sausage

Quaglie con Uva e Salsiccia • Umbria • Italy

Grapes grow all over Italy, so it is not surprising to find them in savory dishes. If wine grapes are unavailable, use table grapes and a bit of lemon juice to balance out their sweetness.

4 quail

Salt and freshly ground pepper to taste

4 fresh rosemary sprigs, plus extra for garnish

2 tablespoons olive oil

4 mild pork sausages

½ cup (4 fl oz/125 ml) dry white wine

1 cup (8 fl oz/250 ml) meat stock

1 lb (500 g) white wine grapes (about 3 cups), stems removed

Serves 4

1 Rinse the quail and pat dry. Sprinkle with salt and pepper. Tuck the wing tips underneath the breasts. Stuff a sprig of rosemary inside each cavity. Tie the legs together with kitchen string.

2 In a large frying pan over medium heat, warm the olive oil. Add the sausages and quail and cook, turning frequently, until the meats are browned on all sides, about 15 minutes. Add the wine and simmer for 1 minute. Add the stock and bring to a simmer. Reduce the heat to low, cover, and cook, turning the sausages and quail occasionally, until the quail are tender, 25–30 minutes.

3 Add the grapes to the pan and cook until hot and slightly collapsed, about 5 minutes. Transfer the quail and sausages to a warmed serving dish. Using a slotted spoon, scatter the grapes over the meats. If the liquid in the pan is thin, raise the heat to high and reduce until thickened. Pour the juices over the meats. Garnish with rosemary and serve at once.

WINE COUNTRY

Grapes have been cultivated in Italy from the earliest times. The Etruscans left evidence that they made and drank wine, and the Greek colonizers are known to have built pipelines for transporting it to the peninsula's southern ports, from which it was shipped to dinner tables in Athens. Today grapes are grown and wine is made in every region of this age-old *paese del vino,* "country of wine."

To ensure their standards of quality, in 1963, the Italian government established the Denominazione di Origine Controllata, a designation granted only to those wines that meet specific requirements in every aspect of grape cultivation and wine production.

In the 1970s, wines of extraordinarily high quality were further distinguished by the institution of a new category, DOCG (the G stands for *garantita,* which means guaranteed authenticity). Wines outside of these two designations are labeled simply *vino da tavola,* "table wine," although the finest of these fall under yet another category, *indicazione geografica tipica,* which classifies them by color or grape variety. Fine wines are produced everywhere, but Piedmont and Tuscany are especially known for their great reds, while the whites that come from the Veneto and Friuli–Venezia Giulia are the most highly prized.

It is not necessary to use an expensive wine for cooking. You should, however, use something that you enjoy drinking and that complements the dish you are making and the wine you will be serving with it.

Italian Sausages with Cannellini

Salsicce con Fagioli all'Uccelletto • Tuscany • Italy

Florentines enjoy eating fresh pork sausages cooked with cannellini beans *all'uccelletto*, or "cooked in the manner of little birds," with garlic, sage, and tomatoes.

2 cups (14 oz/440 g) dried cannellini beans

4 cloves garlic

8 fresh sage leaves

1 tomato, cored and halved

Salt and freshly ground pepper to taste

2 tablespoons extra-virgin olive oil

8 fresh Italian sausages, about 2½ oz (75 g) each

2 cups (12 oz/375 g) crushed canned plum (Roma) tomatoes with juice

Pinch of ground red chile

Serves 4

1 Pick over the beans, discarding any grit or misshapen beans. Rinse well and place in a bowl. Add water to cover generously and let soak overnight.

2 The next day, drain the beans and place in a large saucepan with 7 cups (56 fl oz/1.75 l) water. Bring to a boil and add 2 of the garlic cloves, 4 of the sage leaves, and the tomato halves to the saucepan. Reduce the heat to a very gentle simmer and cook, uncovered, until the beans are tender, 1½–2 hours. Season with salt, then drain the beans. Discard the garlic, sage, and tomato.

3 Crush the remaining 2 garlic cloves. In a large frying pan, warm together the olive oil, the remaining 4 sage leaves, and the 2 crushed garlic cloves. Add the sausages and brown lightly on all sides, about 10 minutes. Add the beans, crushed tomatoes, and ground chile. Simmer, uncovered, stirring gently every so often, for about 15 minutes. Adjust the seasoning with salt and pepper.

4 Spoon the beans onto a warmed oval platter. Lay the sausages on top and serve.

Moorish Pork Kabobs

Pinchos Morunos • Andalusia • Spain

Pincho, or *pinchito,* the diminutive, translates as "little thorn" or "little pointed stick," so roughly translated, *pincho moruno* means Moorish mouthfuls impaled on a thorn or thin, wooden skewer. Of course, the Moors were Muslims and did not eat pork, which means that Christian Spain took the Arab seasonings traditionally used on lamb kabobs (*qodban*) and applied them to their beloved meat in recipes such as this one.

½ cup (4 fl oz/125 ml) olive oil

3 tablespoons ground cumin

2 tablespoons ground coriander

1 tablespoon sweet paprika

1½ teaspoons cayenne pepper

1 teaspoon ground turmeric

1 teaspoon dried oregano

1 teaspoon salt, plus salt to taste

½ teaspoon freshly ground black pepper

2 lb (1 kg) pork, cut into 1-inch (2.5-cm) cubes

2 tablespoons minced garlic

¼ cup (⅓ oz/10 g) chopped fresh flat-leaf (Italian) parsley

¼ cup (2 fl oz/60 ml) fresh lemon juice

Lemon wedges

Serves 8

1 In a small frying pan, combine the olive oil, cumin, coriander, paprika, cayenne, turmeric, oregano, 1 teaspoon salt, and the black pepper. Place over low heat until warmed and fragrant, about 3 minutes. Remove from the heat and let cool to room temperature.

2 Place the pork pieces in a bowl and rub with the spice mixture. Add the garlic, parsley, and lemon juice and toss well. Cover and refrigerate overnight.

3 The next day, preheat a broiler (grill), or prepare a fire in a charcoal grill. Thread the meat onto skewers and sprinkle with salt.

4 Place on a broiler pan or a grill rack and broil or grill, turning once, until just cooked through, about 4 minutes on each side. Transfer to a platter and serve with lemon wedges.

Pork with Figs

Lomo de Cerdo con Higos • Catalonia • Spain

The Moors loved to combine fruit and meat, and Catalan cooks readily embraced the idea. Pork and figs—dried or fresh—make a particularly delicious pairing. If you like, the figs can be cooked the day before, and the sauce made several hours before serving and reheated.

1 lb (500 g) dried black figs or 12–16 fresh figs

1 cup (8 fl oz/250 ml) *oloroso* or *amontillado* sherry

2 lemon slices

1 cinnamon stick

2 whole cloves

PORK AND BASTING MIXTURE

1 boneless pork loin, about 3 lb (1.5 kg), tied

Tiny garlic slivers (optional)

Salt and freshly ground pepper to taste

Pinch of ground cinnamon

½ cup (4 fl oz/125 ml) *oloroso* or *amontillado* sherry

½ cup (4 fl oz/125 ml) fresh orange juice

¼ cup (3 oz/90 g) honey

SAUCE

3 tablespoons unsalted butter

1 large yellow onion, chopped

3 cloves garlic, minced

1 cup (8 fl oz/250 ml) *oloroso* or *amontillado* sherry

1 cup (6 oz/185 g) peeled, seeded, and diced tomato (optional)

1 cup (8 fl oz/250 ml) chicken stock

¼ cup (1 oz/30 g) ground toasted almonds

1 tablespoon grated orange zest

½ teaspoon ground cinnamon

Salt and freshly ground pepper to taste

Serves 4

1 If using dried figs, place them in a saucepan with the sherry, lemon slices, cinnamon stick, and cloves. Add water as needed to cover and place over medium heat. Bring to a simmer and cook until tender, 10–15 minutes. Remove from the heat and set aside to steep for an hour or two. Using a slotted spoon, transfer the figs to a cutting board. Remove and discard the lemon slices, cinnamon stick, and cloves from the cooking liquid and reserve the liquid. Cut the figs in half and set aside. If using fresh figs, proceed as directed but poach them in the sherry mixture for only 3–5 minutes.

2 Preheat the oven to 400°F (200°C).

3 To prepare the pork, trim away any excess fat. If desired, cut a series of evenly spaced slits into the surface of the loin with the tip of a sharp knife and slip a garlic sliver into each slit. Then rub the roast all over with salt, pepper, and cinnamon. Place the pork on a rack in a roasting pan. In a small bowl, stir together the sherry, orange juice, and honey.

4 Roast the pork, basting every 15 minutes with the sherry mixture, until an instant-read thermometer inserted into the thickest part registers 147°F (64°C), 40–45 minutes. Let rest for 10 minutes. Alternatively, test the roast by cutting into it with a sharp knife; the meat should be lightly pink at the center.

5 About 30 minutes before the roast is ready, begin making the sauce: In a frying pan over medium heat, melt the butter. Add the onion and sauté until tender, about 8 minutes. Add the garlic and cook until tender, about 3 minutes longer. Add the sherry, tomato (if using), stock, almonds, orange zest, cinnamon, and reserved fig liquid, raise the heat to high, and cook until thickened, 8–10 minutes. Spoon half of the sauce into a blender and purée, then return to the saucepan. Add the figs and heat through. Season with salt and pepper.

6 Snip the strings on the roast and slice the pork. Arrange the pork slices on a warmed platter and spoon the sauce over them. Surround the slices with the figs. Serve at once.

Sausage, Ribs, and Beans

Salsiccia, Puntini di Maiale e Fagioli · Lazio · Italy

Here, pork ribs are cooked in a sauce until they are so tender that the meat is easily nudged from the bones. Creamy borlotti beans absorb the flavors of the ribs and sausage.

2 tablespoons olive oil

2 lb (1 kg) pork spareribs, cut into individual ribs

1 lb (500 g) Italian sweet pork sausages

1 yellow onion, chopped

1 carrot, peeled and chopped

4 fresh sage leaves, minced

2½ lb (1.25 kg) fresh tomatoes, peeled, seeded, and chopped, or 1 can (28 oz/875 g) plum (Roma) tomatoes, seeded and chopped, with juice

1 cup (8 fl oz/250 ml) water

Salt and freshly ground pepper to taste

3 cups (21 oz/655 g) drained cooked or canned borlotti beans

Serves 6

1 In a large frying pan over medium heat, warm 1 tablespoon of the olive oil. Add the spareribs in batches and cook, turning as needed, until well browned on both sides, about 15 minutes. Transfer to a plate as they are ready. Then add the sausages to the pan and brown them on all sides, about 10 minutes.

2 In a large, heavy pot over medium heat, sauté the onion, carrot, and sage in the remaining 1 tablespoon oil until tender, about 5 minutes. Add the ribs and sausages, tomatoes, water, salt, and pepper and bring to a simmer. Reduce the heat to low, cover partially, and cook for 1 hour. Add the beans and cook until the ribs are fork-tender, about 30 minutes longer. Taste and adjust the seasonings.

3 Spoon into a warmed serving dish or platter and serve immediately.

Pork with Paprika and Garlic

Lomo de Cerdo Adobado • New Castile • Spain

The term *adobado* refers to a traditional cooking method in which the meat marinates for several days in a garlic, paprika, cumin, herb, olive oil, and vinegar or wine mixture. You may roast it in a 350°F (180°C) oven for 45–60 minutes for the loin or 25 minutes for tenderloins.

1 boneless pork loin, 2–3 lb (1–1.5 kg), tied, or 2 pork tenderloins, about 1 lb (500 g) each

2 tablespoons olive oil

1½ tablespoons finely minced garlic

2 teaspoons dried oregano

2 tablespoons sweet paprika

1 tablespoon ground cumin

2 teaspoons fresh thyme leaves

1 bay leaf, crumbled

1 teaspoon salt, plus salt to taste

½ teaspoon freshly ground pepper, plus pepper to taste

½ cup (4 fl oz/125 ml) dry sherry or dry white wine

Serves 4–6

1 Trim off any excess fat from the pork and place in a shallow nonaluminum container.

2 In a small frying pan over low heat, combine the olive oil, garlic, and oregano and heat for 2 minutes to release their aromas. Whisk in the paprika, cumin, thyme, bay leaf, 1 teaspoon salt, ½ teaspoon pepper, and the wine and cook for 1 minute over low heat. Remove from the heat and set aside to cool to room temperature. When fully cooled, pour the marinade over the meat and rub it in well. Cover and refrigerate for at least overnight or for as long as 2–3 days.

3 Prepare a fire in a charcoal grill, or preheat a broiler (grill).

4 Lift the pork from the marinade and pat dry. Sprinkle the pork lightly with salt and pepper. Place on the grill rack or on a broiler pan slipped under the broiler and grill or broil, turning as needed to brown well on all sides, until an instant-read thermometer inserted into the thickest part registers 147°F (64°C), about 10 minutes for the tenderloins and 20 minutes for the loin. Alternatively, test the pork by cutting into it with a sharp knife; the meat should be lightly pink at the center.

5 Transfer the pork to a cutting board and let rest for a few minutes. Slice and then arrange the slices on a warmed platter. Serve at once.

Drunken Pork Chops

Bistecchine di Maiale Ubriache • Tuscany • Italy

Tuscans are wonderfully poetic about their food. These flavorful pork chops are called *ubriache,* or "drunken," because they are cooked in wine. At the dinner table, serve the same young Chianti you use to prepare the chops.

4 center-cut pork chops, each 1 inch (2.5 cm) thick

1½ tablespoons freshly ground pepper

2 tablespoons fennel seed, crushed, plus 1 teaspoon whole seed

2 tablespoons extra-virgin olive oil

Salt to taste

1 cup (6 oz/185 g) crushed canned plum (Roma) tomatoes with juice

½ cup (4 fl oz/125 ml) young red wine, preferably Chianti

Serves 4

1 Generously season both sides of the pork chops with the pepper and the crushed fennel seed. In a frying pan large enough to hold all the chops, warm the olive oil over medium heat. Lay the chops in the pan, turn them over when the meat becomes white, and sprinkle with salt. Raise the heat to high and add the tomatoes and wine. After 1 minute, reduce the heat to medium, cover the pan, and let the chops and sauce simmer, turning once, until the chops are well browned on both sides and pale pink in the center, about 15 minutes.

2 Transfer the chops to a warmed platter and cover them loosely with aluminum foil. Toss the 1 teaspoon whole fennel seed into the sauce and cook for an additional 5 minutes to blend the flavors. Spoon the sauce over the meat and serve immediately.

TUSCAN WINE

The Tuscan year is inextricably bound to the ancient tradition of growing grapes and making wine, from early spring, when the first tender vines are tied down with willow branches, through autumn and the *vendemmia,* when the heavy grape clusters are snipped off the vine and carted off to the wine press. In Tuscany, wine is as essential to a meal as olive oil and bread, and the drinking of wine is free of pomp and snobbery.

Historically, Chianti was the quintessential Tuscan wine: sturdy and inexpensive, sold in potbellied raffia-covered *fiaschi.* But the past twenty-five years brought a wine-making revolution to the entire region, with vintners experimenting with varietals and production methods and crafting truly world-class wines.

Chianti, still the best known Tuscan wine, is made from a mixture of grapes, the most dominant of which is the local Sangiovese. Chiantis range from everyday *vini da tavola* to wonderfully rich and full-bodied vintages. Brunello di Montalcino is one of the greatest Tuscan reds. It is a pure Sangiovese wine made in the hills that surround the town of Montalcino. Running a close second is Vino Nobile di Montepulciano, made from Sangiovese, Canaiolo, and other grapes.

White wines from Tuscany tend to be light and drinkable and, except for the well-known Vernaccia di San Gimignano (made from the Vernaccia grape), are generally pressed from Trebbiano grapes. Much of the recent excitement surrounding Tuscan wines stems from the advent of the so-called Super Tuscans, innovative wines such as Tignanello, Sassicaia, and Ornellaia, created by some of the region's major wine makers.

Pork Chops with Orange and Marsala

Costolette di Maiale all'Arancia • Sicily • Italy

Marsala, traditionally produced in the western Sicilian provinces of Trapani, Palermo, and Agrigento, is generally thought of as a fine dessert wine, but it is also excellent for cooking. A blended wine with a rich amber color, it comes in three basic styles—dry, or *secco;* semidry, or *semisecco;* and sweet, or *dolce.* Sweet Marsala is best used in or as an accompaniment to desserts, while young, dry Marsala makes a superb kitchen wine for savory dishes, as this simple island *secondo* illustrates.

4 pork loin chops, each about 1 inch (2.5 cm) thick

2 tablespoons olive oil

Salt and freshly ground pepper to taste

½ cup (4 fl oz/125 ml) dry Marsala wine

½ cup (4 fl oz/125 ml) fresh orange juice

½ teaspoon grated orange zest, plus orange zest strips for garnish

Orange wedges (optional)

Serves 4

1 Pat the chops dry. In a large frying pan over medium heat, warm the olive oil. Add the chops and cook, turning once, until browned on both sides, about 10 minutes total. Sprinkle with salt and pepper. Reduce the heat to medium-low and continue to cook until the chops are just cooked through but still juicy when cut into the center with a knife, about 15 minutes. Transfer to a plate; keep warm.

2 Add the Marsala and raise the heat to medium-high. Cook, stirring, until the wine is reduced and slightly thickened, about 2 minutes. Add the orange juice and bring to a simmer. Return the chops to the pan and sprinkle with the orange zest. Cook, basting the chops with the pan juices, for 2 minutes.

3 Transfer the chops to individual plates and garnish with orange zest and wedges, if using. Serve immediately.

Pork with Cumin, Lemon, and Cilantro

Rojões à Cominho · Minho · Portugal

Lemon and cumin temper the richness of the meat in this traditional pork dish from Minho. Accompany with sautéed greens topped with toasted bread crumbs.

2 tablespoons ground cumin

1½ tablespoons finely minced garlic

2 teaspoons freshly ground pepper, plus pepper to taste

1 teaspoon salt, plus salt to taste

7 tablespoons (¾ oz/20 g) chopped fresh cilantro (fresh coriander)

2 tablespoons fresh lemon juice

Grated zest of 1 lemon

1 cup (8 fl oz/250 ml) dry white wine

2 lb (1 kg) pork shoulder or butt, cut into 1½-inch (4-cm) cubes

2 tablespoons lard or olive oil

Chicken stock, as needed to cover

4 paper-thin lemon slices, cut into quarters

Serves 6

1 In a small bowl, stir together the cumin, garlic, 2 teaspoons pepper, 1 teaspoon salt, 4 tablespoons (⅓ oz/10 g) of the cilantro, the lemon juice and zest, and the wine. Place the pork in a nonaluminum container, and rub the cumin mixture into the meat. Cover and refrigerate overnight.

2 The next day, drain the pork, reserving the marinade. Pat the meat dry. In a heavy saucepan over high heat, melt the lard or warm the olive oil. Add the pork and sauté until golden, 8–10 minutes. Add the reserved marinade and enough chicken stock just to cover the meat. Raise the heat to high and bring to a boil. Reduce the heat to low, cover, and simmer until very tender, about 45 minutes, adding the lemon slices during the last 10 minutes of cooking.

3 Season with salt and pepper and transfer to a warmed serving bowl. Sprinkle with the remaining 3 tablespoons cilantro and serve immediately.

Roast Loin of Pork with Rosemary

Arista · Tuscany · Italy

A group of bishops assembled in Florence in 1439 to discuss church matters. At a banquet one night, the guests were served a succulent pork roast flavored with rosemary and garlic. The Greek delegates were so impressed that they proclaimed it *aristos*, "the best." The name stuck, and the roast is known by the Italianized *arista*.

4 large cloves garlic

2 tablespoons fresh rosemary

Salt and freshly ground pepper to taste

1 bone-in pork loin roast, about 5 lb (2.5 kg)

¼ cup (2 fl oz/60 ml) olive oil

2 carrots, peeled and chopped

1 celery stalk, chopped

1 cup (8 fl oz/250 ml) dry white wine

Serves 8

1 Preheat the oven to 325°F (165°C).

2 Very finely chop together the garlic and rosemary. Transfer to a small bowl, season with salt and pepper, and mix well to form a paste. Make slits ½ inch (12 mm) deep all over the pork roast and insert some of the mixture into each slit. Rub the roast all over with the remaining seasoning, then rub with the olive oil. Place the meat in a roasting pan just large enough to hold it.

3 Roast the meat for 1 hour. Scatter the carrots and celery around the meat. Continue to roast until an instant-read thermometer inserted into the thickest part of the roast away from the bone registers 155°F (68°C) or the meat is pale pink when cut into at the center, about 1¼ hours longer. Transfer to a warmed platter and cover loosely with foil. Let rest for 15 minutes before carving.

4 Place the pan over low heat. Add the wine and deglaze the pan, stirring with a wooden spoon to scrape up any browned bits from the pan bottom. Pour through a fine-mesh sieve into a small saucepan. Skim off the fat. Reheat to serving temperature, if necessary.

5 Carve the roast and arrange on a warmed serving platter. Pour the pan juices into a warmed bowl and pass at the table.

Polenta with Wild Boar Sauce

Polenta al Sugo di Cinghiale • Tuscany • Italy

Make this thick, flavorful boar sauce the day before serving. Like most stews, it's better on the second day. However, make the polenta right before serving so it stays creamy.

2 lb (1 kg) boneless wild boar

2 teaspoons salt, plus salt to taste

1 cup (8 fl oz/250 ml) extra-virgin olive oil

2 yellow onions, chopped

2 cloves garlic, minced

1 carrot, peeled and chopped

1 celery stalk, chopped

4 fresh sage leaves, chopped

Leaves from 1 rosemary sprig, chopped

1 cup (8 fl oz/250 ml) dry red wine

1 lb (500 g) tomatoes, peeled, seeded, and chopped, or 1 can (14 oz/440 g) plum (Roma) tomatoes, chopped, with juice

Freshly ground pepper to taste

1¼ cups (6½ oz/200 g) coarse-ground polenta

Grated Parmesan cheese

Serves 4–6

1 To make the sauce, rinse the meat in several changes of water, pat dry, and cut into large pieces. Sprinkle the meat with salt and place in a large frying pan over medium-low heat. Cook for 10 minutes, stirring occasionally and draining the pan every few minutes of the water released by the meat. Transfer the meat to a plate.

2 Rinse and dry the frying pan and return it to the stove. Add the olive oil and warm over medium heat. Add the onions, garlic, carrot, celery, sage, and rosemary and sauté until soft, about 5 minutes. Add the meat and brown well on all sides, about 10 minutes. Raise the heat to high, pour in the wine, and deglaze the pan, stirring to scrape up any browned bits from the pan bottom. Cook until the wine has reduced by half, about 5 minutes. Add the tomatoes. Stir well, cover, and cook, stirring occasionally, until the sauce is thick and the meat begins to fall apart, about 1½ hours.

3 Using tongs, transfer the meat to a cutting board. Cut the meat into smaller pieces, then mince using a heavy, sharp knife. Return the minced meat to the pan and stir well to combine with the other ingredients. Adjust the seasoning with salt and pepper.

4 To make the polenta, in a heavy saucepan, bring 6 cups (48 fl oz/1.5 l) water to a gentle boil. Add the 2 teaspoons salt. Pour in the polenta in a thin, steady stream, stirring continuously with a wire whisk so that no lumps form. Reduce the heat to medium. After a few minutes, when the polenta begins to thicken, reduce the heat to low. Cook, stirring nearly continuously with a wooden spoon, until the polenta comes away easily from the sides of the pan, 30–40 minutes.

5 To serve, begin reheating the sauce gently about 30 minutes before the polenta is ready. Spoon the polenta directly onto individual plates. Cover each portion with about 1 cup (8 fl oz/250 ml) of the sauce. Pass the Parmesan cheese at the table.

POLENTA

Since its introduction to Italy after Colombus's voyages to the New World, polenta, or corn ground into meal and cooked into mush, has become so closely associated with northern Italy that southern Italians, who prefer pasta, sometimes call northerners by the disparaging name of *mangiapolenta*, which translates as "polenta eaters."

Today, polenta is enjoyed in many forms, most popularly soft and creamy as a side dish with meats or fish, or chilled and cut into slices to fry or grill as a base for mushrooms, cheese, or a meat ragù. It is also eaten for dessert: in the Alto Adige, polenta is sweetened and then fried in butter and accompanied with baked apples, while in Liguria it is drizzled with extra-virgin olive oil, sprinkled with sugar, and eaten with blood oranges.

Veal Rolls in Tomato and Wine Sauce

Topini in Umido • Tuscany • Italy

The word *topini*, literally "little mice," is used in many parts of Tuscany to refer to gnocchi. In Siena, *topini* most often means little bundles of veal, stuffed with prosciutto and herbs.

8 veal scallops, about 1 lb (500 g) total weight, each about ¼ inch (6 mm) thick

Freshly ground pepper to taste

8 slices prosciutto, each about ⅛ inch (3 mm) thick

8 fresh sage leaves

3 tablespoons extra-virgin olive oil

1 small carrot, peeled and finely chopped

½ small yellow onion, finely chopped

1 small celery stalk, finely chopped

½ cup (4 fl oz/125 ml) dry white wine

½ cup (4 fl oz/125 ml) tomato purée

½ cup (4 fl oz/125 ml) water

Salt to taste

Serves 4

1 Lay each veal scallop between 2 sheets of plastic wrap and place on a work surface. Pound the veal lightly with a meat pounder until no thinner than ¼ inch (6 mm) thick. Remove the top sheet of plastic wrap and grind some pepper over the meat. Lay a slice of prosciutto and then a sage leaf on top of each piece. Roll up each veal scallop, then fold in the sides to make a tight bundle. Secure closed with a toothpick.

2 In a frying pan large enough to hold the rolls, warm the olive oil over medium heat. Add the carrot, onion, and celery and sauté, stirring often, until soft, about 8 minutes. Raise the heat to medium-high and add the rolls. Brown well on all sides. Add the wine and cook until the alcohol evaporates, about 5 minutes. Add the tomato purée, water, and salt, reduce the heat to medium, and cook, uncovered, until the sauce thickens, 15 minutes.

3 Transfer the rolls to a plate. Pool the sauce on the bottom of a warmed serving platter. Remove the toothpicks from the rolls and arrange on top of the sauce. Serve immediately.

Pork Ribs with Black Olives

Rosticciana con le Olive • Tuscany • Italy

This is real food—hearty, flavorful, messy, and delicious. It is often accompanied in trattorias with white beans, a salad of wilted greens, or a soft pile of golden yellow polenta.

4 lb (2 kg) baby back pork ribs, in slabs

Salt and freshly ground pepper to taste

¼ cup (2 fl oz/60 ml) extra-virgin olive oil

2 cloves garlic, crushed

1 fresh rosemary sprig

1 bay leaf

½ cup (4 fl oz/125 ml) dry white wine

1 can (1 lb/500 g) plum (Roma) tomatoes, crushed, with juice

Pinch of ground red chile

½ cup (2½ oz/75 g) pitted black olives

Serves 4

1 Pull away the thin opaque membrane that covers the underside of the rib slabs. Sprinkle both sides with salt and generously with pepper. Divide the slabs into smaller pieces, cutting them into 3-rib sections. In a large frying pan, warm the olive oil over medium heat. Add the garlic, rosemary, and bay leaf and sauté gently until fragrant, about 3 minutes. Raise the heat to high, add the ribs, and brown well on both sides, turning often. This should take about 15 minutes. Drain off most of the fat from the pan.

2 Pour the wine over the ribs, reduce the heat to medium-high, and cook, stirring occasionally and turning the ribs in the pan to coat them in the pan juices, until the wine reduces slightly, about 5 minutes. Stir in the tomatoes and ground chile, cover, and cook over low heat for 2–2½ hours. The sauce should maintain the consistency of a dense tomato sauce. If it becomes too dry, add water, ½ cup (4 fl oz/125 ml) at a time. The ribs are ready when the meat is moist and tender and falls away from the bone.

3 Just before removing the ribs from the heat, discard the bay leaf and rosemary. Add the olives, cooking them just long enough to flavor the sauce, about 3 minutes. Serve the ribs topped with the sauce.

Florentine Steak

Bistecca alla Fiorentina · Tuscany · Italy

Bistecca alla fiorentina is the exception to the general rule that although Tuscans eat meat often, the portions are relatively small. The cooking of these gargantuan steaks is subject to a few easy, but stringent, rules. Each steak, for two people, must weigh between 1¼ and 1¾ pounds (625 and 875 g), be about one inch (2.5 cm) thick, and contain its T-bone, fillet, and tenderloin. You are never asked how you'd like your meat cooked, for an authentic bistecca is well browned on the outside and blood red inside—no exceptions.

1 T-bone or porterhouse steak, cut from the rib with the bone, 1½ lb (750 g)

2 tablespoons extra-virgin olive oil

Salt and freshly ground pepper to taste

Lemon wedges

Serves 2

1 Take the meat out of the refrigerator about 2 hours before cooking it. Prepare a medium-hot fire in a charcoal grill.

2 Rub the meat on both sides with the olive oil. (Do not add any salt at this point.) Using your hands or a pair of tongs so as not to pierce the meat, set the meat on the grill rack about 5 inches (13 cm) above the coals. Cook until browned and juicy on the first side, 5–7 minutes. Turn the meat (without piercing it) and sprinkle with salt. Cook on the second side until browned and juicy, 5–7 minutes longer. Then turn the meat over once again and sprinkle with salt.

3 Transfer the steak to a cutting board and season generously with pepper. Garnish with lemon wedges and bring to the table on the board.

Meatballs in Almond Sauce

Albóndigas en Salsa de Almendra · Catalonia · Spain

These meatballs can be fried and served on toothpicks; cooked in a *cazuela;* fried and tossed in a sauce made of pan juices; or prepared as they are here, fried in olive oil, then briefly simmered in a wine sauce thickened by a signature Catalan almond *picada.*

MEATBALLS

½ lb (250 g) ground (minced) beef

½ lb (250 g) ground (minced) pork

2 slices bread, about 2 oz (60 g) total, weight soaked in water and squeezed dry

¼ cup (1½ oz/45 g) minced yellow onion (optional)

2 cloves garlic, finely minced

3 tablespoons finely minced fresh flat-leaf (Italian) parsley

1 egg, lightly beaten

1 teaspoon sweet paprika

½ teaspoon ground nutmeg or cinnamon

1 teaspoon salt

½ teaspoon freshly ground pepper

Olive oil for deep-frying or sautéing

All-purpose (plain) flour for dusting

PICADA

2 cloves garlic, minced

3 tablespoons ground blanched almonds

2 tablespoons chopped fresh flat-leaf (Italian) parsley

½ teaspoon sweet paprika

A few saffron threads, crushed

Salt and freshly ground pepper to taste

SAUCE

2 tablespoons olive oil

½ cup (3 oz/90 g) minced yellow onion

½ cup (4 fl oz/125 ml) dry white wine

⅔ cup (5 fl oz/160 ml) meat or chicken stock

Serves 6

1 To make the meatballs, in a bowl, combine the beef, pork, soaked bread, onion (if using), garlic, parsley, egg, paprika, nutmeg or cinnamon, salt, and pepper. Knead with your hands until well mixed. Cover and refrigerate for 1 hour.

2 To make the *picada,* in a mini food processor or mortar, combine the garlic, almonds, parsley, paprika, and saffron and process or grind to a paste. Season to taste with salt and pepper. Set aside.

3 In a deep frying pan, pour olive oil to a depth of 2 inches (5 cm) and heat to 375°F (190°C) on a deep-frying thermometer. While the oil is heating, form the meat mixture into 1-inch (2.5-cm) balls and dust them with flour, coating evenly.

4 Working in batches, slip the balls into the hot oil and fry until golden, about 4 minutes. Using a slotted spoon, transfer to paper towels to drain. (Alternatively, in a large frying pan over medium heat, warm a little olive oil and sauté the meatballs until well browned on all sides, 8–10 minutes.)

5 To make the sauce, in a large frying pan over medium heat, warm the olive oil. Add the onion and sauté until tender, 8–10 minutes. Add the wine, stock, and meatballs and simmer over low heat for 5 minutes. Add the *picada* and cook for a few minutes longer to blend the flavors. Taste and adjust the seasonings. Transfer to a serving dish and serve hot.

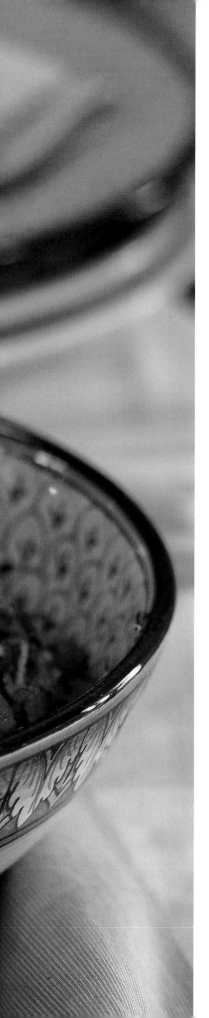

Braised Veal Shanks

Ossobuco • Lombardy • Italy

Thick slices of veal shank are called *ossobuco* in Italian, or "bone with a hole." The tender meat is often served with saffron-flavored risotto, but it is also excellent accompanied with fresh spring vegetables such as peas, asparagus, and baby carrots, cooked in a little butter. Be sure to provide narrow spoons or knives for removing the rich marrow from its hollows.

½ cup (2½ oz/75 g) all-purpose (plain) flour

6 slices veal shank, each 1½ inches (4 cm) thick, tied with kitchen string

2 tablespoons unsalted butter

2 tablespoons olive oil

1 small yellow onion, finely chopped

Salt and freshly ground pepper to taste

1 cup (8 fl oz/250 ml) dry white wine

2 cups (16 fl oz/500 ml) meat stock

¼ cup (⅓ oz/10 g) chopped fresh flat-leaf (Italian) parsley

1 small clove garlic

½ teaspoon grated lemon zest

Serves 6

1 Spread the flour on a large plate and dust the veal, tapping off the excess. In a large, heavy pot over medium heat, melt the butter with the olive oil. Add the veal and cook on the first side until golden brown, about 4 minutes. Turn the meat and add the onion to the pan, scattering it around the pieces of veal. Sprinkle with salt and pepper. Cook until browned on the second side, about 4 minutes longer.

2 Add the wine, bring to a simmer, and cook for 1 minute. Add the stock and bring to a simmer. Reduce the heat to low and cook, covered, turning occasionally, until the meat is tender, 1½–2 hours. (The dish can be prepared up to this point, cooled, covered, and refrigerated for up to 24 hours. To continue, reheat gently over low heat for about 20 minutes.)

3 Combine the parsley and garlic clove on a cutting board and finely chop together. Transfer to a bowl, add the lemon zest, and toss together. Scatter the mixture over the veal. Baste the veal with the sauce and simmer for 5 minutes longer.

4 Transfer to a warmed serving dish or individual plates. Serve at once.

Steak in the Style of the Pizza Maker

Bistecca alla Pizzaiola • Campania • Italy

Ripe, sweet tomatoes and aromatic garlic are the signature ingredients of Neapolitan cooking, often accented with a bit of *peperoncino,* the fiery little red chile beloved by many southern Italian cooks. In Naples, one of the most popular ways to top a pizza is with crushed fresh tomatoes, chopped garlic, and a sprinkling of oregano. The same ingredients can be used as a sauce for simmering small steaks, which is how this dish got its name.

4 small beef chuck steaks or similar small steaks

2 tablespoons olive oil

2 cloves garlic, finely chopped

4 fresh tomatoes, peeled, seeded, and chopped, or 2 cups (12 oz/375 g) seeded and chopped plum (Roma) tomatoes, with juice

2 tablespoons chopped fresh flat-leaf (Italian) parsley

½ teaspoon dried oregano

Salt and freshly ground pepper to taste

Serves 4

1 Pat the steaks dry. In a large frying pan over medium-high heat, warm the olive oil. Add the steaks and cook, turning once, until browned on both sides, about 10 minutes.

2 Reduce the heat to low, scatter the garlic around the steaks, and cook for 1 minute. Add the tomatoes, parsley, oregano, salt, and pepper. Cover partially and simmer, turning the steaks occasionally, until tender and the sauce is thickened, about 30 minutes.

3 Transfer to warmed individual plates and serve.

Meatballs in Tomato Sauce

Polpette al Pomodoro • Tuscany • Italy

Although this is the classic recipe for *polpette* (meatballs), there are infinite variations. They can be made with anything from leftover roasted meat to vegetables or fish, and seasonings can include any combination of onions, garlic, mushrooms, herbs, spices, lemon, cheese, and nuts. *Polpette* are traditionally served on their own.

MEATBALLS

2 slices day-old white bread, crusts removed, torn into pieces

½ cup (4 fl oz/125 ml) milk

1 lb (500 g) ground (minced) beef top round or sirloin

½ lb (250 g) ground (minced) pork

2 eggs, lightly beaten

2 cloves garlic, minced

1 tablespoon finely chopped fresh flat-leaf (Italian) parsley

2 teaspoons finely chopped fresh basil

¼ cup (1 oz/30 g) grated Parmesan cheese

1 teaspoon salt

1 cup (4 oz/125 g) fine dried bread crumbs (page 223)

Vegetable oil for frying

SAUCE

2 tablespoons extra-virgin olive oil

2 cloves garlic, crushed

4 tomatoes, peeled, seeded, and chopped

Salt and freshly ground pepper to taste

1½ teaspoons chopped fresh flat-leaf (Italian) parsley

Serves 4

1 To make the meatballs, in a bowl, combine the bread and milk and let soak for about 10 minutes. Squeeze out and discard the liquid from the bread, then place the bread in a bowl. Add the beef, pork, eggs, garlic, parsley, basil, Parmesan cheese, and salt. Using a wooden spoon or moistened hands, blend the ingredients into a homogeneous paste.

2 Using your hands, form the meat mixture into compact 2-inch (5-cm) balls, then flatten the balls into patties about 1 inch (2.5 cm) thick. Spread the bread crumbs on a plate and, one at a time, coat the meatballs evenly with the crumbs.

3 Pour the vegetable oil to a depth of about ½ inch (12 mm) into a large, heavy frying pan and place over medium heat. When the oil is hot, add the meatballs and fry, turning them every few minutes, until they are cooked through and a deep golden brown on both sides, about 10 minutes. (If desired, to test for doneness, cut into the center of a meatball.) Using a slotted utensil, transfer to paper towels to drain, topping with a second layer of towels to blot the excess oil. Keep the meatballs warm.

4 To make the sauce, in another large frying pan, warm the olive oil over medium heat. Add the garlic and sauté until it becomes fragrant, about 2 minutes. Remove and discard the garlic. Add the tomatoes to the pan and cook uncovered, stirring frequently, until the sauce is thick, about 15 minutes. Season to taste with salt and pepper. Gently set the meatballs in the sauce and cook over low heat for another 5 minutes to blend the flavors.

5 Spoon some of the sauce onto a warmed platter. Place the meatballs on top and cover with the remaining sauce. Sprinkle with the parsley and serve.

Veal Scallopini with Mushrooms and Peppers

Scaloppine di Vitello con Funghi e Peperoni • Lazio • Italy

Veal scallops are one of the nicest cuts because they go with so many different ingredients and cook so quickly. This tasty version is perfect for a quick meal on a busy day. The secret to browning scallopini is to dust them with flour just seconds before cooking them. If the meat is coated in advance, the flour will become gummy and not brown properly.

8 veal scallops, almost 1 lb (500 g) total weight and ⅓–½ inch (9–12 mm) thick

⅓ cup (2 oz/60 g) all-purpose (plain) flour

Salt and freshly ground pepper to taste

2 tablespoons unsalted butter

3 tablespoons olive oil

1 red bell pepper (capsicum), seeded and thinly sliced

½ lb (250 g) fresh white mushrooms, brushed clean and sliced

½ cup (4 fl oz/125 ml) white wine

2 oz (60 g) thinly sliced prosciutto, cut into narrow strips

1 tablespoon chopped fresh flat-leaf (Italian) parsley

Serves 4–6

1 One at a time, place the veal scallops between 2 sheets of plastic wrap and pound gently with a meat pounder until ¼ inch (6 mm) thick. Spread the flour on a plate and season with salt and pepper. Lightly dust the veal scallops, shaking off the excess.

2 In a large frying pan over medium heat, melt the butter with the olive oil. Add the veal and cook, turning once, until browned on both sides, about 6 minutes total. Transfer the veal to a plate.

3 Add the pepper slices and mushrooms to the frying pan over medium heat and cook, stirring occasionally, until the pepper slices are tender, about 10 minutes. Add the wine and cook, stirring, until the liquid evaporates, about 2 minutes. Stir in the prosciutto. Season with salt and pepper. Return the veal to the pan, spooning the vegetables and prosciutto over it, and cook for about 1 minute longer.

4 Transfer to a warmed serving platter or individual plates and scatter the parsley over all. Serve at once.

Breast of Veal Stuffed with Spinach and Mushrooms

Petto di Vitello Ripieno • Lombardy • Italy

An inexpensive cut of veal, the breast is nonetheless full of flavor. Ask the butcher to cut a pocket between the meat and the bones, forming a perfect cavity for a delicious stuffing. The meat is cooked slowly until it is very tender and the flavors of the stuffing permeate it. Serve with mashed potatoes and accompany the meal with a first-rate Barbera wine.

1 In a saucepan, combine the spinach, water, and salt. Cover, place over low heat, and cook until the spinach is wilted and tender, about 5 minutes. Drain in a colander, pressing out excess water with the back of a spoon, and let cool. Wrap the spinach in a clean kitchen towel and squeeze out any remaining liquid. Chop finely and set aside.

2 In a large frying pan over medium heat, melt the butter with the olive oil. Add half of the onions and cook, stirring occasionally, until tender, about 5 minutes. Add the mushrooms and cook, stirring frequently, until the mushrooms are tender and their liquid has evaporated, 10 minutes longer. Stir in the reserved spinach and season with salt and pepper. Remove from the heat and stir in the bread crumbs and raisins. Let cool slightly, then stir in the cheese.

3 Preheat the oven to 450°F (230°C). Oil a large ovenproof pot.

4 Stuff the spinach mixture into the veal pocket, and sew up the opening with kitchen twine. Sprinkle the veal with salt and pepper. Scatter the carrot, the celery, the remaining onion, and the sage in the prepared pot. Add the veal, bone side down.

5 Roast, uncovered, until browned, about 45 minutes. Reduce the heat to 350°F (180°C). Add the stock and wine. Cover and cook, basting the meat occasionally, until it is very tender, about 2 hours.

6 Transfer the veal to a warmed platter and cover to keep warm. Strain the pan juices through a fine-mesh sieve into a small saucepan. Skim off the fat from the surface. Bring the juices to a simmer over medium heat and reduce until the liquid is syrupy, about 3 minutes. Season with salt and pepper.

7 Carve the veal by cutting between the rib bones. Serve with the pan juices.

1 lb (500 g) spinach, tough stems removed

½ cup (4 fl oz/125 ml) water

Salt to taste

2 tablespoons unsalted butter

1 tablespoon olive oil

2 yellow onions, chopped

½ lb (250 g) fresh white mushrooms, brushed clean and chopped

Freshly ground pepper to taste

½ cup (2 oz/60 g) fine dried bread crumbs (page 223)

¼ cup (1½ oz/45 g) golden raisins (sultanas)

½ cup (2 oz/60 g) grated Parmigiano-Reggiano cheese

1 bone-in veal breast (6 ribs), 5½ lb (2.75 kg), cut with a pocket (see note)

1 carrot, peeled and chopped

1 celery stalk, chopped

6 fresh sage leaves

1 cup (8 fl oz/250 ml) meat or chicken stock

½ cup (4 fl oz/125 ml) dry white wine

Serves 6

Veal Cutlets with Garlic and Capers

Cotolette alla Pontremolese • Tuscany • Italy

The small town of Pontremoli is in the northernmost part of Tuscany, close to neighboring Liguria and isolated from the cypresses, vineyards, and olive groves that typify the Tuscan countryside. The town's extraordinary baroque cathedral and crumbling medieval architecture, as well as the surrounding rocky landscape, speak of another Tuscany, one worth exploring. These cutlets flavored with garlic and capers are typical of the area's unpretentious cuisine. The rich sauce begs to be sopped up with good country bread.

⅓ cup (3 fl oz/80 ml) extra-virgin olive oil

1 yellow onion, chopped

1 clove garlic, minced

2 tablespoons chopped fresh flat-leaf (Italian) parsley

1 lb (500 g) tomatoes, peeled, seeded, and chopped, or 1 can (1 lb/500 g) chopped tomatoes

1 tablespoon capers, rinsed

2 olive oil–packed anchovy fillets

4 veal steaks, about 1½ lb (750 g) total weight and each ½ inch (12 mm) thick

Serves 4

1 In a large frying pan, warm the olive oil over medium heat. Add the onion and sauté until soft, about 3 minutes. Add the garlic and parsley and continue cooking until the onion is translucent, about 3 minutes longer. Add the tomatoes, reduce the heat to low, and simmer gently until the sauce is quite thick, about 15 minutes. Stir in the capers and the anchovy fillets, breaking up the anchovies in the pan with a wooden spoon, and cook for 1 minute longer.

2 Push the sauce to the side of the pan and lay the veal steaks in the pan. Cook until the steaks lose their raw color on the first side, about 5 minutes. Turn the steaks, spoon the sauce over the top, cover, and continue to cook until lightly browned on the second side, 4–5 minutes longer.

3 Transfer the veal steaks to a warmed serving platter and spoon the sauce over the top. Serve at once.

Sliced Cured Beef Stuffed with Ricotta and Arugula

Involtini di Bresaola, Ricotta e Rucola • Tuscany • Italy

Bresaola, mild cured lean beef popular in northern Italy but appreciated in Tuscany as well, is ruby red and close in texture to prosciutto. It is available in fine delicatessens outside Italy.

¾ cup (6½ oz/200 g) fresh ricotta cheese

¼ cup (2 oz/60 g) mascarpone cheese

3 tablespoons chopped arugula (rocket), plus whole leaves for garnish

½ teaspoon minced garlic

1 teaspoon grated lemon zest

24 paper-thin slices *bresaola* (see note)

Serves 6

1 In a bowl, combine the ricotta and mascarpone cheeses, chopped arugula, garlic, and lemon zest. Mix well. Scatter the arugula leaves on a serving platter.

2 Lay a *bresaola* slice on a work surface. Dip a spoon into cold water, then scoop out 1½ teaspoons of the cheese mixture and place in the center of the *bresaola* slice. Starting at one end, roll up the slice and place it seam side down on the platter. Repeat with the remaining *bresaola* and filling.

3 Garnish the platter with whole arugula leaves. Cover and refrigerate for 30 minutes before serving.

CURED MEATS

One of the standards of Tuscan cuisine—even though it involves no cooking—is the ubiquitous *affettato misto*. It appears on nearly every buffet table and on trattoria menus in cities and in the countryside. Indeed, it is found just about everywhere but at a formal dinner. And although the two words simply mean "sliced mixed," every Tuscan knows that what is sliced is a combination of cured meats.

First and foremost of all *affettati* is prosciutto. In Tuscany, you will find it *dolce,* referring to the mildly salted varieties from northern Italy, and *toscano,* the highly salted local product, considered a perfect accompaniment to saltless Tuscan bread. Usually it is very thinly cut on a slicing machine, but sometimes it is hand-cut into somewhat thicker pieces.

A Tuscan platter of cured meats will most often include a few slices of *salame toscano,* a full-bodied local salami flavored with peppercorns, garlic, and white wine, and *finocchiona* or *sbriciolona,* delicious soft salamis (the latter so soft that it literally crumbles) flavored with fennel seed. Less common, though no less delectable, is the meat of wild boar. It is often used to make prosciutto, salami, and *coppa,* cured boneless pork—in this case, boar—shoulder. *Prosciutto di cinghiale* has a beautiful deep red cast and an appealing subtle earthiness.

Onion-Smothered Steak

Bife à Cebolada · Estremadura · Spain

Traditionally, the onions and steak in this dish are cooked together slowly until the steak becomes tender. If, however, you use an excellent-quality steak, like the rib-eye called for here, the steak should be quickly panfried and the onion mixture spooned on top.

2 tablespoons red wine vinegar

2 teaspoons minced garlic

1½ teaspoons sweet paprika

½ teaspoon salt, plus salt to taste

½ teaspoon freshly ground pepper, plus pepper to taste

4 rib-eye steaks, about ½ lb (250 g) each

¼ cup (2 fl oz/60 ml) olive oil

2 cups (10 oz/315 g) chopped yellow onion

½ cup (3 oz/90 g) diced canned plum (Roma) tomato

¼ cup (2 fl oz/60 ml) tawny port (optional)

3 tablespoons chopped fresh flat-leaf (Italian) parsley

Serves 4

1 In a mortar or small bowl, combine 1 tablespoon of the vinegar, 1 teaspoon of the garlic, the paprika, and ½ teaspoon each salt and pepper and mix together to form a paste. Rub the paste on both sides of the steaks and set aside at room temperature to marinate for about 1 hour.

2 In a frying pan over medium heat, warm the olive oil. Add the onion and cook, stirring often, until golden, about 25 minutes. Add the remaining 1 teaspoon garlic, the tomato, the remaining 1 tablespoon vinegar, and the port, if using, and simmer, uncovered, over medium heat for 10 minutes to blend the flavors. Season with salt and pepper and stir in the parsley. Remove from the heat and set aside.

3 Place 2 large, heavy frying pans over high heat and sprinkle them both with salt. When the pans are very hot, add the steaks and cook over high heat, turning once, 3–5 minutes on each side for rare, or to desired doneness. Add the onion sauce and heat through, turning the steaks in the sauce to coat.

4 Transfer the steaks to warmed individual plates or a platter and spoon the onion sauce on top. Serve immediately.

Veal Braised in Milk

Vitello al Latte · Tuscany · Italy

In Italy, veal is milk-fed and the meat is a pale pink with no marbling. Gourmet butchers should be able to procure true milk-fed veal for you.

2 lb (1 kg) boneless veal cut from rump, in 1 piece

Salt and freshly ground pepper to taste

½ cup (4 fl oz/125 ml) extra-virgin olive oil

4 large carrots, peeled and finely chopped

1 cup (8 fl oz/250 ml) beef or vegetable broth

½ cup (4 fl oz/125 ml) milk

Serves 4

1 Compress the meat into a cylindrical shape and tie it with kitchen string at 1- to 2-inch (2.5- to 5-cm) intervals along its length. Combine equal portions of salt and pepper in a small bowl. Pat the mixture all over the surface of the meat.

2 Pour the olive oil into a large saucepan and place over medium heat. Add the carrots and cook gently until they soften, 5–8 minutes.

3 Add the veal and turn in the pan to flavor it on all sides. Pour in the broth, cover, and reduce the heat to medium-low. Cook, turning the meat from time to time, until the meat is slightly golden, about 45 minutes. Raise the heat to medium-high and lightly brown the meat on all sides, about 15 minutes. Reduce the heat to medium-low and pour in the milk. Re-cover and cook until the milk is absorbed, about 10 minutes, making certain the meat does not scorch.

4 Transfer the meat to a carving board and let cool for 10 minutes. Snip and remove the strings. Cut the meat into slices ¼ inch (6 mm) thick. Pour the contents of the pan into a food mill fitted with the medium disk and purée.

5 Reassemble the slices into the original cylindrical form, return to the pan, and baste with the purée; this infuses the meat with flavor and keeps it moist.

6 Transfer the slices to a warmed serving platter and ladle the sauce over the top of the meat. Serve at once.

Lamb with Mint and Garlic

Carneiro à Transmontana • Trás-os-Montes • Portugal

There are two ways to prepare this recipe from Trás-os-Montes, a rough mountain terrain where goats and sheep are raised. Some cooks use a bone-in leg of lamb and rub the herb paste over the exterior. Others stuff the mint-garlic mixture into a boneless leg, where the flavors can permeate the meat more intensely, as is done here. Garnish with fresh mint leaves.

1 leg of lamb, 5–6 lb (2.5–3 kg), boned

¾ cup (1 oz/30 g) chopped fresh mint

¼ cup (1½ oz/45 g) finely minced bacon

2 tablespoons finely minced garlic

1 tablespoon paprika

1 teaspoon salt, plus salt to taste

½ teaspoon freshly ground pepper, plus pepper to taste

5 tablespoons (2½ fl oz/75 ml) red wine vinegar

½ cup (4 fl oz/125 ml) olive oil

Serves 6–8

1 Unroll the leg of lamb, fat side down, and trim away all excess fat and sinews. In a mortar or small bowl, combine the mint, bacon, garlic, paprika, 1 teaspoon salt, ½ teaspoon pepper, and 2 tablespoons of the vinegar and mix to form a paste. Rub the paste evenly over the inside of the lamb leg. Roll up the leg and tie securely with kitchen string. Wrap the lamb in plastic wrap and refrigerate for 12–24 hours.

2 Preheat the oven to 400°F (200°C). Unwrap the lamb and bring to room temperature.

3 Put the lamb on a rack in a roasting pan. In a small bowl, stir together the olive oil and the remaining 3 tablespoons vinegar. Brush the lamb lightly with some of the mixture. Sprinkle with salt and pepper.

4 Roast, basting with the oil-vinegar mixture about every 10 minutes, until an instant-read thermometer inserted into the thickest part of the meat registers 120°F (49°C) for rare, 45–50 minutes, or 130°–135°F (54°–57°C) for medium, 55–60 minutes. Alternatively, test by cutting into the leg with a sharp knife; the meat should be rosy or done to your liking.

5 Transfer the lamb to a warmed platter and let rest for 10 minutes. Snip the strings and slice to serve.

Lamb Chops with Port, Mustard, and Cream

Costeletas de Carneiro Escondidinho • Douro • Portugal

This flavorful dish comes from Oporto, the commercial heart of northern Portugal and the center of the port wine trade. The contrast of the nuttiness of the wine, the heat of the mustard, and the richness of the cream works well with lamb chops or lamb loin. Serve with fried potatoes and sautéed carrots with mint.

12 loin lamb chops, each about 1½ inches (4 cm) thick

Salt and freshly ground pepper to taste

2 tablespoons olive oil or unsalted butter

1 cup (8 fl oz/250 ml) dry port

3 tablespoons Dijon mustard

1 cup (8 fl oz/250 ml) heavy (double) cream

Serves 6

1 Sprinkle the lamb chops with salt and pepper. In a large, heavy frying pan over medium-high heat, warm the olive oil or melt the butter. Add the chops and cook, turning once, until well seared and cooked to desired doneness, about 10 total minutes for rare and 14 minutes total for medium-rare. Transfer to a warmed platter and keep warm.

2 Remove the pan from the heat, add the port, and deglaze the pan, stirring to dislodge any browned bits from the pan bottom. Return the pan to medium heat and simmer the port for a minute or so to burn off the alcohol. Whisk in the mustard and cream and continue to simmer until thickened, about 5 minutes. Season with salt and pepper.

3 Return the chops to the pan and swirl them in the sauce. Transfer to warmed individual plates, spooning the sauce over the top, and serve at once.

Grilled Lamb Ribs

Agnello a Scottadito • Umbria • Italy

In an Umbrian trattoria, a roasting fireplace might be used to grill these simple rib chops, bathed with an olive oil, garlic, and rosemary marinade. The crisp chops are best when eaten sizzling hot off the fire, so the Italians call them *scottadito,* meaning "burned fingers."

3 large cloves garlic, finely chopped

2 tablespoons chopped fresh rosemary

¼ cup (2 fl oz/60 ml) olive oil

Freshly ground pepper to taste

8–12 rib lamb chops, well trimmed of fat

Salt to taste

Lemon slices (optional)

Serves 4

1 In a small bowl, stir together the garlic, rosemary, olive oil, and pepper. Place the lamb chops in a shallow dish and brush the mixture over them. Cover and refrigerate for at least 2 hours or as long as overnight.

2 Prepare a fire in a charcoal grill, or preheat a broiler (grill). Brush the grill rack or the rack of a broiler pan with oil. Place the chops on the rack and grill or broil, turning as needed, until browned and crisp on the outside yet still pink and juicy inside, 10 minutes.

3 Transfer to warmed individual plates, sprinkle with salt, and serve immediately with lemon slices, if using.

Braised Lamb Shanks with Rosemary, Olives, and Tomatoes

Brasato di Stinco di Agnello • Abruzzo • Italy

For centuries, raising sheep was the primary occupation in the Abruzzo, where flocks would be driven from the moutains to the more temperate coastal areas each winter.

6 small lamb shanks, about ¾ lb (375 g) each

2 tablespoons olive oil

Salt and freshly ground black pepper to taste

6 anchovy fillets

2 cloves garlic, thinly sliced

1 tablespoon chopped fresh rosemary

Pinch of red pepper flakes

½ cup (4 fl oz/125 ml) dry white wine

1½ cups (12 fl oz/375 ml) meat stock

1 cup (6 oz/185 g) peeled, seeded, and chopped tomatoes (fresh or canned)

½ cup (2½ oz/75 g) Gaeta olives

1 tablespoon chopped fresh flat-leaf (Italian) parsley

Serves 6

1 Pat the lamb shanks dry. In a heavy pot large enough to hold the shanks in a single layer, warm the olive oil over medium heat. Add the lamb shanks and cook until well browned on all sides, about 15 minutes total. Spoon off the fat. Sprinkle the shanks with salt and black pepper. Add the anchovies, garlic, rosemary, and red pepper flakes and cook for 1 minute. Add the wine and bring to a simmer. Then add the stock and tomatoes. Reduce the heat to low, cover, and simmer the shanks, turning them occasionally, until the meat is fork-tender, about 1½ hours.

2 Stir in the olives and heat through. Transfer to a warmed serving platter and sprinkle with the parsley.

COOK'S COUNTRY

The town of Villa Santa Maria in Abruzzo is celebrated as the home of some of the country's greatest cooks. This reputation was established centuries ago when nobles journeyed there to escape the hot Neapolitan summers. The surrounding woods were full of wild game, and hunting became a favorite sport. Local men were employed as guides and cooks, and some returned to the city with their new employers. Soon it became fashionable to have a chef from Villa Santa Maria.

Eventually the town saw the establishment of La Scuola Alberghiera, a restaurant and hotel school for the training of professional chefs. Many of the school's graduates went on to cook for politicians and celebrities and at hotels and restaurants around the world. As the fame of its graduates grew, the town became known as *il paese dei cuochi* (the cooks' country), and every October it hosts a famous culinary competition. Chefs from all over the world participate, and visitors to the two-day festival crowd the streets as they drink the regional wine and sample the cooking of each of the contenders.

Lamb with Lemon and Paprika

Cordero Cochifrito • Navarre • Spain

From the earliest days in Spain and Portugal, lamb played a significant role in the diets of the Jews and Muslims who lived alongside the Christians.

2 lb (1 kg) boneless lamb shoulder, cut into 1-inch (2.5-cm) pieces

Salt and freshly ground pepper to taste

¼ cup (2 fl oz/60 ml) olive oil

2 yellow onions, chopped

4 cloves garlic, minced

1 tablespoon sweet paprika

4 tablespoons (⅓ oz/10 g) chopped fresh flat-leaf (Italian) parsley

⅓ cup (2 fl oz/60 ml) fresh lemon juice

Lemon wedges

Serves 6

1 Sprinkle the lamb with salt and pepper. In a heavy frying pan over high heat, warm the olive oil. Working in batches, add the lamb and brown well on all sides, 5–8 minutes. Using a slotted spoon, transfer the lamb to a heavy pot.

2 Add the onions and garlic to the fat remaining in the frying pan over medium heat and sauté until tender, 8–10 minutes. Add the paprika and sauté for 1 minute longer. Transfer the onions, garlic, and all the pan juices to the pot holding the lamb. Then add 2 table-spoons of the parsley and all of the lemon juice to the lamb and bring to a boil over high heat. Reduce the heat to low, cover, and simmer until the lamb is tender, about 1 hour.

3 Taste and adjust the seasonings. Transfer to a warmed serving dish and sprinkle with the remaining 2 tablespoons parsley. Serve with lemon wedges.

Stuffed Lamb Chops

Carneiro Recheado à Portuguesa • Beira Baixa • Portugal

With the exception of the cilantro, the filling used to stuff these lamb chops resembles a Catalan *picada*, a mixture typically used for enriching and thickening a sauce.

2 tablespoons unsalted butter or olive oil

1 cup (5 oz/155 g) chopped yellow onion

3 cloves garlic, minced

1 cup (2 oz/60 g) fresh bread crumbs

¼ cup (⅓ oz/10 g) chopped fresh cilantro (fresh coriander)

6 tablespoons (1½ oz/45 g) sliced (flaked) almonds, toasted and coarsely chopped

3 tablespoons pitted green olives, coarsely chopped

1 egg, lightly beaten

Salt and freshly ground pepper to taste

12 loin lamb chops, each about 1½ inches (4 cm) thick

Serves 6

1 Prepare a fire in a charcoal grill, or preheat a broiler (grill).

2 In a small frying pan over medium heat, melt the butter or warm the olive oil. Add the onion and sauté until tender, 8–10 minutes. Add the garlic and sauté until fragrant, a few minutes longer. Transfer to a bowl and add the bread crumbs, cilantro, almonds, olives, and egg and season with salt and pepper.

3 Using a small, sharp knife, cut a pocket in each lamb chop as wide and deep as you can before hitting the bone. Spoon the filling into the pockets, dividing it evenly. Skewer closed with toothpicks.

4 Place the chops on an oiled grill rack, or arrange on a broiler pan and slip under the broiler. Grill or broil, turning once, until browned on both sides and cooked to medium-rare when cut into with a knife, 4–5 minutes on each side.

5 Transfer the chops to warmed individual plates and serve immediately.

GLOSSARY

ACHIOTE PASTE This seasoning paste, made from the hard, brick-red seeds of the tropical annatto tree, contributes a mild flowery flavor and a deep yellow-orange color to foods. It is a typical ingredient in the Yucatán.

ANCHOVIES Preserved with salt, which highlights their naturally briny taste, these tiny, silver-skinned fish are used in many European dishes. Look for anchovies sold layered whole in salt; if salted anchovies are unavailable, use fillets packed in olive oil.

To prepare salted anchovies for use, rinse them well under cold running water and scrape off their skins with a small, sharp knife. Split open along the backbone, cutting off the dorsal fins, then pull out the spines and rinse the fillets well. Pat dry with paper towels, place in a nonreactive bowl, pour in enough olive oil to cover with a thin layer, cover tightly, and refrigerate. Use within 2 weeks.

ARMAGNAC Named for the area surrounding Auch, in southwestern France, this fragrant, earthy brandy is distilled from local white wines, then aged in new oak casks.

AVOCADO LEAVES The long, leathery leaves of the avocado tree are used fresh or dried as a savory, aniselike seasoning dishes in south-central Mexico.

To toast avocado leaves, heat a heavy frying pan over medium heat. Place the leaves on the pan, press down on them with a spatula, and cook them briefly, turning once, just until they color lightly and give off their fragrance.

BAMBOO SHOOTS Known as *quinsuin* in Chinese, the tender, horn-shaped shoot of certain varieties of bamboo is hidden under a carapace of tough outer leaves. Ready-to-use shoots are sold fresh, frozen, or canned, either whole or in pieces. Keep fresh in the refrigerator in lightly salted water for up to a week. Salted dried bamboo shoots should be soaked and rinsed thoroughly before use.

BANANA LEAVES The large, pliable leaves of the banana tree are used to wrap tamales, poultry, or meat for steaming, grilling, or roasting. They protect the food and add a mild grassy flavor. Soften them by steaming or passing over a flame before use.

BEAN SAUCES Both broad beans and soybeans provide the base ingredient for many Chinese seasoning pastes and sauces. If refrigerated in sealed jars, they will last for up to 3 months. While each province has its specialties, the most common sauces follow:

BLACK BEAN SAUCE Crushed or chopped fermented black soybeans are soaked in a salt solution. The sauce (*huang jiang*) is available in both thin and thick consistencies.

GARLIC-CHILE SAUCE This salty and hot-tasting combination of crushed garlic, chiles, and fermented beans is known as *suan lajiang*.

HOT BEAN SAUCE Also known as chile bean paste, hot bean sauce (*douban lajiang*) is a thick, salty paste of mashed chiles, fermented yellow beans, seasonings, and oil.

BELL PEPPERS, RED Also called capsicums, large and meaty green bell peppers turn red and become sweeter when fully ripened.

To roast bell peppers, using tongs or a large fork, hold a whole pepper over the flame of a gas burner for 10–15 minutes, turning it to char and blister the skin evenly. Place in a paper bag, close, and leave for 10 minutes. The steam will loosen the skin and allow for easier peeling. When the pepper is cool, peel off the blackened skin, slit the pepper lengthwise, and remove the stem, seeds, and membranes. Cut as directed in the recipe.

BOK CHOY Bok choy (*bai cai*) has fleshy white stems with a delicate flavor and round green leaves, which can be steamed or used raw as a salad vegetable. It is sometimes called Chinese chard or white cabbage.

BOUQUET GARNI The classic bouquet garni includes only three herbs: fresh flat-leaf (Italian) parsley sprigs, fresh thyme sprigs, and bay leaves. When a recipe calls for a bouquet garni, use 3 large parsley sprigs, 2 large thyme sprigs, and 1 bay leaf. For a large bouquet garni, use 4 large parsley sprigs, 3 medium-sized thyme sprigs, and 1 large bay leaf. Lay the thyme and bay on the parsley sprigs, "pleat" the parsley sprigs to hold the other herbs firmly in the center, tightly wind kitchen string around the whole packet, and then tie securely, leaving a tail of string to permit easy removal of the herb bundle from the dish. If a recipe calls for one or more additions to the bouquet, bind them into the bundle with the other ingredients. The sprigs must be fresh, as any sign of mustiness will diminish the flavor.

BREAD, COARSE COUNTRY European-style country bread, also known as peasant bread, has a thick and chewy crust enveloping a tender and moist crumb.

To make bread crumbs, trim off and discard the crusts from a loaf and process the bread in a food processor until the crumbs are the texture desired. To dry the crumbs, spread them on a baking sheet and bake in a preheated 325°F (165°C) oven for about 15 minutes. For toasted crumbs, continue baking, stirring once or twice, until lightly golden, about 15 minutes longer.

CAPERS Growing wild throughout the Mediterranean, the caper bush yields tiny gray-green buds that are preserved in salt or pickled in vinegar to produce a piquant seasoning or garnish.

CARAMEL SYRUP This Vietnamese syrup is added to savory dishes for flavor and sheen.

To make the caramel syrup, in a small saucepan, combine 1 cup (8 oz/250 g) sugar with ¼ cup (2 fl oz/60 ml) water and bring to a boil over high heat; do not stir. Swirl the pan to help dissolve the sugar clinging to the pan sides. Reduce the heat to medium-low and simmer gently for 10–15 minutes. When the syrup turns a deep brown, remove from the heat and slowly pour in ¼ cup (2 fl oz/60 ml) hot water. Return the pan to medium-high heat and cook, stirring continuously, until the caramel dissolves and is thick and syrupy, 3–5 minutes. Stir in 1 teaspoon lemon juice. Let cool, then store in a jar in a cool, dark place. Makes ¾ cup (6 fl oz/180 ml).

CARDAMOM These pale green, three-sided oval pods are about ½ inch (12 mm) long and contain up to 20 black seeds. When ground, they give off an intense camphorlike aroma and a sweet, lemony taste. Loose and ground seeds lose flavor quickly, so buy them whole and remove and grind the seeds as needed.

To toast cardamom, heat whole pods or seeds in a dry frying pan over medium heat for a few minutes until their aroma develops.

CASSIA LEAVES The leaves of the cassia tree, also known as Indian bay leaves, have a slightly clovelike aroma and flavor and are available dried from Indian grocers. Despite their alternative name, they are not related to European bay leaves (*Laurus nobilis*). If cassia leaves are unavailable, the same quantity of European bay leaves may be used, although they will give a somewhat different taste.

CAUL FAT Known in French as *crépine,* this thin membrane, which encases a pig's stomach, is interlaced with a delicate network of fat that resembles a lacy veil. It is also used to wrap delicate veal roasts, keeping them moist in the oven, and to enclose pâtés, terrines, or even stuffed cabbage. Buy caul fresh or dry-salted from a full-service butcher. If it is too stiff to manipulate easily, soak it for about 5 minutes in warm water until pliable.

CHAYOTE A pear-shaped member of the squash family, the chayote, also known as the mirliton, has a mild cucumber-like flavor. Indigenous to Mexico, it comes in varieties ranging from a smooth-textured ivory skin to one that is prickly and dark green.

CHILES, DRIED Buy dried chiles with skins that are flexible rather than brittle in texture, and store them in airtight containers, away from both light and moisture.

ANCHO A dried form of the poblano, anchos measure 4½ inches (11.5 cm) long, with wide shoulders and wrinkled, deep reddish brown skin, and have a mild bittersweet chocolate flavor and a slight aroma of prunes.

ÁRBOL Smooth-skinned, bright reddish orange chile about 3 inches (7.5 cm) long, narrow in shape and fiery hot.

CASCABEL "Rattle" chile, describing the sound made by its seeds when this medium-hot globe-shaped chile is shaken. It is 1½ inches (4 cm) long, with smooth brownish red skin.

CHIPOTLE This smoke-dried form of the ripened jalapeño is rich in flavor and very hot. Sold in its dried form, it is typically a leathery tan, although some varieties are a deep burgundy. It is available packed in a vinegar-tomato sauce (*chiles chipotles en adobo*) and lightly pickled (*en escabeche*).

GUAJILLO Sharp and moderately hot, this burgundy chile is about 5 inches (13 cm) long and tapered, with brittle, smooth skin.

PASILLA Skinny, wrinkled, raisin-black *pasillas* are about 6 inches (15 cm) long, with a sharp, fairly hot flavor.

To seed dried chiles, clean them with a damp cloth, then slit them lengthwise and use a small, sharp knife to remove the seeds.

To toast dried chiles, clean them with a damp cloth, then heat a heavy frying pan over medium heat. Add the whole or seeded chiles, press down firmly with a spatula, turn the chiles, and press down once more before removing. The chiles will change color only slightly and start to give off their aroma.

Caution: The oils naturally present in chiles can cause a painful burning sensation when they come in contact with your eyes or other sensitive areas. After handling them, wash your hands thoroughly with warm, soapy water. If you have particularly sensitive skin, wear latex kitchen gloves or slip plastic bags over your hands before working with chiles.

CHILES, FRESH Choose firm, bright fresh chiles. Smaller chiles are usually hotter. Store them in the refrigerator for 1 week.

ANAHEIM This long green mild to moderately spicy chile is found in most markets.

HABANERO Renowned as the hottest of all chiles, this 2-inch (5-cm) lantern-shaped variety from Yucatán combines its intense heat with flavors recalling tomatoes and tropical fruits. Unripe green as well as ripened yellow, orange, and red varieties are available.

JALAPEÑO This popular chile, measuring 2–3 inches (5–7.5 cm) in length, has thick flesh and varies in degree of hotness. It is found in green and sweeter ripened red forms.

POBLANO Named for the Mexican state of Puebla, this moderately hot chile is 5 inches (13 cm) long with polished deep green skin.

SERRANO Slender chiles measuring 1–2 inches (2.5–5 cm) long and very hot, serranos have a brightly acidic flavor and are available in both green and ripened red forms.

To roast, peel, and seed fresh chiles, see directions for roasting bell peppers (page 223). Roast smaller chiles for 5–8 minutes.

CHOCOLATE, MEXICAN Mexican chocolate, a mixture of cacao beans, almonds, sugar, and often cinnamon and vanilla, is formed into 3 oz (90 g) disks. It has a coarse, grainy texture and is used to flavor sauces or hot drinks.

CINNAMON BARK, TRUE *Canela,* the flaky, aromatic bark of a laurel tree native to Sri Lanka, is true cinnamon. The paper-thin inner layer of the bark is stripped from the trees in layers and then rolled into cylinders about ½ inch (12 mm) in diameter. The cinnamon sticks commonly found in stores and called for in recipes are about 3 inches (7.5 cm). Cassia, a close relative of cinnamon, has a coarser texture and comes from the bark of a Southeast Asian variety of laurel tree. Its flavor is similar, but stronger and more astringent. Products labeled "cinnamon" in the United States and Europe are usually cassia, but in many countries, the two are interchangeable.

COCONUT CREAM AND COCONUT MILK Coconut cream and coconut milk are both derived from an infusion of grated coconut flesh in water or, less commonly, milk. (They are not to be confused with the clear juice inside the whole nut.) The first infusion yields coconut cream, a thick liquid with a high fat content. If the same batch of coconut is steeped again, the resulting liquid is called coconut milk.

CORIANDER Round, gray-brown coriander seeds, used whole or ground, have a bright, citruslike flavor and the combined aromas of lemon, sage, and caraway. The seeds are used to flavor both sweet and savory foods in many cuisines. The leaves of the plant are known as cilantro or fresh coriander.

CORNMEAL Once dried, corn kernels can be ground into a fine, medium, or coarse flour by steel rollers or stone mills. You can use the grinds interchangeably in most recipes. Although white cornmeal is regularly found in the pantries of Southern and Midwestern American kitchens, yellow cornmeal is more readily found on store shelves. Milled with the germ intact, stone-ground cornmeal has a shorter shelf life; store for up to 4 months in the refrigerator. Steel-cut cornmeal can be kept in a cool, dark place for up to 1 year.

CREMA Although *crema* translates simply as "cream," Mexican *crema* is a thick, rich, slightly soured product that can be found in grocery stores specializing in Latin American foods. In its place, use French *crème fraîche,* which is more widely available, or make a substitute by thinning sour cream slightly with whole milk or half-and-half (half cream).

CUMIN A member of the parsley family, cumin has small seeds that are tapered at both ends and lend a warm, earthy, pungent aroma and flavor to dishes. To intensify their flavor, cumin seeds are often roasted in a frying pan set over medium-high heat, stirring to prevent them from burning, for 3–4 minutes.

FATBACK This layer of fat that runs along the back of a pig is used for making lard, for covering roasting meats to keep them moist as they cook, and as an ingredient in sausages, pâtés, and terrines.

FAVA BEANS Slipped from their large, puffy green pods, fresh fava beans, also known as broad beans, have a slightly bitter flavor and a dense texture. Fresh and dried fava beans are markedly different in flavor and should not be substituted for each other in recipes.

To prepare fresh fava beans, split the pods with your fingers and remove the beans. To peel them easily, blanch the shelled beans in boiling water for about 30 seconds. Drain, cool slightly under cold water, and pinch each bean to slip it from its skin.

FISH SAUCE In many Southeast Asian kitchens, fish sauce assumes the same seasoning role played by soy sauce in China and Japan. Made by layering anchovies or other tiny fish with salt in barrels or jars and leaving them to ferment, the dark amber liquid adds pungent, salty flavor to many dishes. The two most common types are Thai *nam pla* and the more mild Vietnamese *nuoc mam*.

FIVE-SPICE POWDER The components of this popular southern Chinese spice blend vary, but star anise, fennel seeds or aniseeds, cinnamon, cloves, Sichuan peppercorns, and sometimes ginger are usually part of the mix.

GALANGAL Similar in appearance to ginger, to which it is related, this gnarled rhizome has a mustardlike flavor. It is available fresh and frozen whole and as dried slices. If only the dried form can be found, use half the quantity you would for fresh. Reconstitute dried galangal by soaking it in warm water for 30 minutes until pliable.

GARAM MASALA This keynote spice mixture of northern India also turns up in Southeast Asian kitchens. The blend—sold commercially or made at home—features coriander seeds, cumin, black pepper, cardamom, cloves, cinnamon, nutmeg, and mace. It is typically used to season dishes at the beginning of cooking and is sometimes sprinkled over finished dishes.

GINGER The edible root or rhizome of ginger is buff colored and smooth when young, and sometimes comes with slender, pink-tipped green shoots attached. When older, it becomes a deep buff color with slightly wrinkled skin; its flavor intensifies and the flesh becomes fibrous. Buy ginger that feels hard and heavy, with a shiny, unbroken peel.

To make ginger juice, peel and finely grate fresh ginger onto a piece of fine cloth, gather into a ball, and squeeze to extract the juice. The pulp can be discarded or used in a soup or stir-fry. One tablespoon of grated ginger will produce approximately 1½ teaspoons of ginger juice.

HAM Many countries boast superb country-style hams that may be served thinly sliced as a first course or used as a distinctive source of flavor in sauces, soups, stews, braises, and other dishes. Portugal's *presunto* has a sweet, smoky flavor and a deep chestnut color. Spain's finely marbled *serrano* ham has an intense, almost sweet flavor. Prosciutto is the famed air-cured ham of Parma, Italy. Other similar hams include French Bayonne, German Westphalian, or American Smithfield.

HERBS Choose fresh herbs that look bright and healthy and are fragrant. Store them in the refrigerator, wrapped in damp paper towels and then placed in plastic bags. Dried herbs should be stored in airtight containers, kept away from both light and heat, and should be replaced after 4–6 months.

BASIL, THAI Three types of basil are used in Thailand: *kraprow, maenglak,* and *horapa. Kraprow* has serrated green leaves with a tint of purple and a hint of anise flavor. *Maenglak,* also known as lemon basil, has smaller leaves and a lemony scent. *Horapa* has purple stems, shiny leaves, and an anise aroma. All three can be used interchangeably.

BAY LEAF The whole glossy leaves of the bay laurel tree are indispensable in savory long-simmered dishes. European bay leaves have a milder, more pleasant taste than the California-grown variety.

CHERVIL Resembling tiny Italian parsley leaves and carrying a hint of sweet anise flavor, this fresh springtime herb is especially popular in France. It goes well with salads, vegetables, eggs, seafood, and chicken.

CHIVE This thin green shoot, a member of the onion family, adds a hint of onion flavor to salads, eggs, cheeses, seafood, and poultry.

CILANTRO This lacy-leafed annual herb, also known as fresh coriander, has a fresh, assertive scent and bright, astringent flavor. Delicate cilantro leaves should be added at the end of the cooking time or used raw.

GARLIC CHIVES Garlic chives have flat, deep green leaves with a strong aroma of garlic. A mixture of peeled, chopped garlic and green (spring) onions can substitute when garlic chives are unavailable.

HERBES DE PROVENCE Dried thyme, marjoram, savory, oregano, basil, rosemary, fennel, and lavender make up this fragrant blend.

KAFFIR LIME LEAVES The kaffir lime contributes its rich, citrusy flavor to curry pastes and other savory and sweet dishes through its dried, fresh, or frozen leaves and its gnarled rind. Its juice, however, is not used. Pesticide-free lemon or lime leaves may be substituted.

LAVENDER Look for small, dried flowers in the bulk herb section of health-food stores or the baking aisle of fine grocers. They should retain a vivid violet hue and flowery fragrance.

MARJORAM Milder in flavor than its cousin, oregano, this herb is used both fresh and dried. It goes well with grilled meats, poultry, and seafood and also frequently seasons vegetable and dried bean dishes.

OREGANO, MEXICAN Although similar in flavor to Mediterranean oregano, Mexican oregano is more pungent and less sweet, making it a perfect match for the spicy, cumin-laden dishes of the American Southwest. Add it at the beginning of cooking to allow time for its complex flavor to meld with others.

ROSEMARY Taking its name from the Latin for "rose of the sea," this spiky evergreen shrub thrives in Mediterranean climates. Its highly aromatic, piney flavor goes well with lamb and poultry, as well as with vegetables.

SAGE Sharply fragrant, with traces of both bitterness and sweetness, this gray-green herb is often used in seasoning pork, veal, game, and sausages.

SALAM LEAVES These aromatic Malaysian laurel leaves are similar to bay and can be used dried or fresh to flavor simmered and stir-fried dishes. Bay leaves can be substituted, but some cooks prefer *kari* (curry) leaves.

TARRAGON Native to Siberia, this heady anise-flavored herb can perfume wine vinegar and Dijon mustards, flavor sauces and dressings, and season seafood, poultry, and eggs.

THYME This low-growing, aromatic herb grows wild throughout the Mediterranean. A key element of many slow-cooked savory dishes, it is often used to season rich meats.

WINTER SAVORY Strong and spicy in flavor, this evergreen Mediterranean herb goes well with robust ingredients such as dried beans, cured meats, pork, cheeses, and tomato sauces.

HOISIN SAUCE Fermented soybeans, vinegar, garlic, chile, and other ingredients are combined in this thick Chinese savory-sweet sauce used as an ingredient and a condiment.

JUNIPER BERRY This slightly resinous dried berry of a small evergreen shrub is a popular seasoning for game, sausage, and pork dishes. Before use, the berries are usually slightly crushed to release their aroma.

LARD Rendered pork fat (known in Spanish as *manteca*) lends a rich taste to many Mexican and Spanish preparations. When cooking, do not use the processed white commercial variety, which lacks authentic flavor. Instead, look for a butcher shop that renders its own.

To render fat into lard, preheat an oven to 300°F (150°C). Spread 1–2 lb (500 g–1 kg) ground (minced) or chopped pork fat in a large roasting pan. Roast until most of the fat has melted, leaving behind light golden scraps, 30–45 minutes. If the lard itself begins to color, reduce the temperature. Remove from the oven and let cool slightly, then pour through a sieve into sealable containers. When completely cooled, seal the containers and keep refrigerated for up to 2 months or frozen for up to 1 year.

LEMONGRASS This stiff, reedlike grass has an intensely aromatic, citrusy flavor that is one of the signatures of Southeast Asian cooking. Be sure to use only fresh lemongrass.

To prepare lemongrass, if a recipe calls for the tender midsection of a stalk, use only its bottom 4–6 inches (10–15 cm). Peel off the tough outer layers of the stalk to reveal the inner purple ring. To release the aromatic oils, smash or chop the stalk before use.

MARSALA An Italian amber-colored fortified wine made in the area around the Sicilian city of the same name. Available in sweet and dry forms, it is enjoyed as a dessert wine and is used as a flavoring in savory and sweet dishes.

MASA HARINA Flour ground from dried corn, used for making tortillas and tamales. Two basic types are available, the fine-ground *masa harina* for tortillas and the coarser-ground *masa harina* for tamales.

MOLASSES Used to add sweetness and depth to sauces and desserts, this full-flavored liquid is derived from the syrupy residue left after sugar crystals have been extracted from fresh cane juice. A light, mild molasses is obtained from the first boiling of the sugar, while the second boiling yields a deep, smoky dark molasses. Blackstrap molasses, strong and bitter, remains after the third and final boiling. Dark corn syrup, black treacle, and maple syrup are all adequate substitutions.

MUSHROOM SOY SAUCE This dark Chinese soy sauce gains extra rich flavor and deep color by adding an extract of straw mushrooms. Some brands also include sugar.

MUSHROOMS, DRIED BLACK Sold fresh or dried in Asian stores, black fungi are also known as wood ear fungi (larger, thicker tree fungi) and cloud ear fungi (smaller, dark, curled fungi). Dried black fungus is sold whole, in pieces about 2 inches (5 cm) square, or shredded. It must be soaked to soften, and woody root sections should be trimmed before use. Store in an airtight container. Fresh fungus should be used within 3 to 4 days of purchase.

NAPA CABBAGE Napa cabbage, also known as Peking cabbage, has a large head of tightly packed leaves with fleshy white bases and crinkled, pale green tops. Its mild flavor, crunchy stems, and tender leaves make it useful in soups, stir-fries, and stuffings.

ONIONS, SWEET Known by the names of places where they are cultivated, sweet onions grow in the fertile, low-sulfur soils of Walla Walla in Washington, Vidalia in Georgia, and Maui in Hawaii. Farmers' markets and specialty grocers carry sweet onions during their peak seasons: the Maui and the Vidalia in spring and the Walla Walla in late summer.

OYSTER SAUCE Used extensively in Chinese cooking, oyster sauce, or *haoyou*, is a thick, salty condiment and seasoning sauce made from fermented soybeans and the liquor drawn off from fermented dried oysters.

PALM SUGAR Derived from the sap of the coconut or other palms, and sometimes called coconut sugar, palm sugar is prized for its fragrant caramel-like flavor and light to dark brown color. The sugar is often sold formed into dark, hard disks or cylinders, which may be grated or shaved for use. Light or dark brown sugar, depending upon the color desired, can be substituted.

PANCETTA A form of unsmoked Italian bacon, this long, flat cut of fatty pork belly is seasoned with black pepper, and sometimes garlic, cinnamon, and nutmeg, then rolled up tightly and salt-cured.

PARMESAN Parmesan is fashioned into wheels and then aged for 1–3 years to develop a complex, nutty flavor and dry, granular texture. "Parmigiano-Reggiano" stenciled on the rind ensures that the cheese is a true Parmesan made in Emilia-Romagna.

PAPRIKA This finely ground brick-red spice is made from a type of dried red pepper. It is available either hot or sweet. Hungarian paprika is considered the highest quality.

PEPPER-SALT To prepare pepper-salt, place a dry wok over medium-high heat. When it is hot, add 2 tablespoons salt and warm for about 40 seconds, stirring constantly. Add 2 teaspoons Sichuan pepper, remove from the heat, and transfer to a shallow dish to cool. Use or serve as directed in the recipe.

PLANTAIN Closely related to the banana, the plantain, or *plátano,* is starchier and firmer. It is always cooked before eating. Fresh plantains have almost uniformly black skins when ripe. Some recipes may call for the texture of an underripe plantain that has yellow-green skin.

POLENTA Both cornmeal and the porridgelike dish made from it, polenta serves as an accompaniment to roast meat or poultry, a base for hearty sauces, or as a meal on its own. If spread in a pan and cooled, polenta becomes firm enough to cut and grill, layer like lasagne, or fry until crisp.

POZOLE The Mexican term for hominy, *pozole* (posole in English) is made commercially by first boiling dried field corn with calcium hydroxide to dissolve its tough hull. The grain is then simmered to make a foundation for robust soups of the same name, usually containing pork and chile, or to add to the tripe stew known as *menudo.* In Mexican markets, pozole is also sold freshly cooked or frozen. Canned white hominy may be used.

ORANGE JUICE, FRESH BITTER The aromatic bitter oranges of Mexico's Yucatán province are seldom found outside their native region. When a recipe calls for their juice, look for similar Seville oranges, which also have a thick, wrinkled peel, or approximate the juice with a mixture of 1 part regular orange juice, 2 parts lime juice, and 1 part grapefruit juice. To intensify the flavor, add a bit of finely grated grapefruit zest.

QUESO FRESCO Fresh Mexican cheeses, or *quesos frescos,* are soft, tangy, lightly salted cow's milk cheeses that are crumbled or sliced to add richness and piquant creaminess.

RICE PAPER Made from rice flour and water, tissue-thin rice paper comes dried in rounds and triangles of different sizes, with 8-inch (20-cm) rounds the most common. Before use, they must be softened with warm water.

RICE WINE Rice wine (*liaojiu*) adds flavor to sauces and stir-fries in Chinese cooking and works as a tenderizer and seasoning in marinades. Those labeled "cooking wine" may contain 5 percent added salt, so check labels before seasoning a dish.

RICOTTA Soft, snowy ricotta is made by recooking the whey left after the making of other cheeses. Outside Italy, ricotta is primarily made from cow's milk, but traditional Italian ricotta comes from the milk of sheep, water buffalo, or goats. Drain commercial cow's milk ricotta in a sieve for 30 minutes before using.

SAFFRON Taking its name from the Arabic word for "yellow," this rare and costly spice comes from the dried stigmas of a purple crocus flower. The best form to buy is saffron threads, the whole dried stigmas. Before the threads are added, they are either toasted in a dry pan over low heat or lightly crushed and then briefly steeped in a warm liquid to release their maximum flavor and aroma.

SAUSAGES, FRESH ITALIAN A variety of fresh pork sausages are made throughout Italy, ranging from the sweet sausages of Emilia-Romagna, to the coriander-spiked links from Lazio, to Calabria's fiery-hot *peperoncini*-seasoned type, to Mantua's simple *luganega,* seasoned merely with salt and pepper.

SESAME PASTE Sesame paste is made from ground whole white sesame seeds and is used to thicken and enrich sauces and dips.

SHERRY Produced exclusively in the Jerez and Manzanilla regions of southwestern Spain, the two main types of this fortified wine are *fino* and *oloroso. Finos,* including the crisp, dry *manzanilla* and the dry, nutty *amontillado,* are pale, fragrant, young aperitif wines often drunk with tapas. *Olorosos,* which are darker and stout, include sweet cream sherry and full-bodied brown sherry.

SICHUAN PEPPER The small, red-brown berries from the prickly ash tree are also known variously as *fagara,* wild peppercorn, or Chinese pepper. Spicy rather than hot, it can have a numbing effect if used to excess. When buying whole peppercorns, look for a bright red-brown color. Store in an airtight jar and use within a few weeks for the best flavor.

SOY SAUCE Typically made by fermenting and aging soybeans with wheat, salt, and water, soy sauce is an indispensable seasoning in Asian kitchens. Dark soy sauce gains its color, consistency, and sweetness from the addition of caramel. Light soy sauce has a thinner consistency and a lighter flavor. Japanese soy sauces tend to be milder tasting, slightly sweeter, and less salty than Chinese varieties.

STAR ANISE Star anise is a star-shaped dried seedpod with five points, each containing one shiny black seed. Its pronounced licorice flavor is particularly good with duck, game,

and pork. It is used whole, broken into individual points, or crushed in a spice grinder. Store in an airtight jar.

TAMARIND The long, brown seedpods of the tamarind tree, native to India, produce a sweet-sour pulp. Tamarind paste and concentrate are also available.

TANGERINE PEEL The thin skin of tangerines can be torn into strips and dried in the sun or oven. The resulting hard brown pieces add a delicious fresh flavor to stewed and braised dishes and the boldly flavored stir-fries of Sichuan. Sold in small packs, tangerine peel should be kept in a cool, dry cupboard, or frozen. Alternatively, dried mandarin orange peel can be used.

TOMATOES During summer, use vine-ripened fresh tomatoes for both uncooked salads and for cooked dishes such as tomato sauce. At other times of year, good-quality canned plum (Roma) tomatoes are best for cooking.

To peel a fresh tomato, use a small, sharp knife to score a shallow X in its flower end. Then, using a slotted spoon, dip the tomato into a saucepan of boiling water for about 20 seconds. Submerge the tomato in ice water to cool. Starting at the X, peel off the loosened skin with your fingers. To remove the seeds, cut the tomato in half crosswise and squeeze gently.

TOMATILLOS Resembling small, unripened green tomatoes, these fruits are actually members of the gooseberry family. They have a tangy flavor and tomato-like texture.

VINEGAR, BALSAMIC While vinegar is most commonly made from wine, Italy's most renowned vinegar, *aceto balsamico,* or "balsamic vinegar," is based on white grape juice that is reduced by boiling it down to a thick syrup, then aged for many years in a succession of barrels made of different woods, each of which contributes its own taste to the final syrupy, sharp-and-sweet product.

VINEGAR, BLACK Black (also labeled brown) vinegar, dark colored and subtly flavored, is distilled from rice. Balsamic vinegar can be used to replace black vinegar.

INDEX

ACKNOWLEDGMENTS

Weldon Owen wishes to thank the following people for their generous support in producing this book: Desne Ahlers, Ken DellaPenta, Carolyn Keating, Andrew William Reccius, Shadin Saah, and Sharron Wood.

CREDITS

Recipe photography by Noel Barnhurst, except for the following by Andre Martin: Pages 72, 75, 77, 80, 82, 85, 89, 90, 91, 95, 96, 99, 101, 102, 103, 106, 110, 111, 114, 115, 117, 118, 119, 120.

Travel photography by William Albert Allard, National Geographic Society Image Collection: ©Page 15 (left); Michael Freeman: Pages 66, ©68 (top), 68 (bottom), 79, 71 (left and right); Sheri Giblin: ©Page 13; James Lemass, Index Stock: ©Page 222; Jason Lowe: Pages 6 (bottom), 8, 70, 125, 126, 168 (top and bottom),170, 171; Madeline Polss: ©Page 12 (top); Steven Rothfeld: 4 (right), 5 (right), 6 (top), 7, 9 (right), 15 (right), 122, 124 (top and bottom), 127 (left and right), 166, 169; Ignacio Urquiza: Pages 9 (left), 12 (bottom), 14; Rachel Weill: ©Page 10

Recipes and sidebars by Georgeanne Brennan: Pages 128, 131, 132, 133, 136, 137, 139, 144, 147, 148, 149, 150, 153, 154, 158, 159, 161, 165; Kerri Conan: Pages 25, 26, 42, 55, 58; Lori de Mori: Pages 175, 181, 184, 191, 197, 198, 200, 205, 209, 211, 213; Abigail Johnson Dodge: Pages 20, 32, 46; Janet Fletcher: Pages 62, 63; Joyce Goldstein: Pages 173, 174, 176, 177, 179, 185, 187, 189, 193, 201, 212, 214, 216, 220; Diane Holuigue: Pages 130, 134, 140, 143, 145, 151, 155, 156, 157, 160, 163, 164; Joyce Jue: Pages 74, 79, 81, 84, 86, 92, 93, 98, 104, 105, 109, 113; Michael McLaughlin: Pages 49, 56, 57, 64; Cynthia Nims: Page 19; Ray Overton: Pages 28, 39, 43; Jacki Passmore: Pages 75, 76, 77, 80, 85, 88, 89, 90, 96, 97, 99, 102, 103, 106, 107, 111, 114, 115, 116, 117; Julie Sahni: Pages 73, 83, 91, 94, 100, 110, 118, 119, 121; Michele Scicolone: Pages 178, 182, 188, 192, 194, 203, 204, 206, 208, 217, 219; Marilyn Tausend: Pages 17, 18, 22, 23, 29, 31, 34, 35, 37, 38, 40, 41, 44, 47, 50, 52, 53, 61.

Page 4 (right): The Italians generally consume less meat than they do pasta and vegetables, and they are highly discerning when they shop at the local *macelleria* (butcher shop). A good butcher must be precise when cutting his customers' selections, be it *vitello* (veal), *manzo* (beef), or *agnello* (lamb). Page 5 (right): This elaborately decorated window in the Alhambra, the exquisite fortified Spanish palace of the Nasrid kings, looks out onto a beautiful garden.

Cover: Steak and French Fries, page 158

Oxmoor
House.

OXMOOR HOUSE INC.

Oxmoor House books are distributed by Sunset Books
80 Willow Road, Menlo Park, CA 94025
Telephone: 650-321-3600 Fax: 650-324-1532
Vice President/General Manager Rich Smeby
National Accounts Manager/Special Sales Brad Moses
Oxmoor House and Sunset Books are divisions of
Southern Progress Corporation

WILLIAMS-SONOMA

Founder and Vice-Chairman Chuck Williams

THE SAVORING SERIES

Conceived and produced by Weldon Owen Inc.
814 Montgomery Street, San Francisco, CA 94133
Telephone: 415 291 0100 Fax: 415 291 8841

In collaboration with Williams-Sonoma, Inc.
3250 Van Ness Avenue, San Francisco, CA 94109

A WELDON OWEN PRODUCTION

Set in Minion and Myriad.
Color separations by Bright Arts in Singapore.
Printed and bound by Tien Wah Press in Singapore.

First printed in 2006.
10 9 8 7 6 5 4 3 2 1

Library of Congress Cataloging-in-Publication data is available.
ISBN: 0-8487-3124-7

First published in the USA by Time-Life Custom Publishing
Originally published as Williams-Sonoma Savoring:
Savoring France (© 1999 Weldon Owen Inc.)
Savoring Italy (© 1999 Weldon Owen Inc.)
Savoring Southeast Asia (© 2000 Weldon Owen Inc.)
Savoring Spain & Portugal (© 2000 Weldon Owen Inc.)
Savoring India (© 2001 Weldon Owen Inc.)
Savoring Mexico (© 2001 Weldon Owen Inc.)
Savoring Tuscany (© 2001 Weldon Owen Inc.)
Savoring America (© 2002 Weldon Owen Inc.)
Savoring Provence (© 2002 Weldon Owen Inc.)
Savoring China (© 2003 Weldon Owen Inc.)

WELDON OWEN INC.

Chief Executive Officer John Owen
President and Chief Operating Officer Terry Newell
Chief Financial Officer Christine E. Munson
Vice President International Sales Stuart Laurence
Creative Director Gaye Allen
Publisher Hannah Rahill

Senior Editor Kim Goodfriend
Assistant Editor Juli Vendzules

Designer Rachel Lopez

Production Director Chris Hemesath
Color Manager Teri Bell
Production and Reprint Coordinator Todd Rechner

Food Stylists George Dolese, Sally Parker
Illustrations Marlene McLoughlin
Text Stephanie Rosenbaum

A NOTE ON WEIGHTS AND MEASURES

All recipes include customary U.S. and metric measurements. Metric
conversions are based on a standard developed for these books and
have been rounded off. Actual weights may vary.